Time Out 1000
Books
to change your life
www.timeout.com

D1056591

Published by Time Out Guides Ltd, a wholly owned subsidiary of Time Out Group Ltd.
Time Out and the Time Out logo are trademarks of Time Out Group Ltd.

© **Time Out Group Ltd 2007**

10 9 8 7 6 5 4 3 2 1

This edition first published in Great Britain in 2007 by Ebury Publishing
A Random House Group Company
20 Vauxhall Bridge Road, London SW1V 2SA

Random House Australia Pty Limited 20 Alfred Street, Milsons Point, Sydney, New South Wales 2061, Australia
Random House New Zealand Limited 18 Poland Road, Glenfield, Auckland 10, New Zealand
Random House South Africa (Pty) Limited Isle of Houghton, Corner Boundary Road & Carse O'Gowrie,
Houghton 2198, South Africa

Random House UK Limited Reg. No. 954009

For details of distribution in the Americas, see www.timeout.com
For further distribution details, see www.timeout.com

ISBN 10: 1-84670-052-3
ISBN 13: 978-1-846700-52-1

A CIP catalogue record for this book is available from the British Library

Printed and bound in Firmengruppe APPL, aprinta druck, Wemding, Germany

The Random House Group Limited makes every effort to ensure that the papers used in our books are made from
trees that have been legally sourced from well-managed and credibly certified forests. Our paper procurement policy
can be found on www.randomhouse.co.uk.

VIDEO ART
AN ANTHOLOGY
IRA SCHNEIDER/BERYL KOROT, EDITORS

Der Zeichner Jean Cocteau — The Graphic Artist

Exterminator!
by William S. Burroughs

FARRAR, STRAUS & GIROUX

Books · Doubleday

THE MAN FROM
U.N.C.L.E.   The Affair of the
                    Gentle Saboteur   TV

Iris   Nuns
Murdoch   and
              Soldiers   Viking

Thousand   ems of
one 2019 Days 2016   POETRY

SKY

Storm De Hirsch   alleh lulleh cockatoo   Brigant Press

JOYCE
CAROL   (WOMAN)
OATES   WRITER   DUTTON

DEATH   KIT
SUSAN SONTAG

FARRAR STRAUS & GIROUX

ACT-E LAWRENCE DURRELL

Visions of the Great Rememberer   Ginsberg   DUTTON

BLUE   monday
                    harper barnes

MARTHA GRAHAM   Armitage

Classic Film Scripts Pandora's Box (Lulu)   G.W. Pabst

EX   Wilhelm
P   Reich Edited by

RANDOM HOUSE

JAPAN   MORTIMER
              MENPES

VOLUME 2, NUMBERS 1 & 2

Hunter S. Thompson   Generation of Swine

The Well-Tempered Angler
Arnold Gingrich

ISAAC BASHEVIS

Time Out Guides Limited
Universal House
251 Tottenham Court Road
London W1T 7AB
Tel + 44 (0)20 7813 3000
Fax + 44 (0)20 7813 6001
Email guides@timeout.com
www.timeout.com

The editors wish to thank the following for advice and assistance: Rosie Blau, Jessica Cargill Thompson, Sarah Guy, Laura Hassan, Tom Lamont, Jonathan Messinger, Michael Miller, John O'Connell, Cath Phillips, Daniel Smith, the staff of the London Library and all the contributors to this book.

Photography page 3 Alys Tomlinson; pages 13, 20, 21, 26, 27, 35, 50, 83, 92, 95, 105, 122, 123, 126, 138, 146,147, 151, 165, 170, 171, 181, 182, 191, 202, 203, 211, 221, 225, 232, 233 Topfoto; pages 16, 17, 70, 76, 102, 103, 119, 141, 154, 155, 166, 167, 199, 222, 244, 245 Getty Images; page 19 Charlie Hopkinson; page 22 Graham Jepson/ Writer Pictures; page 28 A Barrington Brown/Science Photo Library; page 31 OSF/Photolibrary; pages 33, 87, 91, 106, 130, 131, 178, 179 Rex Features; page 36 © Archivo Iconografico SA/Corbis; page 54 BBC/Movie Store Collection; pages 60, 61 Maurice Sendak; page 62 Illustration by Quentin Blake from MATILDA by Roald Dahl, reprinted by kind permission of the Random House Group Ltd; pages 64, 65 © Moomin Characters™; page 65 Illustration from The Tale of Peter Rabbit by Beatrix Potter © Frederick Warne & Co Ltd 1902, 2002, reproduced by permission; page 66 © the Estate of EH Shepard, reproduced with permission of Curtis Brown Group Ltd London; page 68 Illustration by Pauline Baynes © CS Lewis Pte Ltd 1950 taken from The Lion, the Witch and the Wardrobe by CS Lewis © CS Lewis Pte Ltd 1950, reprinted by permission; page 75 Manchester Art Gallery/The Bridgeman Art Library; pages 78, 79, 84, 85 Photofest NYC; pages 96, 117, 137 Courtesy of the Library of Congress LC-USZ62-98767, LC-DIG-ggbain-27631, LC-USZ62-17263; page 111 Don McCullin/Camera Press; page 114 Christina Pabst; page 120 Camera Press; page 129 Superstock; pages 53, 56, 57, 132, 145, 247 Ronald Grant Archive; pages 134, 239, 249 Topfoto/HIP; page 139 Scott Chasserot; page 157 Mary Evans Picture Library; pages 160, 161 akg-images/Erich Lessing; page 162 Mary Evans/Ida Kar; pages 174, 175 Belinda Lawley; pages 184, 185 Laurie Sparham/New Line Cinema; page 200 The Cleveland Museum of Art, Mr & Mrs William H Marlatt Fund; pages 204 Alex James; pages 63, 208 Christie's Images/The Bridgeman Art Library; page 215 Hergé/Moulinsart 2007; page 216 Watchmen™ & © DC Comics 2001; page 236 The Bridgeman Art Library.
All other images kindly supplied by the publishers

Contents

Introduction   7

Birth   10

The age of innocence *Kate Clanchy*   12
Humans and other animals *Kenan Malik*   25
Stranger than fiction *Roz Kaveney*   34

Childhood   38

Telling tales *Adèle Geras*   40
School ties *Peter Watts*   52
Picture perfect *Sarah Guy*   60
The reader as a child *Ali Smith*   69

Adolescence   72

All you need is love? *Sarah Churchwell*   74
Textual liaisons *Sarah Hedley*   87
Teenage kicks *Melissa McClements*   95
Strikes a chord *Barney Hoskyns*   99
De profundis *Brian Dillon*   104

Adulthood   108

Men at war *Michael Hodges*   110
History rewritten? *Tim Newark*   118
Working title *DJ Taylor*   125
Women in war *Juliet Gardiner*   133
Mightier than the sword? *Nick Cohen*   136
Of myths and men *Dave Hill*   140
Poetry in motion *Jason Cowley*   144

Middle Age   148

A moveable feast *Lesley Chamberlain*   150
Words of wisdom *Jonathan Derbyshire*   160
Metropolis *Nicholas Royle*   169
Corridors of power *Iain Dale*   176
Crime and punishment *Maxim Jakubowski*   180
Middle youth *Amanda Craig*   184
Class acts *John Lewis*   188

Old Age   192

Decline and fall *Michael Bywater*   194
In memoriam *Brian Dillon*   207
Novelist, heal thyself *John O'Connell*   210
Low culture, high thought *Nicholas Lezard*   214

Death   218

The art of dying *Mark Thwaite*   220
Life drawing *AC Grayling*   229
Literary haunts *Rebecca Stott*   238
A time to mourn *Daniel Smith*   248

Index

Further reference   251
Contributors   252
Index of titles   254

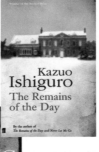

For a fast-growing list of reading group guides to classic and contemporary fiction, resources and further reading, come and browse at

faber.co.uk/bookclub

The Poisonwood Bible / Barbara Kingsolver Snow / Orhan Pamuk / In The Fold / Rachel Cusk / The Remains of the Day / Kazuo Ishiguro / Mrs Fytton's Country Life / Mavis Cheek / Headlong / Michael Frayn Amongst Women / John MCGahern / Real Stephanie Merritt / The Observations / Jane Harris / A Complicated Kindness / Miriam Teows / The Confessions of Max Tivoli Andrew Sean Greer / The Bell Jar / Sylvia Plath / A Fine Balance / Rohinton Mistry / A Married Woman / Manju Kapur / A Black Englishman / Carolyn Slaughter

Introduction

If you've ever set foot in a high-street bookshop you'll have seen them: the multiple volumes of literary snake oil, with coverlines promising to supply the key to changing your life in 'minutes', 'days', or sometimes in just '12 easy steps' (it usually involves reducing your clothes size or eating algae). They're the early 21st-century version of the exhortatory screeds of Victorian 'muscular' Christianity (with the miracle of the makeover standing in for the transforming power of faith) – only much less well written.

Needless to say, this sort of thing is not what we had in mind when we had the idea for a book about life-changing books. But nor were we looking for a straightfoward route to self-improvement through reading. Of course, there are lots of books around that suggest that there is such a route: books that tell you both *how* to read and *what* to read; books that prescribe a canon of great works and then tell you how to go about extracting the ore of significant meaning from them.

But we've no intention of being anywhere near so prescriptive. Not because we're sceptical about the existence of literary value – we're quite sure you can tell a good book from a bad one – but more because we're unsure that most people's reading habits are suited to the kind of strenuous mind-expansion programmes recommended by the latter-day zealots of what used to be called 'improving' literature.

We think Virginia Woolf had it right when she wrote of the 'common reader' that he 'snatches' now this book, now that, 'without caring where he finds it or of what nature it may be'. Woolf chose as the epigraph for her essays on the topic Dr Johnson's paean to the 'common sense of readers uncorrupted by literary prejudices'. Johnson was giving his approval, she thought, to a pursuit 'which devours a great deal of time, and is yet apt to leave behind nothing very substantial'.

Woolf didn't mean by that last remark to cast doubt on the idea that books can change our lives, so much as to suggest that the way in which literature goes to work on us is subtle and not easily quantifiable. Her contemporary TS Eliot made much the same point. We value wide reading, he said, not because it increases our hoard of knowledge (being 'well read' is not the same as having a 'well-stocked mind'), but because it introduces us to 'one powerful personality after another' and so affects us as 'entire human beings'. Eliot was talking about the personality of the authors, whose 'views of life' can transform or expand our own.

However, to move from one book to the next like this is, as Woolf observed, to be 'thrown this way and then that'. Books, especially novels, uproot us and deposit us, for their duration, in a different world. We were reminded of this when thinking about how to organise this volume. As much as we liked the Johnsonian idea of a way of reading untainted by the 'refinements of subtlety and the dogmatism of learning', we could see that some sort of map would be required if we were going to suggest 1,000 books to change your life.

One obvious solution would have been to arrange things by genre. But we were also impressed by something else that Woolf said about how we read. Parcelling our reading out into classes – fiction, biography, poetry and so on – more often than not stops us asking 'from books what books can give us'. And what they give us – and she wasn't just talking about novels – are visions of human life: 'The greater part of any library is nothing but the record of… fleeting moments in the lives of men [and] women'.

With that in mind, we decided that the shape of the book should follow the arc of a human life. And what better guide than Shakespeare's 'Seven Ages of Man' speech from *As You Like It*, a peroration beautifully and wittily compressed into a limerick by the poet and historian Robert Conquest:

'First you get puking and mewling
Then very pissed off with your schooling
Then fucks and then fights
Then judging chaps' rights
Then sitting in slippers – then drooling.'

1000 Books, then, is arranged in seven chapters, from birth to death, 'mewling and puking' to 'mere oblivion'. Each chapter begins with a lead essay either on books about the age in question or, as is the case with Adolescence, Adulthood and Middle Age, books that deal with one of its defining characteristics or preoccupations (and here again, Shakespeare was our guide). The subsequent essays in each chapter unravel these themes further, taking them in all directions. In the chapter on Middle Age, for example, there are investigations of politicians' diaries, and the upper-class twit in fiction; while in Adolescence, we move from love and romance to erotica and melancholy, pausing along the way, in deference to Shakespeare's 'woeful ballads', to consider books about music.

With a few exceptions (AC Grayling's piece about biography, Roz Kaveney's introduction to science fiction and Nicholas Lezard's

reflections on the graphic novel), each essay ranges widely across genres, taking in poetry, prose, history and philosophy as well as novels and plays.

Each of the main essays is accompanied by a list of 20 further books that deal, in different ways, with its theme. These were compiled by the editors with the help of Time Out's team of critics, as were the 'Critics' choice' boxes, on topics from diaries and drugs to nostalgia and decay, that are scattered throughout the book.

Finally, there are 20 short pieces, in which leading writers from Britain and the US – including Jonathan Coe, Jonathan Franzen, Hari Kunzru and Sarah Waters – describe the books that changed their lives. These are little testimonies to the transforming power of literature, to encounters that made writers of those who were once only readers.

In *Words*, a memoir of his childhood, Jean-Paul Sartre composed a hymn to this magic or alchemy. In fact, he turned reading into something very much like a religion. Sartre wrote that his life, or at any rate that portion of it he was able to recall, began among the books stacked like so many Stone Age megaliths in his grandfather's office. Later, once he had learned to read, he was given the run of the library at home and began the 'assault on human wisdom' that would occupy him for the rest of his life. Sartre's childhood memories weren't of digging holes, searching for nests or throwing stones at birds, but of books – 'books were my birds and my nest, my pets, my barn and my countryside; the library was the world caught in a mirror, infinitely various and unpredictable.'

We hope that the essays in *this* book catch something of this variety and unpredictability. We've tried to recreate what Woolf called the 'heterogeneous company' on our bookshelves. By no means all of the books discussed here are great works of art or imperishable classics. Yet each of them, we think, is at the very least capable of satisfying the readerly interest that Woolf compared to the 'curiosity which possesses us sometimes in the evening when we linger in front of a house where the lights are lit and the blinds not yet drawn, and each floor of the house shows us a different section of human life in being'. We trust you'll linger a while. Happy reading!

Seven Ages of Man

All the world's a stage,
And all the men and women merely players,
They have their exits and entrances,
And one man in his time plays many parts,
His acts being seven ages. At first the infant,
Mewling and puking in the nurse's arms.
Then the whining schoolboy, with his satchel
And shining morning face, creeping like snail
Unwillingly to school. And then the lover,
Sighing like furnace, with a woeful ballad
Made to his mistress' eyebrow. Then a soldier.
Full of strange oaths, and bearded like the pard,
Jealous in honour, sudden and quick in quarrel,
Seeking the bubble reputation
Even in the cannon's mouth. And then the justice,
In fair round belly with good capon lin'd,
With eyes severe and beard of formal cut,
Full of wise saws and modern instances;
And so he plays his part. The sixth age shifts
Into the lean and slippered pantaloon,
With spectacles on nose and pouch on side,
His youthful hose, well sav'd, a world too wide,
For his shrunk shank; and his big manly voice,
Turning again towards the childish treble, pipes
And whistles in his sound. Last scene of all,
That ends this strange eventful history,
Is second childishness and mere oblivion,
Sans teeth, sans eyes, sans taste, sans everything.

William Shakespeare

Birth

*'At first the infant,
Mewling and puking in
the nurse's arms.'*

The age of innocence

When it comes to birth and motherhood, canonical writers are often oddly reticent, says **Kate Clanchy** – but times are changing.

The 'mewling and puking' infant, you may notice, gets the least space of all the 'Ages of Man' in that famous speeech. Indeed, Shakespeare has little to say about babies and mothering in any of his works, offering just a few, conspicuously dark, images: Lady Macbeth offering to dash out her metaphorical nursling's brains; the massacre of the Macduff brood, Cleopatra's suckling asp, and the dying Falstaff, snuggled in the arms of Mistress Quickly and babbling of green fields.

But then there is very little about infancy in any canonical literature. Between Homer's account of Hector's little son frightened by the plume on his father's helmet and 'Frost at Midnight', Samuel Taylor Coleridge's 1797 poem for his sleeping baby, pregnancy, birth and infancy merit only the briefest of mentions: the odd carol and elegy, an early exit or bawdy stage joke, a happy end to the story. This is not just because almost all canonical writers were

men, and childbearing is the only experience that belongs exclusively to women, but also because infancy was seen as an animal, speechless stage, belonging to the village rather than the big house, the folk song rather than the book. Coleridge and his fellow Romantics were interested in babies, or at least in the idea of babies, as part of their radical project to bring the folk song and the village into literature – though not many of the infants they wrote about seem to live and breathe as convincingly as Coleridge's little boy, who sleeps 'cradled by my side' and whose 'gentle breathings' are surrounded by the slowly freezing world.

You might hope for more detail from the novel, a form in its cradle at the same time as the small Hartley Coleridge. Here, after all, was an intimate and social way of writing; one bought, read and soon written at least as much by women as by men. But early heroines Pamela and Clarissa are singularly dedicated

The enemy of great art?

delicious noodles | **rice dishes** | **freshly squeezed juices**
wine | **sake** | **japanese beers**

bloomsbury | borough / london bridge | brent cross | camden | canary wharf
covent garden | earls court | fleet street | haymarket | islington | kensington
knightsbridge | leicester square | mansion house | moorgate / citypoint
old broad street / bank | putney | royal festival hall | soho | tower hill
victoria | wigmore | wimbledon

positive eating + positive living

wagamama.com

uk | ireland | holland | australia | dubai | belgium | new zealand | denmark | turkey to avoiding pregnancy at all costs, and while Defoe's Roxanna frequently 'pleads her belly' to get out of jail, she has little to say about the infants she produces. There is only one baby in Jane Austen – the clamorous child in *Persuasion* who is lifted from the back of Anne Elliot by strong and silent Captain Wentworth – and none in Charlotte Brontë, for all her vivid portrayals of older children. Dickens is interested in breastfeeding, though, particularly its absence: one of Pip's deprivations is to be 'brought up by hand' – bottle-fed – by his chilly sister in *Great Expectations*; The Infant Phenomenon is monstrously suckled on gin; and, most movingly, ethereal Paul Dombey is wet-nursed by the earthy Mrs Toodles and begs to see her when he dies.

Dickens was free to value breastfeeding: he did not have to do it. The first great women writers were, almost by definition, childless, because childbearing and child-rearing always took a toll on woman's energies and could easily be fatal. Jane Austen's life was almost hopelessly circumscribed merely by being an aunt and daughter; George Eliot had to add superhuman will to her preternatural intelligence to escape the woman's work she detailed in *The Mill on the Floss*; Emily Dickinson, Emily Brontë and Christina Rossetti sought solitude beyond all else; pregnancy killed Charlotte Brontë where tuberculosis, malnutrition, grief and the Yorkshire damp had failed.

Even when such writers do turn their attention to babies, we may find it difficult to understand them, so different are their concerns and experiences. The early American poet Anne Bradstreet, for example, wrote a poem on marriage that is still popular and immediate – 'If ever two, then we…' – but when she picked up her pen to address the subject of childbirth, produced a sonnet on the fear of death that now seems as mossy and blank as the skull on a Jacobean gravestone. There are very few poems about living babies from the 19th century, but there are numberless elegies, ghost poems and rhymed fables starring children in heaven. An unbearable number of very small children died in our early industrial cities, and the reaction was a Victorian sentimentality about infancy that we now also find unbearable. Charles Kingsley's *The Water-Babies*, the zenith of such feeling,

A book that changed my life

Hari Kunzru

Gravity's Rainbow by Thomas Pynchon

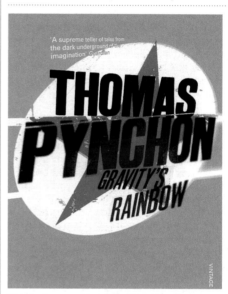

This is the one, the paperback that is held together with tape and probably won't stand another reading; this enormous novel about the chaos of the last days of World War II, with its weird concerns about pigs and bananas and plastics manufacture, its occult structure, its hokey songs, disconcerting scope and flagrant disregard for literary good taste. *Gravity's Rainbow* is a book dumb enough to call a German spa town Bad Karma and clever enough to induce in me, as a 19-year-old would-be writer, a sense of quasi-religious awe that I find slightly embarrassing now, if only because it's not really gone away. After I first read it, I decided most of my considerable problems in life would be solved if only I could learn to make something as pleasurable and complex as this book. It made me abandon most of the other options I was considering to make the time pass, which in retrospect was a good thing.

Hari Kunzru's latest novel is My Revolutions *(Hamish Hamilton).*

BIRTH

for instance, may well strike the modern reader as not just patronising but, with its nudity and suction, actually rather sexualised and perverse.

But then we are all post-Freudian now. Freud's *The Psychopathology of Everyday Life*, published at the turn of the 20th century, and the long, slow revolution it ushered in brought an entirely new way of looking at infancy and motherhood: it became the site of conflict and character formations instead of an animal blank. For the first time, it was seen as worthy of close observation and written record. At the same time, huge improvements in medicine and hygiene meant that both mother and child had more chance of surviving to consider their experience.

All the same, it took a long time for childbirth and pregnancy to be accepted as a suitable subject for literature: TS Eliot, for example, so bold in his own experimentation, was damming about his protégé Anne Ridler's rather lovely sequence 'For a Child Expected' on the grounds of its subject; Joyce, who aspired to go everywhere in *Ulysses*, spends plenty of time on the lavatory but none on the breast. 'There is no more sombre enemy of good art than the pram in the hall,' announced Cyril Connolly in *The Enemies of Promise* (1938). True to his proclamations, the Bloomsberries pursued each other in sterile circles rather than breed; though if you look carefully at their fringes you will find *The Weather in the Streets* by Rosamund Lehmann, a piercing account of an affair, a pregnancy and an abortion in the bleak bohemia of 1930s London, and the poetry of Frances Cornford.

Cornford was a granddaughter of Charles Darwin and a cousin to the artist Gwen Raverat – but her work has none of the neurasthenic quality that pedigree might imply. Her poems, particularly those about children, are tough and thoughtful, penetratingly clean and clear to read: 'How dull our days, how lacking in surprise' she thinks our lives would be without children, without in any way sentimentalising 'the grave, appalling freshness of their eyes'. EJ (Edith Joy) Scovell is another undeservedly neglected poet. Her sequence 'The First Year' is the story of bringing up a baby in the '50s, finding joy in a life lapped by firm routines. Scovell's observations are never less than exact, and may well strike a chord with mothers at home in the age of Gina Ford.

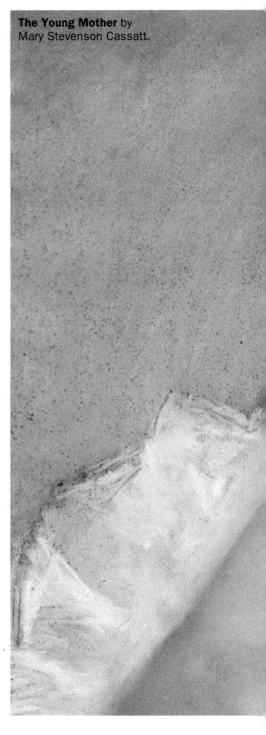

The Young Mother by Mary Stevenson Cassatt.

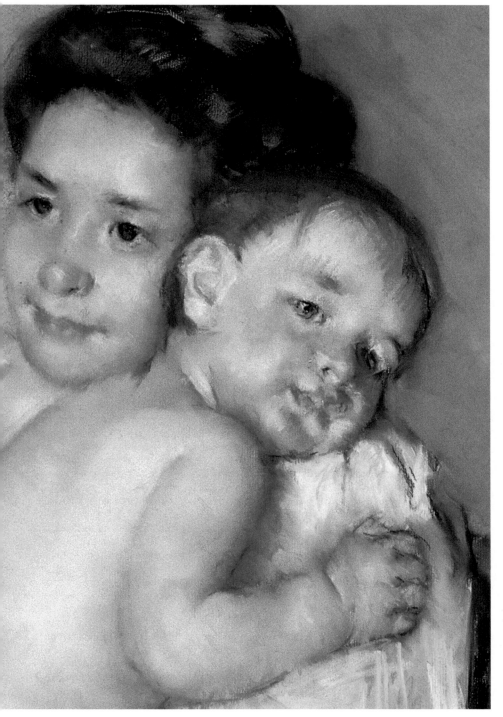

'A generation of women had gone to university and been educated alongside their brothers, only to find themselves married and back in the home, often with babies.'

Scovell's quiet virtues were rather drowned out, however, by the technicolour shriek that was Sylvia Plath's *Ariel* (1965). Plath was always interested in childbearing, and had already written an entire verse-play – *Three Women* – on the subject, but the sheer edge of the *Ariel* poems, their vigour and scale, and the thread of darkness that runs through even the most celebratory, such as 'Morning Song' or 'The Night Dances', caught something particular of its time. A generation of women had gone to university and been educated alongside their brothers, only to find themselves immediately married and back in the home, often with babies. Plath's poems gave voice to the rage, frustration and love of these women, and insisted, for what seemed like the first time, on the many dimensions – physical, mythical, social and literary – of motherhood.

In the same year, Margaret Drabble published *The Millstone*, an account of a young woman entering single motherhood and, to general shock and horror, failing to be bowed by the experience. *Georgy Girl* by Margaret Forster and *The L-Shaped Room* by Lynne Reid Banks cover the same ground: grotty flats and borrowed pints of milk, buses, bosses and fumbled affairs with self-indulgent young men. All three works retain their vigour and conviction, and a freshness that comes from their radical new view of the world, the possibility these novels share and grasp of a woman falling in love – not with a man, as has been recounted so often, but with a baby, an actual, feeding and sleeping baby, unfurling its intricate self at full length for the first time in a novel.

Motherhood, if not infancy, became an important theme of many of the great novels of the last decades of the 20th century – *Beloved* by Toni Morrison, *Breathing Lessons* by Anne Tyler, *Unless* by Carol Shields – and permeates the work of Helen Dunmore, Margaret Atwood, Amy Tan and Tessa Hadley. Among poets, Rita Dove and Adrienne Rich made motherhood a central theme, but childbearing and infancy remained a rare and derided subject. The American poet Sharon Olds, for example, has needed extraordinary courage in the face of critical hostility to hold to what she calls her 'central meanings': sex, birth, children. Her challenge to the literary establishment is explicit:

'I have done what you wanted to do, Walt Whitman,
Allan Ginsburg, I have done this thing,
I and the other women this exceptional
act with the exceptional heroic body,
this giving birth, this glistening verb
and I am putting my proud American boast
right here with the others.'
('The Language of the Brag')

The body, female and breeding, or small and warm 'as laundry fresh from the dryer', is explored and evoked in Olds' work in a way that is indeed startling – but startling because it is so exactly and newly described, not because it seeks to shock. Olds' earlier collections *Satan Says*, *The Dead and the Living* and *The Gold Cell*, in particular, contain poems that evoke all the violent love, loss and rage of pregnancy, miscarriage, birth and early motherhood; several are included in her *Selected Poems*.

The daughters of the Plath and Drabble generation, meanwhile, perhaps mindful of their mothers' experience, took a long time to have children: Sara of *Georgy Girl*, and Octavia from *The Millstone*, born we assume in 1965, would have had a 25 per cent chance of reaching 40 without children. If they did – after, we assume, high-achieving and fulfilling careers – arrive at a typically late child-bed, they would have found themselves undergoing hugely informed pregnancies, brightly illustrated with ultrasound, followed by the greatest physical and mental shock of their entire lives, for theirs is the generation that didn't plan on birth, who expected to love men and work, not babies. Reeling from lack of sleep, maddened by the sudden change in their status, racked by traumatic, medicalised birth experiences, Sara and Octavia would certainly reach for, if not actually write, a 'mum-moir'. Chick lit we have had always with us: the mum-moir, being an autobiographical account of (always late) motherhood, is the original form of the '90s and noughties, penned by mothers as diverse as the feminist intellectual Naomi Wolf and Jools Oliver, wife of the celebrity chef.

As befits a new form, the mum-moir is flexible, which does not mean it is not demanding: Sara and Octavia will be searching for reflections of their own experience and will be outraged by books that seem to portray them inaccurately. Naomi Wolf's *Misconceptions* journeys through medical and cultural history as much as through Wolf's body, and pauses to analyse the flaws in '80s feminism and skewer the middle-class 'equal marriage' on its way. Kate Figes's pioneering work *Life After Birth* is dense with thought and research on the problem of how to integrate the work of children with a woman's career, and touches only briefly on what seem to have been harsh birth experiences.

A Life's Work by the novelist Rachel Cusk, on the other hand, narrows rather than broadens, eschewing argument and statistics in order to focus her story on a few charged, claustrophobic rooms. Hers is a horror story: in prose so formal and clotted that it holds great tension, she shows us the young mother unable to relax at the opera, the visit from the disapproving health visitor, the attempt to join a toddler group, all in slow-motion Gothic close-up. Cusk, like Cyril Connolly or John Osborne, is alienated and appalled not so much by motherhood as by mothers: by older mothers with their *fat arms* and *grey hair*, who nevertheless insist on walking down the street; by mothers who sing, loudly; by mothers who bake and *talk about baking*; and her unflinching exposure of her feelings is, if not sympathetic, at least compelling.

The Irish writer Anne Enright, meanwhile, chooses to use the mum-moir to experiment with the essay, presumably on the principle that a subject new to literature needs to find new forms. *Making Babies/Stumbling into*

A book that changed my life

Sarah Waters

Wideacre by Philippa Gregory

BIRTH

In 1991 I was working as a library assistant at Holborn Library, London. I had recently left university with an MA in English Literature, and was thinking of returning to study for a PhD, but was coasting around for an area to specialise in. One day I came across Philippa Gregory's historical novel *Wideacre* on the library shelves and idly started to read it; soon I was entertaining the staff room with daily updates on its outrageously rococo plot. But I was also tremendously impressed by the points Gregory was making about women, history and power, and *Wideacre* – together with its equally wonderful sequels, *The Favoured Child* and *Meridon* – got me thinking about the subversive potential of the historical novel genre. A year later I started a PhD thesis on lesbian and gay historical fiction; the thesis in turn produced my first novel, *Tipping the Velvet*. I still recommend *Wideacre* whenever I get the chance. I can't honestly say that I would never have become a novelist if I hadn't read it; but I do know that life would have been much less fun.

Sarah Waters's most recent novel is The Night Watch *(Virago).*

Motherhood is elegant, spry and surprising, a collection of pieces ranging in shape and subject from a chapter-length autobiographical reflection on suicide and birth, through the witty literary anecdote to the three-line joke. Ian Sansom's *The Truth About Babies* also invented a form: his book groups memories, reflections and literary quotations in an alphabetical list ('A is for' etc). The shape reflects the disjointed nature of babycare, and wryly echoes the author's attempt to contain the experience within the rickety framework of received knowledge.

Cusk, Enright and Sansom are all serious literary writers, and their work reflects a new contemporary literary seriousness about infancy and parenthood. In the short story form, Helen Simpson's collection *Hey Yeah Right Get a Life* demonstrated that the lives of women surrounded by clamorous small children, women who keep a knife specifically for the purpose of removing vomit from a pillow, can be as rich and intricate a subject as any 'Lady with Lapdog'. The Scottish poet Kathleen Jamie placed an exquisite sequence about pregnancy and birth – 'Ultrasound' – at the heart of a collection about nationhood and family entitled *Jizzen* – Old Scots for 'childbed'. Male poets too are beginning to broach this subject: recent collections by Paul Muldoon, Don Paterson and Simon Armitage are laced with poems about pregnancy and birth, infertility and miscarriage. In the work of these already canonical male writers, as much as in the teeming shelves of 'mummy lit', we can see the first 'stage of man' finally being accepted as a literary subject along with the others, the 'mewling and puking' being transformed, with all the vigour and excitement of the new, into words.

Birth and motherhood in 20 books

Adam Bede by George Eliot

Village beauty Hetty Sorrel is seduced by the dashing Captain Arthur Donnithorne, only realising she is pregnant after he has left. In fear and desperation, she sets off to find him on foot – a journey that ends with her leaving her newborn baby to die, in 'a hole under the nut-tree, like a little grave,' she pitiably confesses.

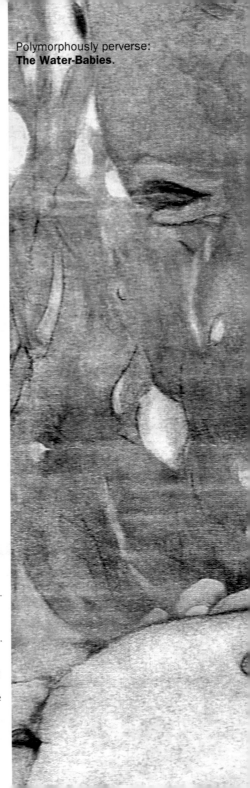

Polymorphously perverse: **The Water-Babies**.

BIRTH

Poet of motherhood: **Frances Cornford**.

Babies and Their Mothers by DW Winnicott

In this collection of essays, Winnicott – a distinguished psychoanalyst – reflects on the peculiar relationship between mothers and their newborn babies. Covering non-verbal communication, breastfeeding and the 'early personality' of newborns, his essential message is one of trust in a mother's instincts.

Baby and Child Care by Benjamin Spock

Dubbed 'the father of permissiveness' by his critics, the good doctor sparked a parenting revolution when his first book was published in 1946. Encapsulated in the famous opening sentence, his message to anxious parents was simple; 'You know more than you think you do.' The book advocated a relaxed, flexible approach to parenting, in contrast to the rigid routines and discipline advised by other experts of the day.

A Chapter from Her Upbringing by Ivy Goodman

Following her first collection of short stories, *Heart Failure*, this second independently published volume chronicles the complex lives of parents and children and the varying relationships between them.

The Child in Time by Ian McEwan

Devastated by the kidnap of Kate, his daughter, Stephen Lewis struggles to make sense of his life and cope with the terrible loss. Repeatedly reliving the mundane events that led to his daughter's disappearance, Stephen drifts in and out of time, eventually 're-experiencing' his own birth.

The Crimson Petal and the White by Michel Faber

The Victorian ideal of the innocent, childlike wife reaches its awful apotheosis in the slender form of Agnes Rackham. Utterly oblivious to the facts of life, Agnes believes her period to be a sign of demonic possession, and is wracked with guilt and disgust. In her confused mind, her pregnancy and delivery was simply a terrible illness – so six-year-old Sophie is hidden away in the nursery, never to be discussed.

The Dollmaker by Harriette Arnow

Forced to move from rural Kentucky to urban Detroit during World War II, Gertie Nevels struggles to keep her family together in harsh and unfamiliar conditions. Arnow's unnerving classic explores the domestic woes caused by isolation and dislocation in a vast, polarised America.

Ghost Story by Toby Litt

A mournful, passionate tale of family contentment brought to a sudden halt. Paddy and Agatha await the birth of their second child when suddenly, unalterably, something goes wrong. As we follow the couple's attempt to recover their lives, Litt conjures a haunting sense of bereavement for the unknown.

Infants Without Families by Anna Freud & Dorothy Burlingham

The last of Sigmund's six children, Anna Freud followed her father's path to become a significant psychoanalyst in her own right. Together with Dorothy Burlingham, she published this study of children under stress based on time spent working in a foster home in Hampstead during World War II.

Macbeth by William Shakespeare

The witches' wily grasp of gynaecology proves Macbeth's undoing, as they assure him that 'none of woman born shall harm Macbeth'. The twist in the tale comes when Macduff reveals that he was delivered by a vicious-sounding Caesarean section, 'from his mother's womb/Untimely ripped.'

Madame Bovary by Gustave Flaubert

This 'Story of Provincial Life' is Flaubert's famous attack on bourgeois complacency. It follows Emma Bovary, bored housewife and listless flirt, and her increasing boredom with her husband, polite society and motherhood. She soon becomes infatuated with more exciting men who offer an escape from the constraining banality of her everyday life.

Newborn by Kate Clanchy

Beginning when her unborn baby is 'perhaps ten cells old', Clanchy's beautifully crafted collection of poems chart her experiences of motherhood. The tone is tender but never lapses into sentimentality; 'At night, in your shift, fine hair upright/you are my tiny Bedlamite,/admonishing the laughing crowd.'

Notes From a Small Island by Andrea Levy

An illicit pregnancy can only be concealed for so long, and Queenie Bligh's secret is revealed in dramatic fashion as she suddenly goes into labour. Her only assistance comes from the bewildered – and faintly repulsed – Hortense, whose only prior experience of birth has been watching chickens laying eggs, and whose first concern is keeping her best dress clean.

Post-Partum Document by Mary Kelly

A touchstone of radical feminism in Britain, this theoretical text is based on Kelly's famous six-part art installation, first exhibited at the ICA in 1976 and published in book form the following decade. A profound and complex work, it kick-started the feminist interrogation of motherhood and birth.

Room Temperature by Nicholson Baker

Taking place over a very short expanse of time (a staple of Baker's fiction, as are his infamous page-long sentences), this tale charts the minutiae of a man's actions as he feeds his baby daughter. Twenty minutes of average daily life – described in exhaustive detail – here becomes compelling, emotive reading.

BIRTH

A book that changed my life

Nicholas Royle

Blind Needle by Trevor Hoyle

Raymond Chandler meets Alain Robbe-Grillet. In the Lake District.

Trevor Hoyle's 1994 novel *Blind Needle* is a chase thriller that turns into a darkly compelling inquisition on the nature and meaning of identity. It's a novel that has a lot of fun with the conventions of the genre, then subverts expectations by going a bit *nouveau roman*, a bit BS Johnson. There are two chapter 15s, for example, which, Hoyle advises in a note at the beginning, should be read concurrently.

Hoyle's publishing record has remarkable range, from *Blake's 7* novelisations to BBC plays and from SF and football hooligan fiction to his three outstanding novels for John Calder, home of Beckett, Borges and Burroughs, among other legends. *The Man Who Travelled on Motorways* is an extraordinary blend of experimental fiction and erotic literature; published in 1984, *Vail* is a speculative

ROYLE ST.

fantasy set in a futuristic Britain that has in part come to exist in the intervening two decades. *Blind Needle* was inspirational to me for its unique mix of experimentation and genre.

With its atmosphere of claustrophobic paranoia generated in a fictitious northern town, it reminds me of David Pirie's 1980 novel *Mystery Story* and JM Morris's later *Fiddleback*, while its exposing of the unlovely Cumbrian underbelly is taken up by Christopher Kenworthy's *The Quality of Light*. But Hoyle's novel is unique, an experimental thriller that is as thrilling for the risks it takes with form as for its twisty-turny plot. When I read it in 1994, its effect was galvanising, because it was not only the kind of book I liked to read, but also the type of novel I was trying to write.

Nicholas Royle's latest book is Mortality *(Serpent's Tail).*

The Shawl by Cynthia Ozick

Through two connected stories – *The Shawl*, a short story set during World War II, and *Rosa*, a novella set 30 years later – Ozick tells a harrowing tale of cruelty, desperation and lost motherhood. In the tragedy of Rosa, we learn how escape from a Jewish concentration camp does not necessarily mean escape from its horror.

Sons and Lovers by DH Lawrence

The story of Paul Morel and his family, set in a working-class mining community in Nottinghamshire, this is Lawrence's most autobiographical work. When Paul falls in love with Miriam, he seeks to break free of his enclosed world, and fierce family conflict is aroused – particularly from his suffocating, emotionally dependent mother.

Tess of the d'Urbervilles by Thomas Hardy

Hardy's compassionate portrayal of a fallen woman and criticism of the sexual double standards of the

day caused a scandal; the outraged Bishop of Wakefield burnt a copy in protest. Bearing an illegitimate baby to the feckless Alec d'Urberville is Tess's ruin – even after her baby has tragically died, there can be no fresh start for Hardy's tragic heroine.

We Need to Talk About Kevin by Lionel Shriver

Shriver's dark tale of reluctant motherhood certainly hit a nerve, inspiring acres of column inches devoted to the time-honoured nature-versus-nature debate. A disturbing depiction of the privations, tedium and traumas of parenting, finally culminating in Kevin's bloody massacre in the school gym, it's not recommended reading for prospective parents.

Woolworth Madonna by Elizabeth Troop

Asking pertinent questions about class and social structure, Troop's little-known tale of tough parenting on a tougher council estate is as political as it is emotional.

BIRTH

Humans and other animals

Science can help us to understand what it is to be human, says **Kenan Malik**.

'I'll never
Be such a gosling to obey instinct, but stand
As if a man were author of himself
And knew no other kin.'

For most of the past 500 years, Coriolanus's paean to human freedom would have been regarded as unexceptional. It was taken for granted by most Western thinkers from the Renaissance onwards that human beings are exceptional creatures, thanks to our possession of reason and consciousness, language and morality. Reason, as Descartes put it, 'is the noblest thing we can have because it makes us in a certain manner equal to God and exempts us from being his subjects.' This was the philosophy at the heart of both the scientific revolution and the Enlightenment.

Today, though, we no longer think in this way. The idea of humans as exceptional beings is seen as both scientifically false and politically dangerous. For most scientists, exceptionalism smacks of mysticism. Their holy grail is an understanding of humans couched in the same language as the rest of physical nature. And politically, human hubris is increasingly seen as the root of most of the world's ills, from global warming to ethnic cleansing. 'We need protection from ourselves,' the biologist Lynn Margulis has said of the human species. This combination of scientific naturalism and political pessimism is helping to transform our understanding of the human condition.

Historically, the question of what it is to be human – who are we? Where did we come from? What defines our nature? – has been the domain of poets and philosophers, theologians and novelists. It was Aristotle and Aquinas, Dante and Descartes, Shakespeare and Schopenhauer to whom people turned in search of answers.

The publication in 1859 of Charles Darwin's *On the Origin of Species* changed all that. Darwin's masterpiece transformed the debate not only by throwing new light on the relationship between humans and the rest of nature, but also by holding out the hope that in understanding that relationship we might also begin to unravel the deepest mysteries of human existence. 'Origin of man now solved,' Darwin wrote in his notebook in 1838. 'He who understands baboon will do more for metaphysics than Locke.'

Thirteen years after *On the Origin of Species*, Darwin published *The Expressions of the Emotions in Man and the Animals*, his most explicit attempt to demonstrate the animal roots of human nature. The emotional stuff of everyday life – love, joy, anger, sulkiness, guilt, disgust, horror, modesty – was, Darwin suggested, common both to all humans and to humans and other animals. This was a challenge both to the creationist idea that emotions are specially bestowed on humans by God and to the racist view that every race has evolved separately. Darwin's argument that human emotions are universal, evolved and derived from those of animals was (and remains) deeply contentious.

The book was a sensational bestseller. Nine thousand copies sold within four months – an extraordinary figure for the time. (*The Origin of Species* had an initial print run of just 1,250.) Yet after its second edition in 1889, the book remained largely forgotten for more than a century. Indeed,

BIRTH

Darwin's voyage of discovery: **HMS Beagle**.

until a new edition appeared to great acclaim in 1998, few would have even known that Darwin had written such a work.

Why did *The Expressions of the Emotions* collect dust for much of the 20th century? Largely because in the decades that followed its publication, evolutionary theory was used to demonstrate not the unity of humankind, but rather the idea that the struggle for existence had created unequal races, and that capitalist exploitation, colonial conquest

and even genocide were simply the working out of the laws of natural selection.

As the racist consequences of social Darwinism became apparent, so psychologists and anthropologists increasingly shied away from any biological explanation of human behaviour. In the wake of Nazism and the Holocaust, the idea that human behaviour was entirely a cultural artefact came to dominate postwar thinking. The very idea of human nature became taboo. 'We knew how politically

loaded discussions of inborn differences could become,' the anthropologist Margaret Mead recalled in her autobiography *Blackberry Winter*. 'It seemed to us that further study of inborn similarities would have to wait upon less troubled times.'

However, the republication of *The Expressions of the Emotions* in 1998 signalled another shift in perceptions of human nature. By the end of the 20th century, sociological explanations of human behaviour had largely fallen into

disrepute, while evolutionary accounts had become fashionable again. Not only are 'claims about human nature less dangerous than many people think', Steven Pinker argued in *The Blank Slate*, his full-frontal assault on cultural relativism, but 'the denial of human nature can be more dangerous than people think.'

It was in the 1970s that the debate about human nature was reignited by two books, neither of which, paradoxically, was primarily about humans, but both of which have

Watson (left) and **Crick**, the discoverers of DNA, examine the building blocks of life itself.

helped to shape the debate about what it means to be human and remain almost as controversial now as they were then: EO Wilson's *Sociobiology* and Richard Dawkins's *The Selfish Gene*.

'Skill in wielding metaphors and symbols,' Dawkins has written, 'is one of the hallmarks of scientific genius.' Whether Dawkins himself qualifies as a scientific genius only history will record. But there have been few scientists – indeed, few writers in any genre – more skilled at metaphor-wielding. And there have been few more evocative metaphors in the modern age than that of the 'selfish gene', nor a scientific book with a greater impact on public consciousness than Dawkins's 1976 work that introduced both the phrase and the author to a non-scientific audience.

The Selfish Gene crystallised the 'gene-eyed view' of evolution developed through the 1960s and '70s by a new generation of evolutionary thinkers, in particular William Hamilton and John Maynard Smith in England and the Americans George Williams and Robert Trivers. Evolution, Dawkins claimed, cares only about the gene, not the individual. Individuals die at the end of their lifetimes, whereas a gene is potentially immortal. Genes are 'selfish' because their only function is to survive at the expense of their rivals. The body is simply a 'survival machine' built by genes to enable them to survive.

The publication of *The Selfish Gene* helped launch the so-called 'Darwin wars'. Critics such as Stephen Jay Gould and Richard Lewontin savaged what they called Dawkins's 'ultra-Darwinism', the belief that 'natural selection regulates everything of importance in evolution'. Many of Gould's criticisms were first aired in the column he wrote for the magazine *Natural History*, and were subsequently collected in a series of books, beginning with *Ever Since Darwin*.

Dawkins bit back and books such as *The Extended Phenotype, Climbing Mount Improbable, The Blind Watchmaker* and *River out of Eden* refined and expanded his argument, challenging both creationists and his Darwinian critics. The fiercest defence of 'ultra-Darwinism' came not from Dawkins but from the philosopher Daniel Dennett, whose 1995 book *Darwin's Dangerous Idea* describes Darwinism as a 'universal acid' that eats away at traditional outlooks and transforms the way we look at the world.

The Selfish Gene, however, was not just a book about Darwinian theory but also, as Andrew Brown puts it in *The Darwin Wars*, 'a book about genes read as a book about people'. The very idea of the selfish gene shocked many critics, as it seemed to attribute agency to genes and deny it to humans – though, in fact, this is to be so dazzled by Dawkins's metaphorical skills as to miss what he is really saying.

The controversy was fuelled by the fact that *The Selfish Gene* was published barely a year after the storm had broken over EO Wilson's *Sociobiology*. Wilson, a Harvard entomologist and world expert on ants, set out to synthesise all the known knowledge about social animals – from corals and jellyfish to ants and bees to birds and primates. But he also tried to show that the same principles of behaviour also apply to humans. 'Behaviour and social structure,' Wilson believed, 'like all biological phenomena, can be studied as "organs", extensions of the genes that exist because of their superior adaptive value.'

Gould and Lewontin (Wilson's colleagues at Harvard) accused him of giving vent to theories that 'led to the establishment of the gas chambers', while the philosopher Mary Midgley, in her book *Beast and Man*, denounced sociobiology as 'biological Thatcherism, romantic and egotistic, celebrating evolution as a ceaseless crescendo of competition between essentially "selfish" individual organisms.' In *Not in our Genes*, a book that Lewontin co-wrote with British biologist Stephen Rose and American psychologist Leon Kamin, Wilson is painted as a 'neoconservative libertarian' and sociobiology as 'yet another attempt to put a natural scientific foundation under Adam Smith'.

Once the initial hysteria had died down, the argument over sociobiology gave way to a debate about nature and nurture: which is more important in shaping human psychology, behaviour and society? The debate generated considerable heat and invective, but behind the straw men attacked by both sides there was a surprising amount of agreement. 'No serious student of human behaviour has denied the potent effect of evolved biology on our cultural lives,' Stephen Jay Gould wrote in *An Urchin in the Storm*. 'Our struggle is to figure out how biology affects us, not whether it does.' The philosopher Janet Radcliffe Richards, a prominent supporter of evolutionary psychology, agreed. 'The disagreement between evolutionary psychologists and standard social science theorists,' she argued in *Human Nature after Darwin*, 'is not about whether the environment influences what we are but only about the extent to which an understanding of evolutionary origins can help show how and to what extent this happens.'

Meanwhile, sociobiology itself transmuted into evolutionary psychology, partly so as to avoid the political opprobrium attached to the old label. In 1992 three academics, Leda Cosmides, John Tooby and Jerome Barkow, edited a collection of papers under the title *The Adapted Mind*, a seminal work that laid the foundations of the new science of human nature. Like Darwin in *The Expressions of the Emotions*, evolutionary psychologists sought both to ground human psychology in animal nature and to demonstrate the universality of human behaviour.

The fieldwork of animal behaviourists has, in recent years, revealed the enormous complexity of the social life of animals, especially primates. For instance, Frans de Waal's fascinating studies of chimpanzees at Arnhem zoo, described in books such as *Good Natured* and *Chimpanzee Politics*, often read like a cross between *Dynasty* and *King Lear*, an invitation to enter a world of generous friendships, treacherous alliances and bitter power struggles. The subtitles of his books – *The Origins of Right and Wrong in Humans and Other Animals* and *Power and Sex among Apes* – tell their own story. For de Waal, the lives of great apes open a window on to the roots of human politics and morality. A stream of books by other primatologists – Andrew Whiten and Richard Byrne's *Machiavellian Intelligence*, David Premack's *The Mind of an Ape*, Richard Wrangham's *Demonic Males*, Robert Sapolsky's *A Primate's Memoir*, Marian Stamp Dawkins's *Through Our Eyes Only?* – have all tried to use the lives of primates to shine a light on the human condition.

If the study of animal lives has provided one source of data for the new science of human nature, the study of human lives across cultural divides has supplied another. Even though human beings are 'morally free to make and remake themselves infinitely,' Matt Ridley argues in *The Red Queen*, 'we do not do so. We stick to the same monotonously human pattern of organising our affairs. If we were more adventurous, there would be societies without love, without ambition, without sexual desire, without marriage, without art, without grammar, without smiles.' Such societies don't exist because love, desire and the rest are evolved traits, and so are common to all humans. Discover universal traits, the argument runs, and you are likely to have discovered evolved characteristics.

Darwin himself had enlisted the help of dozens of missionaries and colonial officers in writing *The Expression of the Emotions*, asking them to describe the way non-Europeans expressed certain emotions, in order to demonstrate that 'all the chief expressions exhibited by man are the same throughout the world'. In the 1960s, Paul Ekman updated Darwin's work by showing photographs of different facial expressions to people in 21 different cultures. Overwhelmingly, Ekman's subjects, irrespective of culture, attributed the same emotions to each expression. Ekman's studies, detailed in a series of books including *The Face of Man* and *Emotions Revealed*, have become classics in the field. More recently, Marc Hauser has posed fiendish moral conundrums to people across different cultures. In his book *Moral Minds*, Hauser argues that not only has 'nature designed a universal sense of wrong and right', but that humans are universally sensitive to the Kantian imperative that one should not treat people solely as means, but primarily as ends.

In the wake of the attacks of 11 September 2001, religion has become a key theme in the new science of human nature. Its universality and persistence has led many writers – notably Sam Harris in *The End of Faith*, Daniel Dennett in *Breaking the Spell* and Richard Dawkins in *The God Delusion* – to see religion as an evolutionary hangover that has become maladaptive. All three books draw heavily on the work of anthropologist Scott Atran who, in his book *In Gods We Trust*, suggests that humans in all cultures possess an evolved desire for supernatural explanations.

However, the universal trait that lies at the heart of evolutionary psychology is sexual difference. As David Buss suggests in *The Evolution of Desire: The Strategies of Human Mating*, men and women can be viewed almost as distinct species. Men and women have different evolutionary strategies and thus have evolved different traits. 'Women's minds evolved to suit the demands of bearing and rearing children and of gathering plant food,' Matt Ridley wrote in *The Red Queen*. 'Men's minds evolved to suit the demands of rising in a male hierarchy, fighting over women and providing meat for a family.' Men tend to be promiscuous, aggressive, risk-taking and spatially aware; women monogamous, co-operative, nurturing and linguistically advanced. For critics of evolutionary psychology, however, such arguments merely confirm the ideological character of the research programme.

By the mid 1990s the map of human nature had been transformed. Where once the idea of human nature was treated with suspicion and ridicule, now there was barely a human activity for which someone did not have an evolutionary account. Human nature had been fully restored to discussions of human behaviour, political policy and social organisation. Darwinism, as former London School of Economics director John Ashworth has put it, has become 'an "ism" for our times'.

But the restoration of human nature to public debate, and the increasing importance of science in defining the boundaries of that nature, has not made any easier the question of how we understand what it means to be human. Few people would deny that humans are animals; evolved beings with evolved bodies and evolved minds. Equally, few would deny that humans are in some fashion distinct

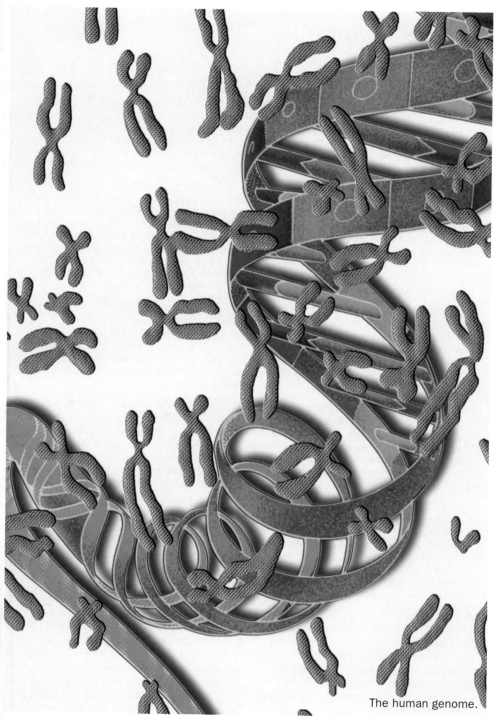

The human genome.

BIRTH

Critics' choice
Innocence

As If by Blake Morrison

After reporting on the trial of the two ten-year-old boys who, in 1993, abducted and killed a toddler, James Bulger, Morrison was haunted by the case. As he explains, 'Murder trials are about Where and When and How, not Why'; As If is his attempt to find some kind of answer, and to unravel a story of innocence lost.

Daisy Miller by Henry James

Daisy's naive, flirtatious ways scandalise European polite society and bemuse her fellow American, Winterbourne. Is she designing and unscrupulous, or simply an innocent abroad? Finding her out alone with an admirer late one night, he finally makes up his mind; by the time her innocence is vindicated, it's all too late.

The Death of the Heart by Elizabeth Bowen

Following the death of her mother and father, 16-year-old Portia Quayne arrives in London to live with her uncle. Here, she falls in love with Eddie, a handsome opportunist; the betrayals she subsequently suffers give the novel its title.

The Inheritors by William Golding

Golding's second novel, an imaginative tour de force, is written from the perspective of a group of Neanderthals. Their innocence is in thrown into sharp relief as they encounter the aggressive, more 'advanced' Homo sapiens for the first time; corruption, it seems, is the price of evolutionary progress.

Innocence by Penelope Fitzgerald

Jewel-like and perfectly formed, Innocence is set in Italy in the 16th and 20th centuries. Two families of contrasting fortune and pedigree collide when Chiara Ridolfi falls for the older Salvatore Rossi. Both lovers are innocents in their way, despite the difference in age.

Oliver Twist by Charles Dickens

Never was a child so constitutionally unsuited to a life of crime as the unfortunate Oliver. Prone to tears and implausibly guileless, at times he seems more of a cipher than a flesh-and-blood boy – and is a positive liability on his one and only pickpocketing expedition.

The Railway Children by E Nesbit

After their father is imprisoned for selling state secrets to Russia, Roberta, Peter and Phyllis are taken to live in a small town in Yorkshire by their mother. There, they discover the innocent pleasures afforded by the nearby railway tracks. They watch trains thunder past, wave at the passengers, and form an important friendship with one regular commuter...

The Social Contract by Jean-Jacques Rousseau

'Man is born free; and everywhere he is in chains.' The social contract, Rousseau argues, is a remedy for the corruption by greed and meanness of the perfect 'state of nature' into which men are born.

Songs of Innocence and Experience by William Blake

Blake's cycle of poems describes 'two contrary states of the soul', embodied in 'The Lamb' and 'The Tyger'. Innocence, in Blake's telling, is a state of childlike immediacy in which man and God are in perfect harmony.

The Way I Found Her by Rose Tremain

Fourteen-year-old narrator Lewis Little and his mother, Alice, move to Paris for the holidays: she to work, he for adventure. Evoking both the heat of a Parisian summer and that of a passionate first love, Tremain's novel is a genuine page-turner.

from other animals. 'We are built as gene machines,' Richard Dawkins wrote in *The Selfish Gene*, but we also possess 'the power to turn against our creators. We alone on earth can rebel against the tyranny of the selfish replicators.' Steven Pinker, meanwhile, has described himself as 'by Darwinian standards... a horrible mistake'. Why? Because he has chosen to remain childless. 'I am happy to be that way,' he adds, 'and if my genes don't like it they can go and jump in the lake.'

But here is the rub. If we are built as gene-machines, how do we possess the power to 'turn against our creators', or to tell our genes to 'go jump in the lake'? If a horse or a chimp told its genes to go take a jump, it would not survive very long in evolutionary terms. So how is it possible for humans to act like this? Pinker explains it like this in *How the Mind Works*: 'The mechanistic stance allows us to understand what makes us tick and how we fit into the physical universe. When those discussions wind down for the day, we go back to talking about each other as free and dignified human beings.'

But freedom and dignity here have no relationship to the physical world, and hence to human nature. They seem to float free in a universe of their own. 'First we are told that our genes know what is best for us, that they control our lives, programming every little wheel in the human survival machine,' Frans de Waal observes in *The Ape and the Sushi Master*. 'But then the same authors let us know we have the option to rebel, that we are free to act differently… These authors want to have it both ways: human behaviour is an evolutionary product except when it is hard to explain.'

The real problem, as neurologist and writer Raymond Tallis suggests in his wonderful book *The Explicit Animal*, is that we lack an adequate framework in which to explore what it is to be human. Like every other organism, humans are shaped by both nature and nurture. But unlike any other organism, we are also defined by our ability to transcend both, by our capacity to overcome the constraints imposed by our genetic inheritance and our cultural heritage.

It is not that human beings have floated free of the laws of causation; rather, humans are more than just the product of a chain of causes, whether natural or environmental. We have developed the capacity to intervene actively in nature and culture, able to shape both to our will. We are biological beings, and thus live under the purview of biological and physical laws. But we are also conscious beings with purpose and agency, traits that allow us to design ways of breaking – or at least easing – the constraints of biological and physical laws. To misquote Coriolanus, it seems that to be human is both to be such a gosling to obey instinct *and* to stand as if a man were author of himself.

Darwinian bulldog: **Richard Dawkins**.

Stranger
than fiction

Roz Kaveney ventures into the realms of science fiction and fantasy.

Stories are born when we ask 'What if?' Finding new ways to say it is how stories are made new. We make stories new by finding new settings in time and space – places beyond the fields we know. Science fiction and fantasy are full of settings endlessly reassembled in configurations that feel new-minted and console with their familiar strangeness. They are fictions that are at once born and reborn.

The great originals of SF and fantasy, from Mary Shelley's *Frankenstein* on, have lives all their own, which lie in part beyond the text. This is particularly true of HG Wells's *The War of the Worlds*, which took late Victorian neurosis about the military build-up in Europe and the imperial smugness that came from knowing we had the machine gun, and people with brown skins and scimitars did not, and shook all those fears and certainties in the air. Vast, implacable intelligences with death rays and walking machines and a taste for our blood kick over London and the Home Counties, and then die, like malarial traders in the White Man's Grave. It is the least obviously literary of Wells's great SF novels – a despatch from the front written out of exhaustion and in horror, shock and awe.

Not all of the grandly influential originals of our dreams are well known, however. Hope Mirrlees's *Lud-in-the-Mist* came out of 1920s Bloomsbury and has remained a quietly lingering flavour ever since in the minds of modern writers like Neil Gaiman and Susanna Clarke. Again, it is a tale of smugness overthrown – the inhabitants of a comfortable bourgeois town in a late medieval/Renaissance neverwhere find that you can't repress the unconscious forever: what has been expelled will always return. Mirrlees's is one of the funniest and most charming handlings of one of fantasy's grand themes, the reconciliation of faerie and the mundane.

Fantasy's other great theme – the quest for the cure of the world's pain – found its classic telling in a book so obvious it is like a mountain range: you can't go round JRR Tolkien's *The Lord of the Rings*, so you just have to accept it as a massive conservative reaction to the trenches and the suburbanisation of the countryside, and read it for its many thrilling moments. And afterwards, as an antidote to the twee that creeps into both Tolkien and Mirrlees, you can read the gritty medieval gloom of George RR Martin's *Song of Ice and Fire*, the decadent bleakness of M John Harrison's *Viriconium* or else the sardonic caper-movie tales of Fritz Leiber's *Books of Lankhmar*, none of which has any damn nonsense about redemption to it.

One of SF's great forms is the planetary romance, in which people go somewhere very different and learn about themselves in the process. Probably the very best of these is Ursula K LeGuin's *The Left Hand of Darkness*, a profound consideration of gender and culture, as well as a gruelling trek through the snow. Another important mode is the space opera, where people hurtle around the galaxy between battles at breakneck speed. The modern master of this sort of thing is Iain M Banks in his *Culture* novels, the pick of which is probably *Excession* (not least because it so bemused Nick Hornby, who was asked to review it for an American literary magazine). Gene Wolfe's vast *Book of the New Sun* combines elements of planetary romance and space opera with a

Orson Welles scares America in the radio broadcast of **The War of the Worlds**.

terrifyingly artistic collage of Borges, Dickens and the traditional folktale, beginning with its hero's training as a torturer and executioner.

The other thing SF does well is awful warnings – Orwell's *1984* and Huxley's *Brave New World* have long been adopted by the genre, though most SF writers would have the resistance bust Winston Smith out before the rats get his soul. Alfred Bester's *The Stars My Destination* is a glossy tale of revenge, war, tattoos and teleportation; it also says some worthwhile things about class, capitalism and their contradictions. John Brunner's *Stand on Zanzibar* is a stunning panorama of what seems like now but was in fact imagined in 1968. Meanwhile, Philip K Dick's many gloriously paranoid novels – *A Scanner Darkly* for example – are about how drugs and robots can both break and liberate our souls.

William Gibson's *Neuromancer*, the grand original of cyberpunk, may be a style icon and accessory these days, but it's also a terrifying book about people struggling to live in a war economy where every skill is a commodity. At its best, cyberpunk was always about class struggle; Pat Cadigan's *Synners* is another good example, as is Kim Stanley Robinson's *Red Mars* trilogy.

Much of the best modern fantasy is about the present and its discontents, whatever the setting. Terry Pratchett's *Discworld* novels are not just about wizards and dragons; they're also scathing satires on religious intolerance and militarism. Elizabeth Hand's *Waking the Moon* is a critique both of patriarchal sexism and the murderous spite that is a possible response to it; it is also a tale of secrets uncovered and scholarship turned to danger that makes Dan Brown's novels read like Ladybird books. Even everyone's favourite quasi-literary fantasy of recent years, Susanna Clarke's *Jonathan Strange and Mr Norrell*, is an intensely moral fiction about taking advantage of other people and what a bad idea that usually turns out to be.

Mary Shelley: the first SF novelist?

Critics' choice
Opening lines

The Adventures of Augie March by Saul Bellow
'I am an American, Chicago born – Chicago, that somber city – and go at things as I have taught myself, free-style, and will make the record in my own way: first to knock, first admitted; sometimes an innocent knock, sometimes a not so innocent.' It was here that Bellow first made Chicago his muse and unleashed the fizzing combination of low slang and high thought that would become his trademark.

Anna Karenina by Leo Tolstoy
'Happy families are all alike; every unhappy family is unhappy in its own way.' Tolstoy anatomises with beautiful and brutal precision Anna's unhappinesses – in her marriage to Karenin and in her affair with Vronsky.

The Bible
'In the beginning God created the heaven and the earth.' The most famous opening line in the Western canon. The cadences of the Authorised Version saturate English literature.

The Communist Manifesto by Karl Marx & Friedrich Engels
'A spectre is haunting Europe – the spectre of Communism.' The end of this celebrated little tract is almost as famous and stirring as that opening, exhorting the proletariat to throw off their chains and claim the world for themselves.

In Search of Lost Time by Marcel Proust
'For a long time I used to go to bed early.' In Proust's seven-volume masterpiece. Marcel, the narrator, does not actively remember his childhood at Combray; he recovers it accidentally when he is transported by the taste of a piece of madeleine steeped in tea.

Invisible Man by Ralph Ellison
'I am an invisible man.' Ellison's narrator is not a spook, he is made of flesh and blood. And he is black. Written in the early 1950s, *Invisible Man* abandons the sober naturalism of the 'negro novel' of the '30s for something altogether richer and more inventive.

Lolita by Vladimir Nabokov
'Lolita, light of my life, fire of my loins.' Lolita is a 12-year-old enchantress in penny loafers.

The author of this paean? Humbert Humbert, a middle-aged admirer as ardent as any pubescent boy – and altogether more lyrical.

Metamorphosis by Franz Kafka
'As Gregor Samsa awoke one morning from uneasy dreams he found himself transformed in his bed into a gigantic insect.' Whatever the allegorical significance of this peculiar tale, you can't help but be mesmerised by the crystalline purity of Kafka's prose.

Middlesex by Jeffrey Eugenides
'I was born twice: first, as a baby girl, on a remarkably smogless Detroit day in January of 1960; and then again, as a teenage boy, in an emergency room near Petoskey, Michigan, in August of 1974.' So begins Eugenides's epic tale of gender change and coming of age

1984 by George Orwell
'It was a bright cold day in April, and the clocks were striking thirteen.' That horological anomaly lets the reader know that an alternative reality obtains in Oceania, one in which 'War is Peace, Freedom is Slavery' and 'Ignorance is Strength.'

Pride and Prejudice by Jane Austen
'It is a truth universally acknowledged, that a single man in possession of a good fortune, must be in want of a wife.' This imperishable first line is entirely typical of the 'playfulness and general epigrammatism' of Austen's style.

The Satanic Verses by Salman Rushdie
'"To be born again," sang Gibreel Farishta tumbling from the heavens, "first you have to die."' Farishta survives a mid-air explosion, only to emerge apparently transformed into the archangel Gibreel. It is Gibreel's delusional dreams of the prophet Muhammad that caught the attention of the mullahs in Tehran.

A Portrait of the Artist as a Young Man by James Joyce
'Once upon a time and a very good time it was there was a moocow coming down along the road and this moocow that was coming down along the road met a nicens little boy named baby tuckoo.' The protagonist of Joyce's early coming-of-age novel, Stephen Dedalus, will later appear in *Ulysses*.

BIRTH

Childhood

'*Then the whining schoolboy, with his satchel And shining morning face, creeping like snail Unwillingly to school.*'

Telling
tales

Adèle Geras suggests page-turners for all ages.

Think of me as a kind of pedlar shouting my wares. The children's book market is a strange one. There are a few books that everyone has heard of (the *Harry Potter* volumes, *Horrid Henry*, *Tracy Beaker*); a few writers who are household names (Pullman, Wilson, Morpurgo) and another handful who'd be recognised if they ventured into their local supermarket. Behind them, the massed ranks of the other children's books – a huge, sprawling, proliferating crowd of them – clamour for attention, and not many people are interested in those. It's my mission to pull a few writers and their works out of the mass and show them off, in the hope that readers will be encouraged to be adventurous – to look beyond the top of the bestseller lists.

Children's books get a raw deal when it comes to criticism. The reason people don't know much about what's available is because the print media, radio and television don't devote much attention to what are perceived

by many as books that are not quite up to scratch, not quite as good as those written for adults. There are a few blogs that take children's books seriously, but the Great British Public is still, mostly, blissfully unaware of the glories awaiting them.

Let's begin, then, with the youngest readers. Many people feel that it must be the simplest thing in the world to write a picture book. They don't contain very many words, after all, so how hard can it be? The answer is: very hard indeed. These are the books that will be read aloud countless times, and every syllable counts.

In *The Big Red Bath* by Julia Jarman (with illustrations by Adrian Reynolds), two children and a whole collection of animals have a bath. Splashy delights all round, with a jaunty, jolly, very catchy rhyming text, accompanied by bold, bright pictures.

Everyone, including Gordon Brown, knows the wonderful *Gruffalo*, and Julia Donaldson and Axel Scheffler, the author and illustrator

Children's author as household name: **Philip Pullman**.

of this classic, are in fact bestsellers and well loved. *Room on the Broom* from the same pair is also a super book, and deserves to be just as famous.

The *Bing* books, written and illustrated by Ted Dewan, ought to be much better known than they are. They're exactly the right size for small hands; there are lots of them, so you can collect the set; and Bing Bunny and his friend Flop have many domestic adventures. There are very few words, but the ones Dewan uses are just right. Bing is a real star and ought to be in every two and three year old's bookshelf. Try *Go Picnic* and move seamlessly on to the others.

Where Are You, Blue Kangaroo?, written and illustrated by Emma Chichester Clark, is also one in a series. The eponymous Kangaroo belongs to Lily, and lives in the most beautifully-coloured world you've ever seen. The heart lifts at the singing shades of pink and blue in this story and the others in the set. You'll want to own them all once you've tried your first one.

Every child needs a good nursery-rhyme book. *The Mother Goose Treasury* by Raymond Briggs is now out of print, but Macmillan has published *Mother Goose's Nursery Rhymes*, a lovely collection illustrated by Axel Scheffler. An anthology of this kind ought to be handed out to all new parents on the National Health. Start saying these rhymes to your child as soon as they're born and keep on saying them. If you can sing them, so much the better. Your offspring will thank you for it.

A book that changed my life

Jasper Fforde

Alice in Wonderland & Alice Through the Looking Glass by Lewis Carroll

Learning to read, like learning to walk and talk, is one of life's Great Expanders. I can remember acquiring this skill, and also the realisation that this was something pretty important. I set about finding a book in my parent's library to flex this newly found power. I didn't want the boring stuff that grown-ups read but a proper book, with chapters, dialogue and pictures. And there it was – *The Complete Alice*. I fell into the books and was immediately dazzled by the virtuosity of the nonsense and the humorous warmth that runs through the pages – from the Red Queen to the Cheshire Cat to the *Jabberwocky*, possibly the finest piece of nonsense poetry ever written. Thus sated, I moved on to other reading adventures, and regarded the series as nothing more than 24-carat juvenilia until a decade or two later, when I discovered to my amazement that the books had changed. Yes, the old stuff I remembered was still there, but there was something else. Something new, subtle, clever and wonderful, hovering in the shadows of the subtext – puzzles of logic, physics and metalanguage. I can't think of a book that has influenced me more. Not simply as an author, but as a person: the value of humour, the boundlessness of the human imagination and how rich life's experience can be, as long as one is willing to look – and be receptive enough to notice when you find it. I still have that very same volume in my library today, and do you know, I think it's still changing.

Jasper Fforde's latest book is First Among Sequels *(Viking).*

ALICE'S ADVENTURES IN WONDERLAND
'Precise, dream-like, subversive'
Quentin Blake, *Independent on Sunday*
LEWIS CARROLL

The much-loved **Gruffalo**.

'When you're young and in a collecting frame of mind, a series is always good.'

Lovers of fairy tales are spoilt for choice. Steer clear of Disneyfications and try the magnificent collection retold by Berlie Doherty, *Fairy Tales*, illustrated by Jane Ray. Then, when your child is familiar with a few of the best stories, try a very enjoyable book called *Tom Trueheart* by Ian Beck, with the author's own illustrations.

This is a story about a family of fairy-tale heroes. Suddenly, they disappear. They're not available to provide happy endings. Before things go really pear-shaped in the land of stories, Tom, the youngest in the family, sets off to see what's become of his brothers and save the day. The book is full of wit and laughter and few thrills and shivers too, and Beck's drawings are just right, as always.

The Sign on Rosie's Door, written and illustrated by the incomparable Maurice Sendak, is a masterpiece. It's about nothing much more than a gang of children playing on a hot day in Brooklyn, but this could be any set of kids from anywhere. The story is funny, perfectly observed and unforgettable. I can't imagine anyone not loving it, and when you've sought it out, there's the rest of Maurice Sendak (including the celebrated *Where the Wild Things Are*) to explore.

Frog and Toad, the protagonists of *The Frog and Toad Collection*, written and illustrated by Arnold Lobel, are two of the most endearing characters in children's fiction. They're friends and have small adventures together. That's it. That's enough. These short, brilliantly written pieces will teach any five year old all she needs to know at that age about life, the universe and everything.

The Quigleys by Simon Mason is about an ordinary family with added humour, madness, originality and fun. These books are just right for newly competent readers and their parents to laugh about together. Again, it's a series, which is always good when you're young and in a collecting frame of mind.

For slightly older children, and by an author who's better known for her excellent books for teenagers, try Linda Newbery's *Catcall*. This deals with sibling rivalry and the fascination we have with wild animals, and observes how families help one another and tear one another to pieces, often at the same time. It's also full of fascinating details about the cat family, both in the wild and in the home, and it's beautifully produced, with a shining golden cover.

Hilary McKay's books about the Masson family are terrific, every one of them. The one that I like best is *Permanent Rose*, but the others are great too, so try them all. The Massons are a bohemian family. The father, an artist, has left home, and the children are making the best of life in a family whose unconventional behaviour is most touchingly portrayed. These books will give anyone over nine many hours of pleasure.

It's high time someone blew the trumpet for Jean Ure, who has been writing every sort of book imaginable for more than 30 years. She can be dark (*Bad Alice* is about child abuse), and she was the first person to write about a boy doing ballet (in *A Proper Little Nooryeff*), but her latest books are funny and sharp, and they appeal to young teenagers who want something with a bit of intelligence to it that is also easy to read. Try *The Secret Life of Sally Tomato* and *Boys Beware*. If you like those, there are many others – Ure is one of the most prolific writers around.

Anne Fine has been writing splendid children's books for years and years, and has won every conceivable prize. Older readers should try *Road of Bones,* a bleak and gripping story about an unnamed country where a terrifying dictatorship is in power. The landscape is Russia-like and the detail and careful accumulation of horrors make this a powerful and readable fable about the consequences of tyranny. Have a warm blanket handy: it's one of the chilliest books in years, and completely unputdownable.

Kevin Brooks's latest exciting thriller is called *Road of Death*. There's a bit of an 'as if' in the denouement, but till you get there you're on the edge of your seat all the way. It's the story of two brothers whose sister has been murdered. It doesn't pull its punches, and the world it depicts is a dark one. This is a very well-written, tense novel that will enthrall both boys and girls.

Once by Maurice Gleitzman is a heart-rending memoir of the Warsaw Ghetto, told in the voice of a boy, Felix, whose parents hid him in a convent for safety. The book is based on extensive research, and it's a good addition to the fiction that deals with the experience of children during the Holocaust.

Anyone looking for a romantic novel that is more than simply a clichéd, run-of-the-mill tale of boy meets girl should try Celia Rees's *The Wish House*. This is a superb coming-of-age novel about sexual awakening, families and art. Rees writes historical novels as well, and *Pirates* is a female take on the buccaneering trade that is both moving and thrilling.

Lovers of historical fiction are spoilt for choice. Ann Turnbull has written two novels about the persecution of the Quakers in the 17th century which are masterly evocations of the time, meticulously researched but written in a simple, direct style that welcomes in readers both young and old. *No Shame, No Fear* and *Forged in the Fire* tell of the love between Will and Susanna, and how they manage to overcome the obstacles that society puts in their way.

Then there's the fast-moving, exciting and exuberant *The Life and Times of Eliza Rose* by Mary Hooper. It takes us into the world of Nell Gwyn, her relationship with King Charles, and very much more besides. *The Whispering Road* and *The Angel Stone*, both by Livi Michael, take us back to Manchester in the days before it became the first industrial city in the world. It's a fascinating fictional universe, and Michael brings it vividly to life.

Mal Peet's *Tamar* won the Carnegie Medal in 2006. It's a novel set both in Holland during World War II and in the present day. The double perspective in fiction is something Peet is fond of, and again uses to very good effect in *Penalty*. The story moves between modern-day Brazil and the same country in the past, when the slave trade was still a flourishing commercial concern. This is a novel about football, voodoo and the past coming back to haunt the present. It's a thriller and a ghost story, and also a story of a young star of the beautiful game who suddenly stops being able to perform on the pitch. This is one to try on boys who think they don't like reading. It's edge-of-seat stuff, but with a heart.

KING
DORK

frank portman

0-385-73291-0 ✳ IN U.S $15.95 (IN CANADA $22.95) ✳ A DELACORTE BOOK

It's easy to see from the books I've chosen that I'm not a lover of fantasy, but unusual versions of fairy tales are quite another matter. *Beauty* by Robin McKinley is beautifully written, and you'll never think of the Beast in the same way again. Fabulous. *Clockwork* by Philip Pullman is amazing, astonishing, breathtaking and spooky in the extreme. It's my favourite of all his books, and no one should miss it. He's managed to do the almost impossible: create a memorable fairy tale from scratch. Carol Ann Duffy, the poet, has also done this. Her postmodern story *The Lost Happy Endings* is perplexing, weird, beautiful and strange, but beware of buying it for very young children. Among Jane Ray's vibrant illustrations are a couple of really disturbing images of a witch that might not go down too well at bedtime.

Humour is very much a matter of personal taste, but here are three books that made me laugh. The first, an oldie-but-goodie by the late, great Jan Mark, is *They Do Things Differently There*. This is a masterpiece of surrealism. No plot summary can do it justice, but try it if you enjoy the seriously weird and hilarious. I don't know why it hasn't become a cult among teenagers. Maybe it still can. *Goldkeeper* by Sally Prue mixes religion, crime, school and celebrity in a very clever book that children will love. It has chases, gangsters, sport and music. What else could you possibly want? *The Pig Who Saved the World* by Paul Shipton is super. I've written two novels myself inspired by the *Iliad* and the *Odyssey,* and so I'm drawn to this very funny and original take on the Homeric oeuvre. The pig who narrates the story is Gryllus, and his work is called the *Grylliad* – well, it would be, wouldn't it? Homer himself appears in this version: a teenage poet with more than a passing resemblance to Bob Dylan. It's great stuff.

Finally, a mention for *King Dork* by Frank Portman. It's a corker. The narrator is King Dork himself, a teenage boy who is having certain problems at school, not least with the book that every American teenager has to read at some stage or another: *The Catcher in the Rye* by JD Salinger. What he has to say about his life, his family, his one friend and the girl he is trying desperately to meet will keep you laughing and crying all the way, and at the end you'll be punching the air in sheer exhilaration. It's a real tour de force.

CHILDHOOD

20 classic children's books

Anne of Green Gables
by Lucy Maud Montgomery

The lives of two staid elderly siblings, Matthew and Marilla Cuthbert, are turned upside down when they adopt an orphaned boy – and are sent a girl instead. Despite 11-year-old Anne's irrepressible chatter ('For pity's sake hold your tongue,' the acerbic Marilla tells her. 'You talk entirely too much for a little girl.'), they decide that she can stay at Green Gables.

Ballet Shoes by Noel Streatfield

Pauline, Petrova and Posy are three orphans, adopted by an eccentric fossil collector, Gum (short for Great Uncle Matthew), and looked after by his great niece Sylvie and her old nurse, Nana. When Gum disappears and money becomes tight, their boarder has an inspired idea: the girls can enrol at the Children's Academy of Dancing and Stage Training, and train for stage careers to keep the family finances afloat.

Black Beauty by Anna Sewell

The story quite literally comes from the horse's mouth in Sewell's equestrian tale, as thoroughbred Black Beauty narrates his life story. Sewell's attempt to draw attention to animal cruelty found immediate success – although the noble beast was later gleefully satirised by Spike Milligan. ('As soon as I was old enough to eat grass, my mother used to stuff it down my throat until it kept coming out the back.')

The Borrowers by Mary Norton

Pod, Homily and Arrietty Clock are the Borrowers: a family of tiny people who live behind the grandfather clock in an old rectory. In their world, a postage stamp is a painting, and stacked match boxes create a roomy chest of drawers. They live in mortal fear of being seen by the 'human beans' they scavenge from – until young Arriety strikes up a forbidden friendship.

Charlotte's Web by EB White

The classic story of the friendship between a lonely pig, Wilbur, and a barn spider called Charlotte. Realising that her friend is destined for a grisly fate, Charlotte concocts an ingenious plan to save his bacon.

The Enchanted Wood by Enid Blyton

Climbing the Faraway Tree takes Jo, Bessie and Fanny into incredible, magical worlds – from the gloriously anarchic Land-of-Take-What-You-Want to the highly unpleasant Land of Dame Slap. At the end of each adventure, they slide to the bottom of the tree on Moon Face's helter-skelter, the Slippery-Slip.

James and the Giant Peach by Roald Dahl

There's no mistaking Dahl's relish for the macabre and grotesque in this splendidly surreal tale. Orphaned after his parents are eaten by a rhino, James is sent to live with his sadistic aunts, Spiker and Sponge. A massive magical fruit and its extraordinary occupants provides our hero with an unlikely means of escape – and fortuitously crushes his aunts on the way.

The Jungle Book by Rudyard Kipling

Abandoned 'man cub' Mowgli is raised by wolves in the Indian jungle. Befriended by Baloo, a sleepy grey bear, and Bagheera, a black panther, his sworn enemy is the evil Shere Khan. The book's combination of moral lessons and derring-do made it a favourite with Sir Robert Baden-Powell, who incorporated its ideas and character names into the Cub Scouts movement.

The Lion, the Witch and the Wardrobe
by CS Lewis

'She took a step further in – then two or three steps – always expecting to feel woodwork against the tips of her fingers. But she could not feel it.' The thrilling moment when Lucy Pevensie's groping fingers find that the musty fur coats in the wardrobe have turned into the prickly, snow-covered branches of Narnia is unforgettable. Generations of children have fallen in love with Lewis's classic story – and blithely failed to detect its theological resonances.

The Little Prince by Antoine de Saint-Exupéry

Grown-ups, in Saint-Exupéry's poetic, beautifully illustrated tale, are foolish creatures, but 'One must not hold it against them. Children should always show great forbearance toward grown-up people.'

Peter Pan by JM Barrie

'All children, except one, grow up.' So begins the timeless story of Peter Pan, the enchanting, adult-hating leader of the Lost Boys, who persuades Wendy and her little brothers to leave their home and fly to Neverland with him. But this is no saccharine fairy tale: Peter's cruel streak and Mrs Darling's distress at finding her children gone are disturbingly dark.

The Phantom Tollbooth by Norton Juster

After driving through a mysterious purple tollbooth in his toy car, Milo finds himself in the Kingdom of Wisdom. Accompanied by the faithful watchdog Tock (who has a clock for a body), he embarks on a quest to rescue the princesses Rhyme and Reason.

The Secret Garden
by Frances Compton-Burnett

Brought up in India, the spoiled and sickly Mary Lennox is sent to live with her uncle in Yorkshire after her parents die. She hates it – until she finds the key to an overgrown, abandoned walled garden.

The Silver Sword by Iain Seraillier

In the chaos of World War II, the Balicki family is torn apart. When the war is over, Ruth, Edek and

Critics' choice
Scary children

Bad Influence by William Sutcliffe
Ben and Olly are ten and best friends. Their north London suburban idyll is destroyed when Carl arrives in the street. Carl doesn't go to school, he 'attends a unit'. Soon, he has Ben and Olly under his spell.

Border Crossing by Pat Barker
When the novel opens, Danny Miller, now an adolescent, is succumbing to the icy waters of the River Tyne. He is saved by Tom Seymour, a child psychologist who'd been a witness at the ten-year-old Danny's trial for murder.

deadkidsongs by Toby Litt
Andrew, Paul, Matthew and Peter are in a gang – not just any gang, but 'Gang'. They're a quasi-military outfit, goaded by Andrew's extremely sinister father, whom they call the 'Major-General'. Gang swears revenge when Matthew dies suddenly from meningitis.

Lord of the Flies by William Golding
Golding's astonishing literary debut, published in 1954, has lost none of its power to shock. What happens when a group of boys are left stranded on an island following a plane crash, with no adult authority? Nothing very pleasant, it emerges, as their attempts at creating a democracy break down and savagery prevails.

The Midwich Cuckoos by John Wyndham
The village of Midwich is inexplicably cut off from the outside world for 24 hours, and its inhabitants fall unconscious. Nine months later, all the women give birth to blonde, golden-eyed children – the ruthless 'cuckoos' of the title.

Spies by Michael Frayn
Stephen Wheatley looks back 50 years to his wartime childhood. His only friend is Keith Hayward, whom he quietly idolises. Things take a decided turn for the worse when Keith denounces his mother as a German spy.

The Turn of the Screw by Henry James
When a governess arrives at a country house, she is struck by the charm of her new charges, Flora and Miles. That impression is undone when the ghost of a former valet appears.

We Need to Talk about Kevin by Lionel Shriver
Biased as Kevin's mother might be, she paints a damning picture of her infant son, who cries from sheer malice, shows an uncanny ability for manipulation from an early age, and quickly learns that caring about nothing makes him all-powerful. In retrospect, buying him a crossbow for Christmas wasn't a wise move.

Bronia set off on a desperate journey across the desolate, war-torn landscape, accompanied by the orphaned Jan, to try to find their mother.

Stig of the Dump by Clive King
Rooting around a disused chalk pit one day, Barney comes face to face with a rather fierce-looking boy in an animal pelt, who carries a bow and arrow. Stig is a caveman – and the fact that he can't speak doesn't prevent him and Barney from becoming firm friends.

Swallows and Amazons by Arthur Ransome
Holidaying beside a lake, the Walker children sail a dinghy named Swallow. The Blackett offspring, who live nearby, take to the water in Amazon. They meet for adventures on a sylvan idyll, Wild Cat Island.

Tom's Midnight Garden by Philippa Pearce
When the grandfather clock in the hallway strikes 13, time miraculously shifts back to the 19th century. Night after night, a pyjama-clad Tom creeps down to explore the huge sunlit garden that appears in place of the small back yard. It's here that he befriends the lonely Hatty – the only person who is able to see him.

Treasure Island by Robert Louis Stevenson
Henry James was among the admirers of Stevenson's swashbuckling tale of pirates, parrots and pieces of eight. Stevenson also came up with the convention of an X marking the location of buried treasure.

Watership Down by Richard Adams
A group of rabbits leave their warren in search of a new, safer home, with tragic consequences. The animated film traumatised a generation of children – just hum 'Bright Eyes' and watch them well up.

Winnie-the-Pooh by AA Milne
The irresistible adventures of 'a Bear of Very Little Brain'. Pooh's encounter with a Heffalump, attempts to track a Woozle and search for the morose Eeyore's lost tail make for excellent reading at any age.

ties School

CHILDHOOD

Peter Watts examines the enduring appeal of the school story.

Wellington might not have actually said that the 'Battle of Waterloo was won on the playing fields of Eton', but as misquotations go, it's not a bad place to begin an essay about school in English fiction. This sentiment – of the public school as the training ground for a certain kind of Englishman – has influenced almost all fiction written on educational institutions since Thomas Hughes kicked it all off with *Tom Brown's Schooldays*. It has been celebrated by some and criticised by others, parodied and rhapsodised over. Orwell and Larkin debated it – though not with each other, sadly – while Americans adapted it. Schoolchildren, meanwhile, have more or less ignored it, and simply got on with the serious business of enjoying the wizard japes, priceless pranks and assorted capers of the various 'swots, bullies, sissies, milksops, greedy guts and oiks' (*pace* Nigel Molesworth) who make up the alumni of the English school story.

Based on Hughes's experiences under Dr Arnold at Rugby, *Tom Brown's Schooldays* is set, fittingly, at the dawn of the Victorian era (something that is ruthlessly and brilliantly exploited by George McDonald Fraser's *Flashman* novels). Almost unbearably moralistic, it follows Tom's progress at Rugby, where, along with his great friend Scud East, he clashes with louche bully Flashman and mentors the sickly George Arthur, while developing into the sort of young gentleman who was starting to shape a third of the world in his own image. Brown became the genre's archetypal hero – one with a well-developed sense of fair play, who knows his place but retains a whiff of independence, is honest to

a fault, dogged, sporting and sporty, hard-working but never too clever. This was the muscular Christianity that shaped an Empire.

Hughes was a Christian Socialist, and while some of his egalitarianism seeped into the text, the establishment understood the value of *Tom Brown*. 'It is difficult to estimate,' a reviewer in *The Times* enthused, 'the amount of good which may be done by *Tom Brown's Schooldays*. It gives in the main a most faithful and interesting picture of our public schools, the most English institutions in England, and which educate the best and most powerful elements in our upper classes. But it is more than this; it is an attempt… to Christianize the society of our youth through the only practicable channel – hearty and brotherly sympathy with their feelings; a book, in short, which a father might well wish to see in the hands of his son.'

A rather different reception awaited Rudyard Kipling's contribution to what became an established genre after the popularity of *Eric, or, Little by Little* (1858) by Frederic Farrar and Talbot Baines Reed's *The Fifth Form at St Dominic's* (1887). 'An unpleasant book about unpleasant boys at an unpleasant school', said George Sampson of *Stalky & Co*, and his was not the only dissenting voice. Somerset Maugham believed that 'a more odious picture of school life can seldom have been drawn', while another critic believed it 'impossible to show by mere quotation the horrible vileness of the book describing these three small fiends in human likeness… The vulgarity, the brutality, the savagery… reeks on every page.'

It's hard to understand today why *Stalky* so repelled such critics. Kipling's three heroes are manifestly the men who defined the Victorian era – the book is full of references to the characters' later imperial adventures. But Kipling writes openly about bullying, money and cold-hearted revenge, and his characters are adventurers rather than missionaries, as close to Flashman as they are to Tom Brown. Writes Isabel Quigly in the introduction to the Oxford World Classics edition: 'It took an empire not just to contain Stalky but to provide scope for his energy and qualities… *Stalky & Co* shows school as a direct preparation for life. Most others actually make the world outside school seem irrelevant, an anticlimax, an unimaginable void.'

The latter is a fine description of those weekly school stories directly inspired by *Stalky & Co* but stripped of Kipling's darker intent. Appearing in the boys' magazines of the early 20th century, the most memorable were the St Jim's stories of the *Gem* and the Greyfriars series featuring Billy Bunter in the *Magnet*.

Both were written by Charles Hamilton, who, using the pseudonyms Frank Richards and Martin Cliffords, produced school stories by the yard, earning a place in the *Guinness Book of Records* as the most prolific author of all time. While Hamilton borrowed the slang and atmosphere of Stalky, he placed it within a cosy, closeted England that later attracted the scorn of old Etonian George Orwell, who complained: 'In so far as Greyfriars and St Jim's are like real schools at all, they are much more like Tom Brown's Rugby than a modern public school… but without doubt the main origin of these papers is *Stalky and Co.*'

The stories are harmless enough, but Orwell was appalled that something so anachronistic – 'sodden in the worst illusions of 1910' – could be so popular, and alarmed that English boys should be 'absorbing a set of beliefs which would be regarded as hopelessly out of date in the Central Office of the Conservative Party'.

Tom Brown's Schooldays, the original tale of public school life...

CHILDHOOD

... and the **Ripping Yarns** spoof.

A book that changed my life

Jonathan Coe

Tom Jones by Henry Fielding

Henry Fielding's *Tom Jones* seems to have fallen out of fashion lately. I remember being shocked when some newspaper conducted a poll of international writers, asking them to name the greatest novels of all time, and *Tom Jones* didn't make the top 100. Today's readers seem to prefer Fielding's contemporary Samuel Richardson – perhaps because he does psychological realism in a way that Fielding doesn't; perhaps because he was in touch with his feminine side, and *Tom Jones* is now seen as a bit blokey. For me, anyway, this was the book that threw the door wide open on the novel's infinite possibilities. The plotting is complex, astonishing and perfect. The scale of the book takes your breath away. It brims with good nature and generosity of spirit. It is (and people tend to forget this) formally radical: throughout the novel, Fielding keeps up a running commentary on his own procedures as a writer, without once forfeiting our precious suspension of disbelief. At the same time, it excels at all the thrillingly vulgar devices without which a novel is dead on its feet: it's full of jokes, suspense, cliffhangers, narrative reversals and pathos.

It's years since I reread it (there are some books that you don't need to reread – they simply take up residence in your psyche), but I always keep a copy on the shelf above my desk, just so that, whenever a writing challenge looks too daunting, I can always ask myself: 'How would Fielding have done this?'

Jonathan Coe's latest novel is The Rain Before it Falls *(Penguin).*

CHILDHOOD

Doubtless Orwell would have been equally surprised by the appearance of *Jennings Goes To School* in 1950, the year he died and Atlee's Labour government began its second term. Anthony Buckeridge's books have a reputation for waywardness, but in truth they are mired in Bunteresque conservatism; watered-down Stalky with a dash of Tom Brown's earnestness. Here the familiar schoolboy code is writ in full: loyalty to school and friends; honesty without sneaking; and no room for snobbery, albeit from within the comfort zone of a fee-paying public school. While Jennings himself is often regarded as a rebel, in truth he is little more than high-spirited, displaying an unhealthy respect for teachers and an unnatural fondness for school: '[They]… were all very happy at Linbury, they liked all the masters and they knew that the rules of the school were made for their own enjoyment.'

Liked their masters! For their own enjoyment! Compare such contemptuously vanilla behaviour with that of English fiction's greatest schoolboy, William Brown, an anarchic ball of dirt and fury who spends almost every page of Richmal Crompton's *Just William* series in a state of outright war with the grown-up world, like an Edwardian ASBO waiting to happen. William, of course, benefited from never being sent to boarding school, and even in the recent school-centred collection, *Just William at School*, it's impressive how infrequently our hero actually attends class – indeed, he spends more time breaking into teachers' houses in search of confiscated items than he does studying. Whereas the stolid Jennings 'was no genius, but he did his best and managed to hold his own about halfway down the form', William had a rather different attitude to schoolwork, as we discover when 'Mr Strong set, for homework, more French than it was convenient for William to learn'.

Doubtless schooled in the classics of the genre, William's dutiful mother nonetheless remains ever hopeful, and in *Finding A School For William*, she tries to send her son to boarding school. 'Mrs Brown,' we learn, 'had a vague idea that some mysterious change of spirit came over a boy on entering the portals of boarding school transforming him from a young savage to a perfect gentleman.'

William, of course, is a cunning if ignoble savage, and the irony of it all is that while Jennings might present schoolchildren with

the better case study for the young English gentleman, Crompton's stories undoubtedly make for a more challenging, interesting and entertaining read. This has much to do with her recognition that, for most children, school is something to avoid as much as celebrate, an attitude that would have proved anathema to her female contemporaries playing it safe with the girls' school story.

Starting with Angela Brazil's *The Fortunes of Phillipa* in 1906, the girls' school story was not far removed from the boys'; the busy Charles Hamilton even tried his hand at them for a while, writing as Hilda Richards in *The School Friend* in a series that featured Billy

Girls rule at **St Trinian's**.

Bunter's sister, Bessie. Elsie Oxenham, Elinor Brent-Dyer and Dorita Fairlie Bruce were all widely read, but the best-known writer of girls' school stories is Enid Blyton, whose *Malory Towers* series following a pupil from first year to last was surely an influence on JK Rowling.

The schoolgirls' code was not much different from the schoolboys', and Rosemary Auchmuty puts up a robust defence of the genre in her critical study *A World Of Girls*. 'Loyalty and the team spirit had to fit into a scheme of teaching which represented a compromise between femininity and feminism... the girls' school stories reflect this uneasy compromise; they show how these values, hitherto seen as

masculine, were absorbed into the schoolgirl culture, but also how the feminine world refined and manoeuvred around them.'

This has led to the sort of sniggering epitomised by Julie Burchill writing about *Malory Towers*: 'Pashes, petulance, pillow fights – and the heroine is called "Darrell"! Hel-LO? Sub-textual dyke action ahoy.' Philip Larkin was aroused enough to pen the not-very-good semi-spoof *Trouble at Willow Gables* under the pen name Brunette Coleman, with much attention given to uniforms, French lessons and punishment. He also wrote an essay, in character, analysing the genre, rejecting Orwell's earlier criticism of the boys' version as 'ephemeral chatter', laying out the formula and lamenting the lack of real bitchiness: 'Let the villainess be vicious and savage,' he pleaded. 'Let her scheme to overthrow games-captaincies and firm friendships, and spread slackness throughout the Hockey XI. Let her hate the heroine wholeheartedly, and refuse, yes, even on the last page, to take her hand in forgiveness.'

He'd probably have approved of Ronald Searle's gin-soaked, knuckleduster-wielding St Trinian's schoolgirls. Searle's venomous cartoons attracted the support of a number of writers, including Wyndham Lewis, Robert Graves and Cecil Day Lewis, as well as the comic duo Flanders and Swann. For her part, Auchmuty does not regard parody as the sincerest form of flattery: 'What is being knocked here is, put simply, women: and an all-female world, where men are unnecessary and irrelevant, is the most obvious target for patriarchal fear and anger […] But laugh at masculine institutions? Never! […] Not only is there nothing self-evidently funny about institutions which exclude women […] but such institutions cannot be touched, since they are sacred to the patriarchal ruling class: men.'

Strong stuff and, as any fule kno, completely wrong. There is a fine history of boys' school parody, the best of which is Searle's own companion to *St Trinian's*, *Molesworth*. Written by Geoffrey Willans and illustrated by Searle, *Molesworth* is the fictional journal of schoolboy Nigel Molesworth, 'the curse of St Custard's', who spends four books casting an increasingly withering and dyslexic eye over his low-rent post-war public school. Molesworth is no fool, but in the best traditions of the

Critics' choice
Siblings

Atomised by Michel Houllebecq

Bruno and Michel are half-brothers. Michel is a geneticist; Bruno a sexual obsessive, whose frustrations are the vehicle for Houellebecq's vicious and brilliant critique of modern life.

The Brothers Karamazov by Fyodor Dostoevsky

Fifty-five-year-old Fyodor Pavlovich Karamazov is a lying, penny-pinching womaniser, and a cold, indifferent father to his three sons. So when he is found murdered, which of his offspring is to blame?

The Cement Garden by Ian McEwan

After their mother dies, Julia, Jack, Sue and Tom are left orphaned. Afraid of being separated, they keep her death a secret. In the sticky summer heat, free from adult authority, the days take on a dreamlike – or rather nightmarish – quality. Four-year-old Tom regresses back to babyhood, while 15-year-old Jack's infatuation with his beautiful sister Julie slowly intensifies.

The Corrections by Jonathan Franzen

Franzen reinvents the sprawling family saga for the 21st century. Chip Lambert is a failed professor of cultural studies. His brother Gary is a suburban pater familias and sister Denise a celebrity chef. They each feel helpless when their father's health fails.

East of Eden by John Steinbeck

The story of Cain and Abel was at the forefront of Steinbeck's mind as he plotted his bleak family saga. Brotherly rivalry in two generations tears the Trask family apart – although the novel ends with the hope of redemption.

Franny and Zooey by JD Salinger

Franny and Zooey are the precocious offspring of the Glass family. The novel is written as two discrete stories: Franny's is set on a weekend date with a college boyfriend; in Zooey's, the siblings discuss their dead brother Seymour.

The God of Small Things by Arundhati Roy

Rahel is so close to her twin, Estha, that she sometimes dreams his dreams and shares his memories. 'They thought of themselves together as Me, and separately, individually, as We or Us'. But when an act of shocking violence brings their childhood to an end, Estha is sent away. Years later, Rahel travels home to find him.

The Mill on the Floss by George Eliot

It's hard to see what the affectionate, impulsive Maggie Tulliver sees in her insensitive, narrow-minded brother Tom – who generally treats her with indifference or contempt. But love him she does, and their estrangement and eventual reunion form the emotional core of Eliot's novel.

Tales of a Fourth Grade Nothing by Judy Blume

This classic, comic children's book describes the trials of living with an irrepressible, aggravating little brother – who everyone else thinks is 'cute'.

A Thousand Acres by Janet Smiley

Wealthy, tyrannical Iowan farmer Larry Cook is a 20th-century King Lear in Smiley's Pulitzer Prize-winning recasting of Shakespeare's tragedy. As the battle over his three daughters' inheritance intensifies, dark family secrets come to light.

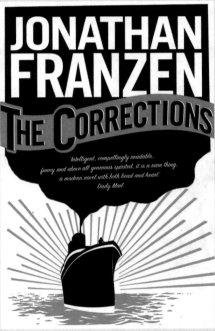

JONATHAN FRANZEN
THE CORRECTIONS

'Intelligent, compellingly readable, funny and above all generous spirited, it is a rare thing, a modern novel with both head and heart.'
Daily Mail

CHILDHOOD

well-trained fictional public schoolboy, he also considers himself a 'young Elizabethan', ready to reshape the world and the ragged remains of an empire in the wake of World War II, albeit with slightly more scepticism than his contemporary, Jennings. While the *Molesworth* books are less, well, evil than *St Trinian's*, there is an underlying cynicism and borderline sadism that sit surprisingly easily alongside the wit and whimsy. Critic Thomas Jones suggests that the books lack edge because they were only read by – and thus confirmed the prejudices of – those who boarded at prep schools themselves, but Orwell understood that such stories appealed to all classes: 'It is quite clear that there are tens and scores of thousands of people to whom every detail of life at a "posh" public school is wildly thrilling and romantic.' This is as true of the *Molesworth* parodies as it is of the Bunter rhapsodies, and the prejudices that are confirmed – physical violence, child abuse and apathetic parents – are not always self-aggrandising. That said, one fancies that the girls of St Trinian's would eat Molesworth and co for breakfast.

Considerably bleaker is *Tomkinson's Schooldays*, from Michael Palin and Terry Jones's *Ripping Yarns* TV series, which also appeared in superbly annotated script form. Riffing on the *Molesworth* theme, Palin and Jones added a dash of *If...* by way of *Monty Python* to the pastiche. It's set at Graybridge School, 1912, a brilliantly cruel spoof of Tom Brown's Rugby, where children are nailed to walls as punishment and to which young Tomkinson is sent by a mother too busy attending to numerous affairs to bother with parenthood (his father is exploring Antarctica, and has been absent for years). Graybridge's resident bully is Grayson, whose fondness for casual violence, alcohol and naked Filipino women recalls the genre archetype Flashman, himself the anti-hero of a series of books by George MacDonald Fraser in which he frequently rails against the hypocrisy of Dr Arnold's Rugby. Fraser's Flashman, by turns a snivelling coward and thundering bully, with an eye for the ladies and a talent for receiving unwarranted acclaim, is every bit a product of Victorian schooling as Scud East and Stalky.

While the UK school story focuses on the ongoing warfare between cads and 'proper sorts', the American tradition favours jocks

'Hogwarts sits proudly within a tradition that values the brave as much as the bright, and where sport plays a leading role in developing the young body and mind.'

versus nerds. One recent exception is Tobias Wolff's *Old School*, about life at the sort of East Coast establishment Holden Caulfield was fleeing in *The Catcher in the Rye*. Wolff's novel is about a scholarship boy trying to fit in at an elite New England prep school in the 1960s, but good though it is, it has none of the grab of the more familiar American high schools portrayed by populists such as Stephen King. King has Stephen Spielberg's uncanny gift for simultaneously locating both the romance and horror of childhood – *Carrie* being the epitome. The opening scene in which Carrie has her first period during her gym class is a classic piece of school writing, and King's influence can be seen in superior American school-set narrative television series such as *Buffy the Vampire Slayer* and *Freaks and Geeks*.

Today, the British fictional school lives on in *Harry Potter*. JK Rowling's books are distinguished by their clever mixing of various fictional staples – Blyton's mystery, Narnia's fantasy and *Tom Brown's Schooldays* – and Hogwarts (whose name, coincidentally, appears in *Molesworth* as the title of one of Nigel's cod-Latin plays) sits proudly within a tradition where courage is valued as highly as intelligence (Harry and his friends are in Gryffindor House, which favours the brave over the bright) and sport plays a leading role in developing the young body and mind. Wellington might not have quite grasped the complexities of quidditch, but he'd certainly have embraced the sentiment, and saluted the schoolboy spirit.

CHILDHOOD

Picture
perfect

The best illustrations can bring a book to life, says **Sarah Guy**.

Everyone has a favourite children's book. Fond memories linger of books that were read and re-read, transporting the reader back to childhood. No matter if they've lost the habit of reading in later life; it's a rare adult who doesn't have a residual tenderness for a defining work, whether it's *The Story of Babar*, *A Bear called Paddington* or *Ballet Shoes*. Sometimes it's the text that attracts, but more often than not it's the illustrations that draw in the young reader – and they're also what takes up permanent residence in our imaginations. Often the names of the artists – Edward Ardizzone or Quentin Blake, Shirley Hughes or Helen Oxenbury – are better known than the titles they illustrate. Here we've chosen a small selection of the greats.

In the best instances, words and pictures work some kind of alchemy together. In *Where the Wild Things Are*, Maurice Sendak created both memorable text and magical illustrations, and the book became an almost instant classic. Published in 1963, it has a timeless quality, thanks to the fairy tale images and near poetic prose. These are qualities shared by the Moomintroll books, a series aimed at older children but with great appeal for adults. Tove Jansson wrote and illustrated these books about

Where the Wild Things Are by **Maurice Sendak**.

Quentin Blake's inimitable rendering of Roald Dahl's *Matilda*.

the lives of the Moomintroll family and their friends, a group of unlikely-looking creatures with very human characteristics, set in a land that's both fantastical and familiar. *Comet in Moominland* is the first book in the series (first published in Jansson's native Finland in 1946). These aren't picture books, but the drawings

are so important in creating the mood and setting the scene that it's impossible to imagine the books without them.

An earlier and more famous example of the author-illustrator is Beatrix Potter. Her first and probably best-known book, *The Tale of Peter Rabbit*, published in 1902, was followed

Alice in Wonderland by **Arthur Rackham**.

The Tale of Peter Rabbit by **Beatrix Potter**.

by many other tales, and eventually by ballets, films and all manner of merchandising – but the original stories and drawings have endured.

Of course, the author and illustrator don't have to be the same person for the magic to work. The happy marriage of Roald Dahl's words and Quentin Blake's illustrations was repeated time and time again, in books such as *James and the Giant Peach, Charlie and the Chocolate Factory, The Twits* and *Matilda*. Though Quentin Blake has successfully collaborated with many other authors, notably Michael Rosen (most movingly on *Michael Rosen's Sad Book*), as well as writing many

Moomintroll, Snuffkin and Sniff, from
Comet in Moominland by **Tove Jansson**.

books himself, for many readers he will always be associated with the stories of Roald Dahl.

Arthur Rackham (1867-1939) and EH Shepard (1879-1976) are similarly famous in their own right, yet both will forever be identified with certain books. Rackham's work included illustrations for *Fairy Tales of the Brothers Grimm* and many other tales and fables (his French contemporary Edmund Dulac, 1882-1953, illustrated many of the same fairy tale titles – both have classic status), but most people now associate him with Lewis Carroll's *Alice's Adventures in Wonderland* (though Sir John Tenniel's drawings from the original 1865 edition are equally well known).

EH Shepard is linked with two of England's best-loved children's classics: *Winnie-the-Pooh*

(by AA Milne) and *The Wind in the Willows*. The latter, written by Kenneth Grahame in 1908, was originally published without illustrations. EH Sheperd's drawings were added in 1931, and it is this version that has won a place in the nation's affections. The characters of Ratty, Mole, Badger and Mr Toad are so delightfully drawn, and the illustrations so full of detail and incident, that it's now impossible to imagine the story without them.

Some stories are less intimately entwined with their illustrations in the reader's imagination, but are nonetheless enhanced by visual accompaniment. Pauline Baynes's delicate drawings for CS Lewis's *The Chronicles of Narnia* series, for instance, are less well known than the text, but any adult returning to

EH Shepard's illustrations for *The Wind in the Willows*.

The White Witch confronts Edmund in **Pauline Baynes**'s drawing for the *Narnia* books.

the books after the 2005 film *The Chronicles of Narnia: The Lion, the Witch and the Wardrobe* will be seduced by the rather elegant, decidedly 1950s illustrations.

Altogether less subtle, though just as popular, are the Dr Seuss books (Dr Seuss being the pen-name of Theodor Seuss Geisel). *Green Eggs and Ham, The Cat in the Hat, Fox in Socks* – all display an ineradicable connection between the

linguistic invention of the text and the graphic, cartoonish nature of the drawings. There's an antic quality in the language that's matched by the visual element, and the combination is timeless and imperishable.

There are countless other examples of this mutually enriching relationship of word and image; and all the best and most enduring illustrated children's books share it.

The reader
as a child

A bookish childhood was to shape the course of **Ali Smith**'s life.

I learned to read early; I was three years old. According to my father, I learned by pairing the heard names of programmes to the words in the TV listings in the paper, and I can actually remember working out the link between the spoken and written words 'fine' and 'woman' on the Beatles double-A-sided 45, 'She's a Woman/I Feel Fine'. By the age of eight I'd read everything in the house; it felt fine, to read.

I was precocious, because I was born at the end of a family of five children, with my closest brother seven years older than me. This meant the cupboard above the bed in the bedroom, which I shared with my two much older sisters, was full of the books they and my brothers were reading, mainly secondary-school set texts, I suppose now, though there were rogue copies of unexpected things, and there was certainly a lot of Georgette Heyer up there (belonging to my sister Anne, who had the ability to remove herself so deeply into a book that you could be shouting her name right next to her ear and she'd not hear you).

I wasn't much for historical romance (though I quite liked the horses in it). I ignored the piles of Heyer and read all the other books in the cupboard. It wasn't till I was in my twenties and reading for a university degree that I realised I'd read my way through a lot of Joyce, Orwell and Swift before the age of ten.

My parents quite literally had no time for reading. My mother worked in my father's tiny electrical shop; my father was, before the advent of Thatcherism and Dixons, one of the main electrical contractors in the north of Scotland, and had had more chance to read, he says now, when he was in the Navy, under age, in the middle of the sea, and recovering after the bombing of the ship he was on, in World War II. *And Quiet Flows The Don*, that's a great book, he says. Both my parents were clever children to whom history denied chances. Both had won scholarships for further education, which neither could take up; both were made fatherless young, and were expected, of course, to go out to work at the age of 13 or 14 to bring money home.

Both held the notion of books in high regard, as if books were a gift from another, unthinkable, unreal universe where things would be allotted their real worth, and they tolerated my alien status with great affection, because I was impossibly bookish, more and more so as I grew older, reading HG Wells and DH Lawrence when I should have been watching TV or baking or doing the dishes or going out with boys.

They worried when I developed a penchant for writers who were women who, they thought, all seemed to have committed suicide. 'No, only one of them did; Stevie Smith didn't commit suicide,' I told my mother. 'She died normally, and Muriel Spark isn't suicidal, she's still alive, she's a Catholic.'

My mother was kind. She knew I wanted to buy Sylvia Plath's short stories, which had just been published in a cover the bright orange sheen of which I couldn't get out of my head, and she knew there was a copy at Melvins, the local bookshop, and she knew it was a bit expensive, and she got her purse out and gave me what it cost.

I know now that all of us born here in the 1960s inhabited a time of real choice, a

CHILDHOOD

The young reader: **The Hon. Frederic Wellesley,** by Lord Leighton.

time when education could be nothing to do with money, and when, in my sixth year at school, more of us from my year (the school had become comprehensive a couple of years before I went, and was full of energetic, bright, generous teachers) went to university than ever before; a time when Melvins, the one bookshop, on Union Street in Inverness, had opened its basement and filled it with shiny new Penguin classics. You always met interesting people in the basement. They always loved books.

If I didn't spend the £10 a week I earned serving chips in the Littlewoods café there, I spent it at Leakey's, a new second-hand bookstore tucked away in the market, which my English teacher Ann McKay had tipped me off about; you'll love it, she'd said. John Wyndham, Simone de Beauvoir, Albert Camus all mixed in together, nestling up against the different editions of *Palgrave's Golden Treasury*.

There was Paris in Inverness, there was poetry from all the centuries. Sweet lovers love the spring; everyone suddenly burst out singing; yes, I remember Adlestrop. The whole world was possible, and a whole lot of other worlds eddying out beyond it.

A book that changed my life

John Burnside

Collected Poems by Marianne Moore

I remember Corby Library, where I used to hide out after school, sitting in the reference library reading Poe and Dostoevsky, or gazing at the works of great photographers and painters, or maybe studying the atlases, imagining the place where I would one day disappear: some little town in Canada, say, or northern Norway, a grown man walking off into the cold, finally arriving at a blessed solitude.

All those books changed me, in various ways, but the one that altered the direction my life was taking in a decisive way – and by decisive, I mean as decisive as an addiction – the one that decided how

The Poems of Marianne Moore

Edited by Grace Schulman

I would spend my adult years, was Marianne Moore's *Collected Poems*.

The first poem, 'The Steeplejack', struck me as extraordinarily clear-sighted and well made, and it seemed to slow time, or perhaps to make time to take a more attentive look at the world than I had ever thought possible. All at once, I realised what poetry was about – this lyric slowing of time to pay a proper, reverent attention to the given world – and I knew, without a doubt, what I wanted to do with the rest of my life.

John Burnside's most recent novel is The Devil's Footprints *(Jonathan Cape).*

Adolescence

*'And then the lover
Sighing like furnace,
with a woeful ballad
Made to his mistress'
eyebrow.'*

All you need is love?

There's more to romance than happy endings, argues **Sarah Churchwell**.

'Love loves to love love,' James Joyce wrote mockingly near the end of *Ulysses*, a sentence that plays with grammar to suggest the sentimental excesses that romantic passion so often has prompted – as well as the way attempts to parse it risk banality. Writers tackle love at their peril, and many teachers of creative writing warn students against using 'four-letter words' such as 'love' and 'soul': in modern literature, sentimentality is the ultimate obscenity.

As ee cummings declared, 'since feeling is first,/who pays any attention/to the syntax of things/will never wholly kiss you.' The syntax of romance always puts feeling first, and can easily skip physical consummation; this is why romance comprehends erotica but draws the line at pornography. By definition, romance cares. As long as its emotional needs are met, however, literary romance can be a fickle form, embracing not only sexual love, courtship and the marriage plot, but also magic, mythopoeia,

legend, glamour, imagination, fancy, fantasy, pleasure, sensuality, hallucination, vision, even the workings of fiction itself. Its impulse can be tragic or comic, but romance is generally serious rather than ludic. It may strive for verisimilitude and plausibility, but romance resists realism: it is characterised by imaginative intensity, and intuition is its mode.

Romance is perpetually in flight from conceptual, physical or social constraints, towards hope and ambition. Romance can fulfill daydreams (*The Sheik*) or prompt nightmares (*The Mysteries of Udolpho*), but it belongs in the realm of reverie and vision, of phantasmagoria and fantasy. In his 14th-century elegy *The Book of the Duchess*, Chaucer seeks 'a romaunce' to 'drive the night away': he finds a tale that he 'thoughte a wonder thing'. Romance offers him escape into an imaginative world of marvels, of 'queens lives, and of kinges', of courtly love and 'wonder'; it is, essentially, a fairy tale.

A Victorian depiction of seventh-century Greek poet **Sappho**.

He could be reading Charles Perrault's 'The Sleeping Beauty in the Wood', Alfred, Lord Tennyson's *The Idylls of the King* or Danielle Steel's *H.R.H.* Fairy tales remain our most familiar romances, the prototype for most love stories, which recount comfortingly familiar fables: indeed, romance can seem as obsessive as any lover, compulsively following the routes of previous tales. The contours of *Cinderella* can be traced across the literary map, from 'classics' (*Jane Eyre, Pamela, Evelina*) to 'trash' (*Forever Amber, The Wide, Wide World, A Little Princess* and *Little Lord Fauntleroy*) and everything in between (*Little Women, Rebecca*).

For all their differences, these stories share an emphasis upon idealised, usually distant worlds, peopled by heroes and heroines who must overcome trials and obstacles on the quest to find a happiness that is nearly always represented through sexual union or reunion. 'Romance' could potentially encompass most of Western literature: Keats's poem 'Endymion', Nathaniel Hawthorne's *The House of the Seven Gables* and Susan Sontag's *The Volcano Lover* were all subtitled 'A Romance'.

Even if we define 'romance' reductively as sexual love, it is difficult to imagine a literary text that does not at least flirt with Eros in one guise or another. As a consequence, the history of writing about love and romance is more or less coeval with the history of writing. The most defiantly lapidary and abbreviated of modernist lyrics, such as Ezra Pound's 'In A Station of the Metro' ('The apparition of these faces in the crowd;/Petals on a wet, black bough'), can easily be interpreted in erotic terms, while the classic epics of nationalism, such as *The Aeneid* or *The Iliad*, have sexual entanglements at their hearts.

Milton cannot 'justify the ways of God to man' in *Paradise Lost* without justifying the ways of man to woman – and, given that the Old Testament is one of the most sexually various of our culture's foundational texts, this shouldn't come as a surprise. A great deal of biblical sex may be transgressive, but when the Bible celebrates the erotic, it uses romance to do so: the Song of Solomon glorifies the erotic connection between a bride and a bridegroom as a perfect love, an allegory for the relationship between human and deity.

Shakespeare's reputation rests in large part on his treatment of romantic love (which shapes not only all the comedies and tragedies, but also most of the histories and all of the 'problem plays' – or, as they are also known, the 'romances'). And before Dante wrote *The Divine Comedy*, he composed *La Vita Nuova*, a collection of poetic love letters to Beatrice. Soon after, Petrarch published a sequence of love poems addressed to the idealised Laura.

By the time of the English Renaissance, the sonnet had become virtually an obligatory mode for addressing lovers, and many of its lines remain cultural clichés: Christopher Marlowe's arcadian panegyric 'Come live with me and be my love/And we will all the pleasures prove' is nearly as familiar as Elizabeth Barrett Browning's question from 'Sonnet from the Portuguese', written 300 years later: 'How do I love thee?/Let me count the ways.' Some of the oldest formulas in romance writing remain the most tenacious: the work of Sappho, the Greek poet who wrote in the seventh century BC, survives only in fragments, but her imagery and themes – love as illness, or the ubiquity of fire metaphors, for example ('When I look on you a moment, then I can speak no more, but my tongue falls silent, and at once a delicate flame courses beneath my skin, and with my eyes I see nothing, and my ears hum, and a wet sweat bathes me, and a trembling seizes me all over') – flourish in the work of such spiritual descendants as Barbara Cartland and Danielle Steel.

'Even if we define "romance" as sexual love, it is difficult to imagine a literary text that does not flirt with Eros. The history of writing about love is coeval with the history of writing.'

Doomed love: **Anna Karenina**.

Romance's association with formula, sentimentality and women is the primary reason for its declining reputation from the later 19th century on. The connotations of frivolity and self-indulgence were already sufficiently well established by 1878 for Russian critics to deride *Anna Karenina* on publication as a 'trifling romance of high life'. Up until then, what readers today would consider romances – that is, love stories – predominate on any list of 'classic literature'. Only epics and devotional literature can compete for space with romance, and both include their own versions of love. Indeed, 'love and romance' must take their place with the other intrinsic themes of literature across the ages: death, religion, power, the nature of identity; all overlap with love in one way or another. And even a story 'purely' about sexual love must by definition comprehend other aspects of existence, including the nature of identity and consciousness.

To take just one example: the supposedly simplistic and consolatory marriage plot nonetheless requires a violent rupture, almost always in the form of a crisis of faith, on the road from self-delusion to self-knowledge. In comic and gothic romances, self-knowledge brings reconciliation and consummation; in tragic novels, the crisis of faith leads to the death of one or both of the lovers. Such plots figured in virtually every novel written during the 18th and 19th centuries, and the writers who played variations on the romance theme include some of history's most eminent novelists: Samuel Richardson, Henry Fielding, Jane Austen, the Brontës, George Eliot, Charles Dickens, Nathaniel Hawthorne, Charles Flaubert, Thomas Hardy and Leo Tolstoy (to name just a few). Even in the 20th century, romance creates the most unlikely of bedfellows: Ernest Hemingway's *A Farewell to Arms* and Erich Segal's *Love Story*, for example, have more in common than might at first appear: both were immensely popular romances that relied on the death of the heroine to generate the intense emotion upon which romance feeds, while encouraging readers to identify with a hero whose pain seems to derive as much from his lost illusions as from his lost lover. Similar romantic impulses can be seen in writers as different as J-K Huysmans and JK Rowling, DH Lawrence and Joyce Carol Oates, Joseph Fielding and Helen Fielding.

A book that changed my life

Andrew O'Hagan

The Great Gatsby by F Scott Fitzgerald

MODERN CLASSICS

F. Scott Fitzgerald
The Great Gatsby

Everything that can happen to a writer happened to Scott Fitzgerald – success, failure, Hollywood, alcohol and the crack-up, but the most important thing that happened to him was that he was able to create in one novel an absolutely perfect marriage of style and subject. Like all good artists, Fitzgerald's style changed as he changed, and as the world changed and his subject deepened, but *The Great Gatsby* is the high point of everything, because it is the book in which he managed to capture the meaning of his times in a very American language that is quite unafraid of its own beauty. Like the best tragedies, *The Great Gatsby* is also a romance – not only that hopeless one that exists between the mysterious Gatsby and Daisy Buchanan with the green light at the end of her wharf, but between Gatsby and the possibilities of America itself. Nick Carraway, the narrator, is rather quietly possessed of a poetic vision, one that yearns to understand how it is to live and dream in the America of those days, among a people both blessed and tortured perhaps by their 'capacity for wonder'. For Scott Fitzgerald there was something very personal in that sort of possession: he lived with it, and one suspects his own blood is mingled with the flow of sentences in this story of Long Island hedonists. It remains the task of a serious writer to enter his or her times with an appetite for the uncanny, the beautiful and the true, which might also mean the ugly. *The Great Gatsby* shies away from nothing and risks everything in order to be what it is – the perfect American novel.

Andrew O'Hagan's most recent novel is Be Near Me *(Faber).*

Although romance novels developed in part out of the far more respectable gothic romance, today they are often derided as the most formulaic of formula fiction. Critics attack their conservative gender and sexual roles and their tendency to nourish dangerous illusions and raise unrealistic expectations. And it is no coincidence that these are exactly the same fears that novels raised in their infancy. But whatever its significance, romance is one of the most successful genres in Anglo-American publishing, accounting for around a third of all annual popular fiction sales.

Furthermore, our dismissive equation of 'romance' today with predictable plots that pander to 'the emotionally impoverished' itself represents an impoverished understanding of the term. The meaning of romance has significantly narrowed over time: early paradigms such as Sir Thomas Malory's *Le Morte d'Arthur* (held by some to be the first novel in English), Ariosto's *Orlando Furioso* and Cervantes's *Don Quixote* exemplify medieval romance, which focused upon aristocratic tales of courtly love and heroic quests. This mode of romance, which persists in fairy tales, was revived in the 19th and 20th centuries in the works of Sir Walter Scott (*Ivanhoe* is also subtitled 'A Romance'), James Fenimore Cooper and Robert Louis Stevenson. It was commonplace enough to be lampooned in Mark Twain's *A Connecticut Yankee in*

King Arthur's Court, before being reinvented in 20th-century popular fiction, in such successful novels as *When Knighthood Was in Flower*, which would be spoofed in turn.

If courtly love among aristocrats dominates medieval romance, the seduction or marriage plot was a staple of the early bourgeois novel, with its emphasis on sexual economics, social mobility and individualism. Over the 18th and 19th centuries, marriage acquired increasing ideological importance in puritan middle-class culture as a paradigmatic social structure; narratives of courtship consequently gained ascendancy, and helped tighten the bonds between private and public virtue. Romances could be exemplary (*Sense and Sensibility*, *Evelina*) or cautionary (*Clarissa*, *The Coquette*, *Charlotte Temple*), concerned with courtship or seduction. Either way, romance offers as much instruction as wish-fulfillment, and archetypally achieves closure through the reconciliation of difference as it unites genders, classes and, eventually, races and sexualities through the ideal of the couple.

Romance, therefore, does not merely satisfy sexual appetites: economic or social desires are often realised through the institution of marriage, as marrying advantageously motivates heroines and anti-heroines alike. Everyone from Becky Sharp to Bridget Jones seeks a man whose ideal qualities are reinforced by his wealth and status. As Jane Austen sardonically observes in the opening sentence of *Pride and Prejudice*: 'It is a truth universally acknowledged that a single man in possession of a good fortune must be in want of a wife.'

Despite its mordant acknowledgement of the uses of wealth, *Pride and Prejudice* is the most romantic of Austen's novels, considered by many to epitomise the form: not only are its protagonists her most idealised, but their reconciliation is her most lingering, suggesting the emotional weight given to their union. The satisfactions offered Lizzie Bennet are sweeping: emotional, physical and material desires are all fulfilled by the *beau idéal* of Mr Darcy. *Mansfield Park*, by contrast, must be Austen's least romantic book, given the prosaic nature of its central couple and the dismissive way that their long-deferred union is handled. Edmund has been genuinely 'attached' for several hundred pages to someone else, before he rather abruptly transfers his affections to the heroine, Fanny. *Mansfield Park* is also widely regarded as Austen's least popular novel, though its treatment of love more nearly typifies Austen's general attitude towards it. Like most of the best-known 19th-century writers of romance, she seems to hope but not quite to believe. Emma may win her 'Knightley', but he hardly carries her off on a white charger; instead, he tells her off, before moving in with her and her father. Sisters Marianne and Elinor are 'rewarded' with husbands whom *Sense and Sensibility* seems to find somewhat deficient.

Even at her most romantic, Austen prompts doubt: one need think only of poor Mr Bennet, fearing that his favourite daughter will repeat his mistake of marrying for the wrong reasons and regretting it for life, to realise the grim possibilities that haunt even the most idealised stories. Jane Eyre finds happiness with Rochester only after they both nearly die, his manor is destroyed and his first wife immolated. Charlotte Brontë's rather less optimistic sister Emily wrote an even more sombre romance in which the central couple repeatedly avow their mystical, spiritual fusion but whose only physical consummation comes when Heathcliff crawls into Cathy's grave and embraces her corpse. Despite this rather gloomy outlook, *Wuthering Heights* continues to be regarded as one of the most romantic novels ever written.

'*If courtly love among aristocrats dominates medieval romance, the marriage plot was a staple of the early bourgeois novel, with its emphasis on sexual economics and social mobility.*'

Bleak House is, in one sense, not bleak at all in its insistence that love overcomes all obstacles; but some might see Dickens's decision to disfigure his pretty heroine to test her lover's character as adding rather a caustic edge to his tale. The ending of *A Tale of Two Cities* probably constitutes Dickens's single most romantic moment in print, but once again the perfect love of Sidney Carton is realised only by his self-immolation: 'It is a far, far better thing that I do, than I have ever done. It is a far, far better rest that I go to, than I have ever known.' If the romantic mood is intensified by death, which it so often is, then romance as a genre is not quite so consolatory as popular opinion might hold. It is the idea of romance that is the consolation, not necessarily the story it tells.

Gone with the Wind, probably the most popular romance of the 20th century, defiantly refused its readers the satisfaction of a reconciliation between Scarlett O'Hara and Rhett Butler: when Scarlett finally realises that she loves Rhett it's too late, and for the most anti-romantic of reasons – Rhett wearily informs Scarlett that she wore his feelings out.

The reputation of romance for determined, unrealistic optimism, disingenuous fantasy and fatuous sentimentality is in many ways undeserved. Shakespeare spared no one in his investigation of the illusions of love throughout the human lifespan, from the adolescent (*Romeo and Juliet*) to the middle aged (*Antony and Cleopatra*) to the senescent (*A Winter's Tale*). As *A Midsummer Night's Dream* shows, love makes asses of us all. Shakespeare's sonnets, meanwhile, often touted as among the most 'romantic' instances of English poetry, are by turns brutal, excoriating and bitter in their denunciation of the follies and betrayals of love, while at the same time subverting the conventions of the form. The love poems in praise of beauty and merit, for example, are addressed to a man, while those written to a woman are nearly all as acidic as Sonnet 147, which declares that 'desire is death' and finds in it only madness and delusion: 'For I have sworn thee fair and thought thee bright,/Who art as black as hell, as dark as night.' Even his compliments are determinedly back-handed: 'My mistress' eyes are nothing like the sun … If snow be white, why then her breasts are dun.' Shakespeare inaugurated a tradition of

reversing the clichés and expectations of the form that has been followed by everyone from Dorothy Parker, who concluded her 'General Review of the Sex Situation' with the question, 'What earthly good can come of it?', to the Irish poet Nuala ni Dhomhnaill. In the latter's comic carpe diem, 'Nude,' a female speaker informs a male love object that:

'when you come with me to the dance tonight
(though, as you know, I'd much prefer
to see you nude)

it would probably be best
for you to pull on your pants and vest
rather than send
half the women of Ireland totally round
the bend'

The hortatory poems of John Donne and Andrew Marvell, while great instances of comic rationale, nonetheless figure love in terms of hastening death and disease, as in Donne's 'The Flea', which humorously likens the loss of virginity to a flea-bite, or Marvell's 'To His Coy Mistress', which argues for immediate sex on the basis that time is running out and death is imminent.

If romance is darker than conventional wisdom holds, however, it is also true that hope never dies in it; salvation is always possible. Romance can work almost like faith itself in its capacity for redemption. Nick Carraway, who narrates *The Great Gatsby*, Fitzgerald's masterclass on American romance, declares in his final summation on Gatsby's character that despite being a gangster and a fraud, he was redeemed precisely by his 'romantic' capacity for hope and wonder: 'It was an extraordinary gift for hope, a romantic readiness such as I have never found in any other person and which it is not likely I shall ever find again. No – Gatsby turned out all right at the end.'

The Great Gatsby is archetypally romantic, despite the fact that its central love story is unconsummated (except by a kiss that creates the novel's cosmology), delusional, implicitly materialistic and explicitly pathetic, and ends tragically. The romance in *Gatsby*, too, lies less in its plot than in its belief; its two central characters are equally hopeless romantics in their tendency to see the world, and other people, through the rosy tints of glamour and desire.

Emily Brontë's only novel, *Wuthering Heights*, remains a classic of romantic fiction.

Medieval romance in **Don Quijote de Orson Welles**, starring Francisco Reiguera.

The narrator of *Wuthering Heights*, Lockwood, similarly romanticises Heathcliff, an even less promising model than Gatsby. Belief may, in the end, be the secret of romance. Shakespeare ruefully admits: 'When my love swears that she is made of truth/I do believe her, though I know she lies.' Why do lovers believe, even in full sight of evidence to the contrary? Perhaps because love is faith, a master narrative that gives order and meaning to lives that otherwise might flounder. Or perhaps it is because love loves to love love.

Love and romance in 20 books

The Accidental Tourist by Anne Tyler

In the aftermath of his son's death, middle-aged travel writer Macon Leary's relationship with his wife Sarah falls apart. Macon is left with only his ill-behaved dog Edward and eccentric siblings for company – until he meets Muriel, a garrulous, pushy dog trainer. She is determined to win his affections, despite being his opposite in every way – but his ex-wife has other ideas.

The Age of Innocence by Edith Wharton

Unfulfilled love is the theme of Wharton's Pulitzer Prize-winner, set against the glittering backdrop of 1870s New York high society. Newland Archer stays in his loveless marriage for his children's sake – and to conform to society's dictates. Years later, after his wife's death, he arranges to meet the woman he truly loved in Paris, only to leave without seeing her; the reality can never live up to his long-cherished ideal.

Any Human Heart by William Boyd

Despite debating books with Joyce, going to war with Hemingway, trading sketches with Picasso and playing golf with the Duke of Windsor, the most significant encounter in Logan Mountstuart's life is meeting Freya Deverell. She is young, witty, glamorous, and everything Logan's wife is not…

Doctor Zhivago by Boris Pasternak

The Russian poet was awarded a Nobel Prize for his story of love, loneliness and loss, set in war-torn turn of the century Russia, but was forced to turn it down after the Soviet authorities objected. Haunted by guilt at his betrayal of his wife, Tonya, Zhivago is powerless to resist his infatuation with the beautiful Lara – a role played to perfection by Julie Christie.

Idylls of the King by Alfred, Lord Tennyson

Tennyson's epic poem traces the rise and fall of King Arthur's Round Table fellowship, charting the

ADOLESCENCE

adulterous love between Queen Guinevere and Sir Lancelot that will prove its undoing. The seeds of ruin are sown from the start, as the young king asks 'his warrior whom he loved/And honoured most, Sir Lancelot' to ride and fetch his future queen to Camelot.

The Letters of Abélard and Héloïse

Twelfth-century philosopher Peter Abélard was sorely punished for eloping with and impregnating his student, the beautiful and fiercely intelligent Héloïse. For his transgression, her uncle had Abélard castrated in his bedchamber. The *Letters* capture the early – less turbulent – phase of their relationship.

Love in the Time of Cholera by Gabriel García Márquez

Florentino Ariza's all-consuming, unreciprocated love for Fermina Daza torments him for over half a century – but eventually his persistance pays off.

Love's Work by Gillian Rose

In this brief, limpid autobiographical work, written shortly before she died from cancer, the philosopher Gillian Rose reminds us that for the ancient Greeks, love was *agape* as well as *eros*. It is God's love for man, or the everyday fellow-feeling of friends and comrades, as well the charged, blind intensity of erotic love.

Loving by Henry Green

Green's best-known novel is set in an Irish country house. Charley the butler is in love with Edith the housemaid. Edith's friend Kate loves the stable-hand. And Mrs Jack, whose husband is away in the army, is having an affair with a neighbour.

Oscar and Lucinda by Peter Carey

Incapable of expressing their love, Lucinda Leplastrier, an impulsive heiress, and Oscar Hopkins, a shy, awkward clergyman, place a bet on whether Oscar can transport a glass church to the wilds of the Outback – an insane endeavour that ends in tragedy.

The Passion by Jeanette Winterson

Lyrical and dreamlike, Winterson's grand tale of Napoleonic Venice follows Henri, chef and romantic, and Villanelle, pickpocket and cross-dresser. Their intertwining story allows the author to explore war, survival and the crushing effect of a broken heart.

Possession by AS Byatt

Love and scholarly obsession fuse in Byatt's erudite romance. Post-doctoral researcher Roland Michell finds letters recording an illicit relationship in an original copy of a book by (fictitious) Victorian poet Randolph Henry Ash. While trying to unravel the mystery, Roland falls for Maud Bailey, a feminist academic who specialises in the work of Christabel LaMotte – who, it emerges, was Ash's secret correspondent…

The Rainbow by DH Lawrence

Lawrence's fourth novel tracks the erotic entanglements of three generations of the Brangwen family, from Tom Brangwen's successful marriage to Lydia Lensky to their granddaughter Ursula's engagement to army officer Anton Skrebensky. The relationship is eventually broken off – but only after Ursula has unpicked the mysteries of physical love.

The Remains of the Day by Kazuo Ishiguro

The emotionally repressed narrator has spent his life putting his duties as a butler above everything else, including his unspoken love for the housekeeper, Miss Kenton. Years later, he journeys to visit her – to remember an age unspoiled by war and, perhaps, to articulate the feelings he has held back for so long.

A Room With a View by EM Forster

Will stolen kisses with the bohemian, free-spirited George Emerson tempt Lucy Honeychurch away from her bookish, pretentious fiancé, Cecil Vyse?

The Scarlet Letter by Nathaniel Hawthorne

It is Boston in the 17th century, and the scarlet letter is an 'A' worn by Hester Prynne as a punishment for adultery. One contemporary reviewer wrote that Hawthorne's examination of forbidden love was touched by the 'miraculous vitality of genius'.

A Suitable Boy by Vikram Seth

Set against the turbulent backdrop of post-colonial India, Seth's epic saga details the interweaving stories of four families, centering on the indomitable Mrs Rupa Mehra's quest to find a good match for her younger daughter, Lata.

The Unbearable Lightness of Being by Milan Kundera

Tomas, a libidinous doctor living in Prague, meets Tereza on a visit to a provincial town. A week later she turns up at his flat, her life packed into a suitcase. When she leaves, Tomas is faced with a choice: should he ask her to return, and sacrifice the 'lightness' of a libertine lifestyle for the weighty responsibility of love?

The Well of Loneliness by Radcliffe Hall

Published in 1928, Hall's groundbreaking depiction of lesbian love caused a furore. 'I would rather give a healthy boy or a healthy girl a phial of prussic acid than this novel,' declared one outraged journalist.

The Woodlanders by Thomas Hardy

Giles Winterborne, a simple woodsman, adores his childhood playmate, Grace Melbury. When Grace's ambitious father persuades her to marry the dissolute, dashing Dr Fitzpiers instead, tragedy ensues. A silent, agonised background to the drama is occupied by Marty South, whose love for Giles is all the more profound for its quiet, unpretentious faithfulness.

Textual liaisons

For literature that changed the world, look under 'Erotica', says **Sarah Hedley**.

I f I say two words – *Kama Sutra* – what's the first thing you think about? Go on, admit it, you're thinking about sex positions. In fact, only four of the 200 pages of this world-famous sex manual translated by Sir Richard Burton back in 1883 cover 'acts of congress'. The rest feature tips on how to acquire wives and courtesans and be an upstanding member of society in ancient India cAD100-600, when Vatsyayana originally composed the Sanskrit text.

There are also chapters on passionate scratching, smacking and biting – 'All the places that can be kissed are also the places that can be bitten, except the upper lip, the interior of the mouth and the eyes' – proving the Victorians didn't invent S&M.

Credit can also be given for the earliest-known labelling of lovers based on the size of their *lingam* (penis) or *yoni* (vagina): men were either hare (small), bull (medium) or horse (large), while women were either deer (small),

Kama Sutra: the first sex manual.

THE
JOY OF SEX

EDITED BY ALEX COMFORT, M.B., Ph.D.

A Gourmet Guide to Lovemaking

**Mitchell
Beazley**

mare (medium) or elephant (large). While being told you have a vagina like an elephant is not considered a positive message by modern-day sex manual standards, at the time these categorisations were made without judgement or disgust. Sadly, times have changed, but the *Kama Sutra* remains a seductively open window into the bedroom of an ancient civilisation, through which we are all free to peep.

Publishing illicit material back in the day was not without risk; over 100 years before the *Kama Sutra* emerged in the West, John Cleland wrote the first erotic novel of our times, *Fanny Hill*, in 1748, for which he was consequently arrested one year later.

Country girl Fanny is tricked into working at a town brothel where she receives a sex education spying through holes in walls – but she likes what she sees: 'For my part, I will not pretend to describe what I felt all over me during the scene; but from that instant, adieu to all fears of what a man could do unto me; they were now changed into such ardent desires, such ungovernable longings, that I could have pull'd the first of that sex that should present himself, by the sleeve, and offered him the bauble, which I now imagined the loss of would be a gain I could not too soon procure myself.' And pull she did, taking flight with Charles, the man who was to become her true love, but he is then sent abroad by his father, and Fanny is left to rely on a succession of new lovers to survive.

What's so remarkable about this book, indicated in the alternative title *Memoirs of a Woman of Pleasure*, was that Cleland's Fanny actually enjoyed sex, and, for a woman of that era, sexual pleasure – particularly at the hands of men – was rarely a consideration.

In court Cleland denounced the book and was pardoned. He consequently released an expurgated version and several other works, but none lived up to this landmark in libertine literature. Perhaps he should have accepted that stint in the clink – *Fanny Hill* is said to have been written while Cleland was incarcerated in Fleet Prison for non-payment of debts.

Another notorious magnum opus created in the slammer was *120 Days of Sodom*. The term for inflicting pain – sadism – was coined after its author, the Marquis de Sade, Donatien Alphonse François, a French aristocrat and purveyor of philosophy and porn.

And while *120 Days* is filed under 'Erotica' in bookstores, it is the stuff of nightmares.

In a remote castle in the darkest depths of the Black Forest in the early 1700s, four wealthy aristocrats embark on a four-month-long orgy of depravity, rape and murder with a harem of victims including eight well-endowed studs, 16 child virgins, four old hags and their own daughters.

Weathered prostitutes hold court, telling tales of sexual atrocities they have witnessed, including abuse, torture and coprophilia (the eating of faeces), which the protagonists then re-enact with their captives. Victims are whipped, sodomised and penetrated with hot pokers – if they're lucky. Far worse befalls others, such as Augustine: 'The Duc thrusts his hands into her cunt and cuts through the partition dividing the anus from the vagina; he throws aside the scalpel, reintroduces his hand, and rummaging about in her entrails, forces her to shit through her cunt.'

While imprisoned in the Bastille, the Marquis wrote *120 Days* in just 37, on rolls of paper he kept hidden in the wall of his cell. The roll eventually measured 49 feet in length, but the text was never completed; only the first instalment was written, with detailed notes for the remaining three. Then without warning, ten days before the storming of the Bastille in 1789, he was moved to another fortress. Though his wife had managed to smuggle earlier works out of the Bastille, Sade never saw this one again.

Later the manuscript was discovered and kept in private hands until it was made available to doctors studying sexual aberration in the early 20th century. Finally, Jean-Jacques Pauvert published de Sade's work and was prosecuted for it in 1957, but acquitted on appeal the following year. Today many feminists would still like to see the book banned, though not Camille Paglia, who famously stated that 'no education in the Western tradition is complete without de Sade. He must be confronted, in all his ugliness.'

In a time when every second person with a web connection is publicly spewing the minutiae of their sex lives via a blog, it's easy to disregard the bravery of diarist forefathers such as Victorian gentleman 'Walter', who compiled *My Secret Life* in 1888. The Obscene Publications Act of 1857 was in force, frivolities such as sodomy were punishable by law, and society was quick to make an outcast of anyone who didn't adhere to the puritan ideals of the time. Though it's possible that, with 11 volumes covering over 1,000 sexual conquests, 'Walter' was too busy to give it a second thought.

His contribution to erotica is by no means a masterpiece: the sex scenes are monotonous and his writing style treacherous, yet *My Secret Life* gives a fascinating insight into the sex lives of our Victorian ancestors, even if, as some have conjectured, the work is fictionalised. (This may account for the chapter on the woman with two vaginas, though medical science doesn't rule it out – just Google 'uterus didelphys'.) However, Walter claimed, 'I determined to write my private life freely as to fact, and in the spirit of the lustful acts done by me, or witnessed; it is written therefore with absolute truth and without any regard for what the world calls decency.'

Enhancing the appeal of this diary is the long-running debate over the true identity of the author. At present it's thought that Walter was in fact Henry Spencer Ashbee (1843-1900), respected society gent, husband and textile trader, whose circle of friends included none other than fellow sex explorer and *Sutra* translator Sir Richard Burton. It's a small world.

Just as Walter's *Secret Life* was banned in most countries for many decades, the same fate befell DH Lawrence's classic *Lady Chatterley's Lover* when it was released 30 years later – that was until Penguin Books decided to publish it in the UK as part of the company's 25th anniversary celebrations in 1960. This led to a six-day trial at the Old Bailey in which the jury, to their eternal credit, decided the book did not contravene the Obscene Publications Act. The publisher won the right to reproduce the book

A book that changed my life

Julie Myerson

South of the Border, West of the Sun by Haruki Murakami

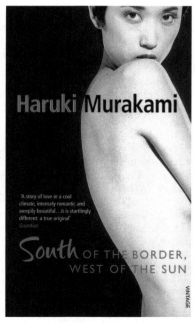

I admire nearly everything that Murakami has written, but this slim novel – which seems to shake up every reader who encounters it – has moved me more than almost anything I've read in my entire adult life. At his best Murakami is somehow both straightforward and eerie, innocent and dark, childlike yet sexy, and this novel is all of those things. It tells the story of Hajime and the deliciously named Shimamoto, childhood sweethearts who've spent years apart then meet again, with destructive and life-changing consequences. I am haunted by this novel. It's told in an apparently passive, reasonable, deadpan prose, yet it's one of the most emotionally shattering things I've ever read. It has all the stillness and lyricism of a poem, yet one of my favourite things about Murakami is the way he's unafraid to write about the normal stuff of everyday life – pasta, condoms, socks, face cream – as if they were every bit as weighty and worthy as all the more abstract ideas and passions. But more than anything, this novel is about a desire that seems to go beyond love or sex or death itself. I've read it three or four times, and I still don't understand it. It transfixes me and amazes and upsets me. It's a great, great book.

Julie Myerson's most recent novel is The Story of You *(Jonathan Cape).*

Anaïs Nin proved that erotica was not the preserve of the male writer.

in its entirety. With help from the trial's extraordinary publicity, Lawrence's tour de force became an overnight success, shifting two million copies in the run-up to Christmas that year, outselling the Bible and doing as well as Dan Brown's *The Da Vinci Code* today.

Despite the fuss, it is in fact a most tender book, charting the tale of Connie, wife of war-wounded, wheelchair-bound Lord Clifford, who finds an outlet for her passions in Mellors, the Chatterley estate's gamekeeper. Their illicit encounters bloom from the page as a reminder of what sexual love can be like: 'All her womb was open and soft, and softly clamouring, like a sea-anemone under the tide, clamouring for him to come in again and make a fulfilment for her. She clung to him unconscious in passion, and he never quite slipped from her, and she felt the soft bud of him within her stirring, and strange rhythms flushing up into her with a strange rhythmic growing motion, swelling and swelling till it filled all her cleaving consciousness.' Hardly obscene, though obscenely beautiful.

At the same time, across the pond in America, *Lady Chatterley* was fighting another landmark censorship battle against the US Supreme Court – joined by Cleland's *Fanny Hill* and Brooklyn-born Henry Miller's *Tropic of Cancer*, which had first been published in France in 1934.

Literature finally won out: a new freedom of expression was granted to all American writers, and *Tropic of Cancer* made it into America's Modern Library top 50 Greatest Books of the 20th Century, with its depictions of 'shaved twats', sex in the 'shit-house' and erections 'light and heavy at the same time, like a piece of lead with wings'.

The novel is in fact a semi-autobiographical account of Miller's first two years in Paris, written in what he called 'the first person spectacular' and filled with what were then precedent-shattering descriptions of sexuality, set against a backdrop of his true longing for his wife, Mona.

Tropic of Cancer may never have been published at all if it wasn't for financing from Miller's fellow author and lover, Anaïs Nin.

An 'allegorical portrait' of the **Marquis de Sade**.

Like I said: small world. Her groundbreaking collection of erotic fantasies *Delta of Venus* was written in the 1940s, for an anonymous client who requested that she 'leave out the poetry and descriptions of anything but sex'. Nonetheless, exquisite sensuality flows through her words, along with a wily, mocking humour.

In the story of Mathilde, she writes of a sailor's tale about a rubber sex doll his shipmates have made and shared between them to help while away time and satisfy desires during their months at sea. 'The sailors found her untiring and yielding – truly a marvellous companion. There were no jealousies, no fights between them, no possessiveness. The rubber woman was very much loved. But in spite of her innocence, her pliant good nature, her generosity, her silence, in spite of her faithfulness to the sailors, she gave them all syphilis.'

Nin earned a dollar a page for these commissions and in creating them became the first noted female author of erotica, whose books continue to be published around the globe in over 20 different languages to the enduring delight of both men and women.

Another book that took the world by its love-handles and gave it a good shake was *The Joy of Sex*, written by Dr Alex Comfort, a physician and human biologist with a beautifully matter-of-fact turn of phrase.

It discusses just about every heterosexual sex act from postures (sexual positions) to *postillionage* ('Putting a finger in or on your partner's anus just before orgasm – popular in French erotic books, and works on some people'). Sadly, the now fashionably retro line drawings of the original print run have been replaced with less amusing modern offerings. But that merely dents rather than destroys the joy of this tome.

To date, Comfort's sex manual extraordinaire has sold over eight million copies, and when it was first published in 1972 it enjoyed 11 weeks at the top of the *New York Times* bestseller list, heralding a major milestone in the sexual revolution then under way. 'People today, who never experienced the freeze on sexual information, won't appreciate the proportions of the transformation,' Comfort wrote. 'It was like ripping down the iron curtain.'

A year later the term 'zipless fuck' became common parlance. 'The zipless fuck is absolutely pure. It is free of ulterior motives. There is no power game. The man is not "taking" and the woman is not "giving". No one is attempting to cuckold a husband or humiliate a wife. No one is trying to prove anything or get anything out of anyone. The zipless fuck is the purest thing there is. And it is rarer than the unicorn,' wrote Erica Jong in *Fear of Flying*.

She went on to explain that 'zipless' wasn't a reference to European men and their button-flies, but rather a term meant to connote zippers that fell away 'like rose petals'. The criteria for this sort of encounter lay in knowing very little about your lover, lest knowledge quell passion, as it does in lead protagonist Isadora's own marriage.

The US ban on books like *Tropic of Cancer* had not long been lifted, and writers such as John Updike and Philip Roth had, to Jong's mind, taken advantage of their newfound freedom to delve deeply into the male erotic psyche. In *Fear of Flying* she wanted to do the same for womankind. 'I was determined to slice open a woman's head and show everything happening inside,' she said, 'but the fantasy of the "zipless fuck" was what caught the fancy of the generation.'

Indeed, 1973 was a good time for female sexuality. Nancy Friday's *My Secret Garden* – a collection of real women's fantasies – was hot off the press that same year. Thousands of copies were passed around schools and pored over by teenaged girls lucky enough to be exonerated for their own sordid thoughts. Women everywhere breathed a sigh of relief on discovering they weren't the only ones dreaming up dark rape scenarios and bestiality bonanzas like Rosie's ('one day, while I was playing with my dog, I suddenly wanted it to lick my cunt').

In the foreword, Jill Tweedie wrote: '*My Secret Garden* is a livid jungle sliced by the screams of the Monkey God; a dark forest lit by burning tigers; an English woodland marked by the hooves of Pan; a smooth lawn broken by the craziest of paving. *My Secret Garden* is Bacchus rampant in the head, and whatever its meaning, the body revels in it.' And so it does, arousing readers at the same time as vindicating them in their fantasies. And therein lies the basis of successful erotica: words which change lives by changing attitudes – as well as making us feel as horny as hell.

ADOLESCENCE

Critics' choice
Illicit liaisons

Anna Karenina by Leo Tolstoy

Anna's impassioned affair with Count Vronsky begins to sour once lust and desire are replaced by the consequences of flouting 19th-century Russian convention. Snubbed by society, Anna's dependence on Vronsky increases, as does her depression – with dreadful consequences.

Asylum by Patrick McGrath

Psychiatrist Max Raphael's marriage is falling apart. As he channels his frustrations into his work, his wife begins an affair with a patient – the charismatic, unstable Edgar.

Closer by Patrick Marber

This iconic 1990s play explores the tangled lusts and loves of four confused Londoners. Alice loves Dan, who leaves her for Anna, who is married to Larry, who lusts after Alice. They spar and seduce until all four have had their hearts well and truly bruised.

Dangerous Liaisons by Pierre Choderlos de Laclos

In this story of decadence and cruelty, first published in 1782, the Vicomte de Valmonte and Marquise de Merteuil plot the seduction of virginal debutante Cécile de Volanges.

The End of the Affair by Graham Greene

Deeply in love, Maurice Bendrix makes a daily pilgrimage across Clapham Common to meet Sarah Miles, the wife of a colleague with whom he is having an affair. When Sarah calls off their liaison, Maurice obsessively tries to discover who has replaced him in her affections.

The English Patient by Michael Ondaatje

The Patient, disfigured in a plane crash during World War II, tells the story of his Saharan affair with Katharine, the wife of a fellow desert explorer. War breaks out just as her husband discovers the truth; the result is an injury to the Patient more painful than any external wound.

An Equal Music by Vikram Seth

A decade after ending their relationship in Vienna, violinist Michael Holme catches sight of Julia on a London bus. She is now married, but their affair is rekindled, imbuing Michael's empty life with a new sense of purpose and harmony – destined, alas, to be short-lived.

The French Lieutenant's Woman by John Fowles

Detailing the illicit love between Charles Smithson and Sarah Woodruff, a 'fallen woman'. In his pursuit of her, Charles risks the wrath of a repressive and hypocritical Victorian society.

The Go-Between by LP Hartley

Young Leo enjoys his role as messenger between the beautiful, aristocratic Marian and local farmer Ted – until he realises that their love letters are more than just a game. Embroiled in the messy world of adult relationships, Leo's innocence is lost.

The Golden Bowl by Henry James

The study of an affair between Prince Amerigo and Charlotte Stant, a former lover who marries the Prince's father-in-law. His wife, Maggie, becomes suspicious, concocting a plan to separate the lovers.

The Good Life by Jay McInerney

An affair that takes place in the unlikely setting of post-9/11 New York. Luke is helping to clear the rubble when he meets Corrine, who volunteers in a soup kitchen – in part to escape the confines of a loveless marriage. Soon, altruism is simply an excuse for them to meet.

Laughter in the Dark by Vladimir Nabokov

This deeply depressing (yet grimly funny) tale follows the woes and humiliations of Albert Albinus, as he conducts an ill-fated affair with the beautiful but utterly vacuous Margot.

The Return by Joseph Conran

Alvan Hervey arrives home from work to discover a letter from his wife, revealing that she has left him for another man. Before he knows it, she has returned – offering one last desperate chance to salvage their marriage.

The Severed Head by Iris Murdoch

Everything in Martin's life is perfect: he is just as satisfied with his sensible wife Antonia as he is with his exciting mistress Georgie. Then the unthinkable happens: Antonia announces that *she* is having an affair with her psychiatrist – and intends to leave Martin. In a complex tale of bedswapping, this is just the beginning of his trauma.

ADOLESCENCE

Teenage kicks

Angry, isolated and misunderstood; it's no wonder adolescents make the best narrators, says **Melissa McClements**.

'*What really knocks me out is a book that, when you're all done reading it, you wish the author that wrote it was a terrific friend of yours and you could call him up on the phone whenever you felt like it.*'

So Holden Caulfield – the wise-cracking, angst-ridden 17-year-old narrator of JD Salinger's 1951 novel *The Catcher in the Rye* – describes the novels he loves best and, inadvertently, how readers the world over feel about him. Exuberantly funny yet deeply troubled, he has become an icon of teenage alienation and insecurity.

As Holden amply demonstrates, adolescents make exceptional narrators. The intensity and egotism of teenage experience lend themselves beautifully to the first-person form. Teenagers have a unique perspective on the world: caught between childhood directness and adult complexity. Being in transition, however, can mean feeling ostracised, and Holden is not alone in feeling alone.

Marisha Pessl's electrifying novel *Special Topics in Calamity Physics* is the literary equivalent of American high-school movies, but with a precocious intellectual – called Blue van Meer – as the geeky wallflower who seeks to befriend the cool kids' clique. The narrator of Jeanette Winterson's lesbian coming-of-age novel, *Oranges Are Not The Only Fruit*, faces even greater isolation. As the daughter of evangelical Christians who want her to become a missionary, Jeanette provokes scandal when she falls in love with her friend Melanie.

Another teen struggling with religious fanaticism is 15-year-old Kambili in Nigerian writer Chimamanda Ngozi Adichie's powerfully compelling *Purple Hibiscus*. The daughter of a wealthy businessman – widely celebrated for his philanthropy, but feared at home for his violence and Catholic zeal – she is initially cowed by his controlling presence. With the help of her aunt and cousins, however, she manages to assert her own identity.

In the overwhelming confusion of such rites of passage there is often a gap between the immature narrator's understanding of events and that of the reader. When her father runs off with her aunt, Marsha – the ten-year-old protagonist of Suzanne Berne's *A Crime in the Neighborhood* – is so traumatised that she links this personal betrayal to the horrific, sexually motivated murder of a young boy in her Washington suburb – and even the wider political events of the ongoing Watergate crisis.

MJ Hyland's gripping *Carry Me Down* is the story of 11-year-old John Egan. Already over six feet tall, he is a gangling man-child who has such a fine awareness of the physical detail of human behaviour that he can spot when anyone is lying. Tragically, he has no comprehension of the complex motivations behind people's untruths, and the reader shudders as he unwittingly destroys his own family.

Shedding a harsh light on the compromises and hypocrisies of the adult world, young narrators with special needs widen the gap between storyteller and reader even further. The wonderfully moving *The Curious Incident of the Dog in the Night-Time*, by Mark Haddon, is written from the perspective of Christopher Boone, a 15-year-old with Asperger's syndrome, who struggles to interpret social behaviour.

ADOLESCENCE

The original American teen: **Huckleberry Finn**.

Similarly, Sparky, the burger-chain worker narrator of Alan Bissett's *The Incredible Adam Spark*, is 18, but has a mental age of eight. The reader cringes at his misinterpretation of those around him in this effervescent, bittersweet tale of moral dilemmas and sibling dependency.

Sparky's raw Caledonian council-estate idiom is riveting. It follows in a long line of authentic teen voices that goes back to Mark Twain's *The Adventures of Huckleberry Finn*, which was written in 1885 using the earthy dialect of the American Deep South. Huck's free-spirited, colourful voice leaps off the page as he describes his escape down the Mississippi from 'sivilised' society.

More recent examples of virtuoso teen literary linguistics include the eponymous narrator of *Vernon God Little* by DBC Pierre, who tells of how he was wrongly accused of a Texan high-school massacre with gutter-mouthed, demotic aplomb. Living in the near future, 15-year-old Tom Boler in Daren King's *Boxy an' Star* comes from a dynasty of ecstasy-popping hedonists. In his ingenious, childlike, urban patois he describes his bewildered life with his girlfriend – in which they have to write notes to remind themselves to eat.

In the teen world, peers are of central importance and friendships are all-consuming. Jeffrey Eugenides's mind-blowing slice of modern gothic, *The Virgin Suicides*, illustrates this uniquely communal side of adolescent experience with its highly unusual narrative voice. The narrator is not one but several adolescents – an anonymous group of boys, obsessed with five sisters who all kill themselves.

Two classic novels deal, in very different ways, with teen gangs. SE Hinton wrote *The Outsiders* in 1967, when she was just 16. It is a violent and bleak story of two gangs separated by a vast economic divide, but it does offer a glimmer of hope as its 16-year-old narrator, Ponyboy, begins to realise the similarities between himself and his rich kid enemies. Anthony Burgess's *A Clockwork Orange* offers a stark vision of a hypothetical future in which Alex, a brutal 15-year-old 'Droog' gang leader, takes his mob on a horrifying spree of robbery, rape, torture and murder before being locked up and subjected to scientific experimentation.

Other disturbingly dark teenage narrators that cannot be ignored include Francie Bradie, the psychotic slaughterhouse worker of Patrick McCabe's remarkable *The Butcher Boy*. Written in a stream-of-consciousness monologue, this novel – peppered with hilarious anecdotes and hallucinogenic invention – describes Francie's savage murder of his friend's mum in small-town Ireland in the early 1960s. Seventeen-year-old Frank Cauldhame in Iain Banks's dazzlingly grotesque *The Wasp Factory* lives on a tiny and remote Scottish island, where he enjoys mutilating animals and enacting eccentric rituals.

But sometimes teens crave the reassuring boundaries of the adult world. Sixteen-year-old Piscine Molitor Patel, the narrator of Yann Martel's unforgettable *Life of Pi*, is set adrift on the ocean after the ship on which he and his family were sailing from India to Canada sinks. His lonely survival is so harrowing that he can only tell his story by dressing it up in the fantasy of magical folklore – transforming the murderous sailor he shares his lifeboat with into a Bengal tiger.

In Ian McEwan's beautifully written *The Cement Garden*, the absence of grown-up society makes teenagers seek to emulate it. After burying their mother, the narrator Jack and his three siblings are left to fend for themselves. Bizarrely, Jack ends up in an incestuous, mock-parental relationship with his sister Julie – showing that sometimes adults are needed after all.

'Adolescents make great narrators. The intensity and egotism of teenage experience lend themselves beautifully to the first person form. They have a unique perspective.'

Critics' choice
Drugs

Artificial Paradise by Charles Baudelaire

'At first, a certain absurd, irresistible hilarity overcomes you. The most ordinary words, the simplest ideas assume a new and bizarre aspect [...] The demon has invaded you.' That demon is hashish, whose effects Baudelaire analyses with singular precision.

Confessions of an English Opium Eater by Thomas de Quincey

The classic 19th-century examination of the 'pleasures' and 'pains' of opium. De Quincey denies the drug is a narcotic, describing instead its many 'exciting and stimulating' effects – as well as the torments of cold turkey.

The Doors of Perception by Aldous Huxley

Huxley's record of his experiments with hallucinogens. The 'mescaline visionary' sees what a disastrous mistake Plato made when he separated being from becoming: 'He could never, poor fellow, have seen a bunch of flowers shining with their own inner light'. Poor fellow, indeed.

Fear and Loathing in Las Vegas by Hunter S Thompson

The semi-fictionalised author and his mentally unstable attorney drive to Las Vegas to write about a motor convention. Their trunkful of dangerous narcotics operates as both a catalyst to the ensuing insanity, and as a metaphor for Thompson's vision of the American Dream: hallucinatory, destructive and dangerous.

Naked Lunch by William Burroughs

Naked Lunch offers a hit (possibly overdose) of torture, sexual depravity, serious drug abuse and, most memorably, a Talking Asshole, the novel's strongest anti-consumerism metaphor. At the book's 1965 obscenity trial, Norman Mailer called Burroughs an artist who has 'come back from Hell with a portrait of its dimensions'.

On Hashish by Walter Benjamin

Benjamin, like his hero Baudelaire, partook of hash, opium and sundry hallucinogens. He argues that such intoxicants offer the prospect of 'profane illumination' in a modern world that has been abandoned by the gods.

A Scanner Darkly by Philip K Dick

Undercover narcotics agent Bob Arctor himself becomes addicted to Substance D, and falls in love with his drug dealer. But in Dick's classic science fiction novel, nothing is quite as it seems...

The Sign of Four by Arthur Conan Doyle

'Sherlock Holmes took his bottle from the corner of the mantel-piece and his hypodermic syringe from its neat morocco case. With his long, white, nervous fingers he adjusted the delicate needle, and rolled back his left shirt-cuff'. The fictional super-sleuth indulges in his cocaine habit with undeniable panache.

Trainspotting by Irvine Welsh

Welsh's darkly comic, no-holds-barred tale of a group of Scottish heroin addicts – and the slickly shot film adaptation that followed – were a defining moment in 1990s pop culture.

ADOLESCENCE

Strikes
a chord

Barney Hoskyns picks the best literary explorations of rock 'n' roll.

Since I've spent the last five years building an online library of seminal rock articles (at www.rocksbackpages.com), you'd think I'd be able to write about music books in my sleep. But, of course, the task is dreadfully daunting, 'rock' now being an engulfing umbrella for way too many (sub-) genres of modern popular music. I'm focusing, therefore, on the tomes that have most excited and illuminated me as a fan.

Going back to a personal dawn, I have to cite *The Sound of the City*, Charlie Gillett's groundbreaking 1970 account of pop's rise and dissemination: I owe much of my early rooting in rock history to this superbly researched book.

In tandem with Gillett, Greil Marcus's *Mystery Train* was my introduction to what we now call Americana: essays on Elvis, Sly Stone, The Band and others through the prism of what it meant to be American. The work of Peter Guralnick in this area – the 'trilogy' that is *Feel Like Going Home*, *Lost Highway* and *Sweet Soul Music* – is more personal and elegiac than *Mystery Train*, but no less compelling. Guralnick himself would want me to mention the masterful prose of Brit veteran Bill Millar, whose *Let the Good Times Rock* contains his best writing on the legends of R&B and rockabilly.

Other sacred Americana texts are the late Robert Palmer's *Deep Blues*, Anthony Heilbut's *The Gospel Sound*, Gerri Hirshey's *Nowhere to Run*, Nicholas Dawidoff's *In the Country of Country* and – more iconoclastically – Nick Tosches's *Country*. Tosches, whose outrageous Jerry Lee Lewis biography *Hellfire* was No.1 on the *Observer Music Monthly*'s

all-time Best Music Book chart in 2006, may be the finest writer on popular music of all of them. 'I like [Tosches],' remarked Tom Waits. 'If you write about music, you've got to be musical in the way you write.' As readers of *Dino*, *Unsung Heroes of Rock and Roll* and *Where Dead Voices Gather* will know, Tosches is nothing if not that.

The so-called 'Noise Boys' of gonzo rock journalism – Tosches, Richard Meltzer and the late Lester Bangs – are well represented by anthologies: Bangs's *Psychotic Reactions and Carburetor Dung* and *Mainlines, Blood Feasts and Bad Taste*, and Da Capo's Tosches and Meltzer readers. If those *Creem* stars have a true heir, it is the Chuck Eddy of the entertaining *Stairway to Hell* and *The Accidental Evolution of Rock 'n' Roll*.

On this side of the pond, the key '70s writers were Nick Kent, Charles Shaar Murray and – more cerebrally – the late Ian MacDonald. The latter's painstaking Beatles study *Revolution in the Head* brought him back into prominence in 1994, but the pieces collected in *The People's Music* put him on a par, critically, with the likes of David Thomson, Robert Hughes and James Wood.

Kent's *The Dark Stuff* is half in love with easeful (or at least premature) rock death, but establishes the pantheon of lost boys tottering along rock's wild side. Murray's Hendrix biog *Crosstown Traffic* did more than justice to its extraordinary subject. The best punk books are Jon Savage's definitive *England's Dreaming* and Legs McNeil's riveting oral history *Please Kill Me*. The key grunge text is Gina Arnold's *Route 666: The Road to Nirvana*, but Charles

A book that changed my life

Maggie O'Farrell

The Yellow Wallpaper
by Charlotte Perkins Gilman

The Yellow Wallpaper by Charlotte Perkins Gilman was first published in 1892. It is a portrait of a young woman's marriage to a doctor, and her gradual mental disintegration under his treatment. She has just had a baby and is suffering from 'nervous depression'. Her husband confines her to a room with barred windows and heavily patterned wallpaper. Although she craves stimulation and freedom to 'work' (that is, write – there are more than a few autobiographical parallels), he insists that she must 'rest' and will not allow her to do anything or see anyone.

For a piece of writing only 30 or so pages long it possess an astonishing, febrile power. The narrator is a person going slowly mad, crippled and suffocated by the wrong kind of love and care. She becomes fixated by the 'sinuous' patterns of the yellow wallpaper – 'when you follow the lame uncertain curves for a little distance they suddenly commit suicide' – and begins to imagine that she can see 'a woman creeping' behind these patterns, shaking 'the bars'.

Maggie O'Farrell's most recent novel is
The Vanishing Act of Esme Lennox *(Headline).*

Cross's Cobain biography *Higher than Heaven* is essential too.

I read Nik Cohn's trailblazing *Awopbopaloobop Awopbamboom*, published in 1969, after I'd read Gillett's *The Sound of the City*, but I still dig its hip, flip irreverence – not least with regard to that most sacred of all cows, Bob Dylan. *Rock Dreams*, the book on which Cohn collaborated with Belgian illustrator Guy Peellaert, also helped to shape my teenage musical psyche.

On the same seamy side of the pop subconscious, you can't beat Fred and Judy Vermorel's *Starlust*, verbatim fantasies of sex with pop stars from David Bowie to, er, Bruce Foxton. Actual sex with musicians is the principal theme of Jenny Fabian's *Groupie*, a rather less starry-eyed confession than Pamela Des Barres's bestselling and oddly innocent *I'm With the Band*.

The most bracing and demystifying studies of Rock as Big Bizness are Fredric Dannen's *Hit Men*, Simon Garfield's *Expensive Habits* and Fred Goodman's *The Mansion on the Hill*. The latter should be mandatory for anyone prone to deifying musicians.

I've also always felt that Albert Goldman, the merciless biographer of Elvis and Lennon, got an unfairly bad rap before his passing. Nelson George's Motown history *Where Did Our Love Go?* and Craig Werner's *A Change Is Gonna Come* are important socio-cultural studies of black American pop.

Though he's often derided for being an ivory-tower rock prof, Mercury Prize chairman Simon Frith in his *Sound Effects* made me think hard about pop as a cultural-capitalist construct. I also greatly admire Simon Reynolds' and Joy Press's *The Sex Revolts*, a jolting, unsparing study of gender in rock, as well as Reynolds's subsequent *Energy Flash* and *Rip It Up and Start Again*. Two other tomes that have dazzled me as intellectual feats are David Toop's *Ocean of Sound* and Evan Eisenberg's all-but-forgotten but deeply fascinating *The Recording Angel*.

Essay collections by favourite prose stylists include Richard Williams' elegant *Long Distance Call* and Glenn O'Brien's dryly brilliant *Soapbox*. Williams was my first editor – at *Melody Maker* – and his taste remains unerring after three and a half decades. Sweeping scenic narratives I've

NICK KENT
THE
ff DARK
STUFF

SELECTED WRITINGS ON
ROCK MUSIC 1972–1993
WITH A FOREWORD BY IGGY POP

'I COULD TELL YOU STORIES
ABOUT NICK KENT THAT
WOULD UNCURL THE HAIR
IN YOUR AFRO'
MORRISSEY

Bob Dylan: the sacred cow of rock writing?

loved include Joel Selvin's evocative Haight-Ashbury history *Summer of Love* and David Cavanagh's Creation Records annals *My Magpie Eyes Are Hungry for the Prize*. The best books of rock conversations are NME bête noire Paul Morley's *Ask*, Bill Flanagan's *Written In My Soul* and Kristine McKenna's *Book of Changes*.

As for straight rock (auto)biography, I don't think I've enjoyed any example of the genre more than *Faithfull*, the Marianne memoir concocted by the delightful David Dalton. Dylan surprised us all with the vivid and poetic detail of his *Chronicles, Volume One* in 2004, and we await the next instalment with bated breath.

The best jazz autobiographies are Charles Mingus's fiery, defiant *Beneath the Underdog* and Art Pepper's bleakly real *Straight Life*. Jerry Wexler's *Rhythm and the Blues*, written with superior ghoster David Ritz, is as passionate and erudite as you'd expect from the Atlantic Records avatar.

Jimmy McDonough's *Shakey: Neil Young's Biography* is also a masterpiece of engagement with its subject, wrestling with the enigma that is Neil in way that never shirks irreverence when it's required. A unique musical memoir is James Young's *Songs They Never Play on the Radio*, a tragicomic account of life as Nico's keyboard player. Joe Boyd's *White Bicycles* boasts riveting memories of Syd Barrett et al, along with shrewd insights.

Among the proliferation of book-length studies of individual albums, the slim but superior tomes in Continuum's *331/3* series are always worth a punt. The pick of the litter? Erik Davis on the fourth Zeppelin album, and John Niven's uncanny 'novella' inspired by the Band's *Music from Big Pink*.

With what you will agree is admirable humility, I've cited none of my own books. But there's a feast of great writing in *The Sound and the Fury*, the anthology of seminal pieces by such Rock's Backpages contributors as Dalton, Marcus, Toop, Reynolds, Frith and O'Brien from the last four decades. From Al Aronowitz's account of the Beatles' arrival in America to Jon Savage's journey into the fractured mind of Kurt Cobain, *The Sound and the Fury* sums up how central writers have been in communicating the power and danger of rock 'n' roll.

ADOLESCENCE

De profundis

Depression has ever been a source of artistic inspiration, says **Brian Dillon**.

What exactly does melancholia look like? The question was easily answered for the artists of the Renaissance: in Albrecht Dürer's engraving *Melancolia I*, a winged angel sits slumped, head on its left hand, with eyes downcast, regarding the ruins of human endeavour. The iconography has hardly altered since: the contemporary depressive has only to substitute a duvet for the angel's folded wings, and daytime TV for the detritus at its feet, to assume the unmistakable attitude of the morbidly sad. Music, too, has no problem conjuring the melancholic's pain: a baritone moan courtesy of Leonard Cohen or Nick Cave, a spectral whimper from Nick Drake or Thom Yorke, and we know we're in the presence of intractable angst. But writing requires more than mere mood or pose. It has to deal in the tricky stuff of story, context, character: the literature of melancholy is, accordingly, infinitely varied.

The first classic on the subject is Robert Burton's *The Anatomy of Melancholy*, published in 1621: a book so vast and digressive it seems to want to say everything there is to say about mental suffering, and then tackle the modest matter of the rest of human knowledge. Burton wrote, he said, to cure himself of his own depression; he revised his study for nearly 20 years, till it became 'a rhapsody of rags … raw, rude, phantastical, absurd'. He simply couldn't stop adding causes, symptoms, cures, anecdotes, wildly erudite conjectures. Melancholia might be caused by black bile, excessive exercise, too much study, heat or cold, idleness or ardour. It might manifest as sadness, paleness, swarthiness, windiness, weeping, sighing or swooning.

The cure might be found in diet, climate or employment. With its labyrinthine sentences, low comedy and baroque display of learning, Burton's book makes it sound as though the whole world has become melancholic.

Which is, after all, from *Hamlet* onwards, a favoured fantasy of the depressive, who imagines that the universe itself shares his cosmic dolour, his 'obstinate condolement'. In Romantic poetry, that vision becomes a marker of some special sensitivity on the melancholic's part. The young and sickly John Keats, in his 'Ode on Melancholy', advises his reader to 'glut thy sorrow on a morning rose', to savour death and decay as the mirrors of life and beauty. Charles Baudelaire goes further in *The Flowers of Evil*; in the poem entitled 'Spleen', there is no redemptive union of grief and joy, just the lowering sky of melancholia, of hopes vanquished, while 'despotic despair/Plants its black flag on my bowed head'.

In the 20th century, the name given to such prodigious displays of languor, sloth and lassitude was, of course, adolescence. Depressives, like teenagers (with whom they share some biochemical aberrations), always think they know better than others: both about themselves and the parlous state of the world. In JD Salinger's *The Catcher in the Rye* or Sylvia Plath's *The Bell Jar*, teenage depression is the same thing as sincerity or authenticity: it's the rest of the (adult) world that is false and phony, toxic to the hero's sense of self. Late in the century, while subject to all manner of psychotherapeutic and pharmacological experiments, it's actually the late-adolescent depressive – typified by

Democritus Abderites.

THE
ANATOMY OF
MELANCHOLY.

*What it is, With all the Kinds causes,
symptomes, Prognostickes, & severall cures of it.*

*In three Partitions, with their severall
Sections, members & subsections.*

*Philosophically, Medicinally,
Historically, opened & cut vp.*

By.

Democritus Junior.

*With a Satyricall Preface, Conducing
to the following Discourse.*

*The fourth Edition, corrected and
augmented by the Author.*

Omne tulit punctum, qui miscuit vtile dulci.

Democritus

Iunior

Elizabeth Wurtzel's *Prozac Nation: Young and Depressed in America* – who diagnoses the ills of the society around her.

Freud would have agreed, up to a point. In his 1917 essay on 'Mourning and Melancholia', he points out that the depressive's self-estimation – useless, ugly, unpopular – is quite likely to be accurate, given, after all, that he or she is clinically depressed. For Freud, melancholia is mourning gone wrong: instead of grieving for the loss of another person, we feel bereft of our own selves. Freud's is a compelling and

Sylvia Plath, life-long depressive and suicide.

influential account, but William Styron's memoir, *Darkness Visible*, is perhaps the best, or even the only, book the truly melancholic ought to read. It has the virtue of brevity: depression is bad enough for one's concentration, but once the drugs kick in you're nodding out after half a page. Styron's is also the most uncannily accurate account of just what the disease feels like: 'one does not abandon, even briefly, one's bed of nails, but is attached to it wherever one goes.'

There is also, of course, the literary aversion cure, of which the Romanian aphorist EM Cioran is about the most caustic exponent. His 1949 book *A Short History of Decay* is bracingly grim, though couched in such elegant prose that you find yourself lulled into agreeing with Cioran that happiness is indeed for dolts, procreation a mistake and insomnia a gift from the gods. He does not, however, recommend suicide: a quick tour of the nearest cemetery will, he says, put paid to such thoughts. Like Nietzsche, he aspires to be light-hearted at the edge of the void. Then again, Cioran, it is said, was so lugubrious in person that even his friend Samuel Beckett had to put a stop to their regular dinners, such was the dismaying effect on his mood of a few hours in the company of the author of *The Trouble with Being Born*. Left unchecked, Cioran once wrote, his depression would attack his entire being, and eat away even his fingernails.

But Cioran is also frequently hilarious, and Beckett himself averred that 'nothing is funnier than unhappiness'. Despite their varied circumstances, what comedy and depression share is an unfortunate propensity for repetition: an overfamiliar inability to escape the cliché of one's own being, a certain cyclical pratfall tendency. David Foster Wallace's bravura short story 'The Depressed Person', from his collection *Brief Interviews with Hideous Men*, recounts with deadpan detachment the extent of the depressive's endless, wheedling, exhaustive and exhausting monomania. She just cannot shut up about her desperate needs, her inexpressible pain, her comically predictable family history, all of it couched in the feeble language of self-help: 'support systems', 'quiet time', 'inner-child-focused experiential therapy'. Which is terribly funny, and also simply terrible.

Critics' choice
Unrequited love

Astrophil and Stella by Sir Philip Sidney
Sidney's trendsetting sonnet sequence recounts the tormented feelings of Astrophil (literally 'star-lover') for the unobtainable Stella ('star') – alas, to no effect. In the end, he is forced to admit defeat; 'Leaue, me, O loue which reachest but to dust,/And thou, my mind, aspire to higher things.'

Breakfast at Tiffany's by Truman Capote
'Never love a wild thing,' is Holly Golightly's drunken advice to Joe Bell. 'The more you do, the stronger they get. Until they're strong enough to run into the woods.' Sadly, none of her admirers takes heed of her advice, and all are heartbroken when, inevitably, she vanishes from their lives.

Enduring Love by Ian McEwan
The dark side of unrequited love is explored in McEwan's tense, disturbing thriller. After a chance encounter, the clearly unhinged Jed Parry begins stalking Joe Rose. His unwanted attentions gradually destroy Rose's marriage – and start to unbalance his mind.

Notes on a Scandal by Zoë Heller
Lonely, frumpish Barbara Covett is distraught to discover that her fellow teacher Sheba Hart is engaged in an illicit affair with a 15-year-old pupil. Having long harboured her own secret crush on Sheba, she's bitterly jealous – and out to exact revenge for the 'betrayal'.

The Sorrows of Young Werther by JW Goethe
Driven to despair by his love for the happily married Lotte, the eponymous hero finally kills himself. So great was the readerly empathy inspired by Werther's romantic angst that a spate of copycat suicides followed the book's publication.

Villette by Charlotte Brontë
There's no happy-ever-after for Charlotte Brontë's unhappy heroine, Lucy Snowe – the object of her affections first prefers the vain, self-centred Ginevra Fanshawe, then marries another woman. The ambiguous ending hints at further heartbreak for Lucy, leading the novelist Harriet Martineau to disapprovingly declare *Villette* 'almost intolerably painful'.

ADOLESCENCE

Adulthood

'Then a soldier.
Full of strange oaths,
and bearded like the pard,
Jealous in honour, sudden
and quick in quarrel,
Seeking the bubble
reputation
Even in the cannon's
mouth.'

Men
at war

Michael Hodges enters the fray.

My own experience of combat is limited to hiding under tables in Baghdad and behind armoured cars in Basra, and running away from Israeli helicopters in Palestine. These are not heroic battle honours, but I have seen enough to realise that war smells of excrement, piss and sweat, and that most of its victims are not combatants.

This has been the case since the birth of the industrial age, when it first became possible to level cities from a distance. The war book is itself a creation of that age. The first modern war book, Stephan Crane's 1895 novel *The Red Badge of Courage*, was a product of the American Civil War, the first conflict to be fought with iron ships, trenches and artillery barrages. Yet its central narrative follows a pattern as old as fighting itself: a boy, Henry Fleming, goes off to fight for the cause, is almost overwhelmed by fear on the eve of battle, somehow survives his first encounter with the enemy and finally becomes a man.

This format influenced nearly all the war books that followed, though the story is not always an uplifting one: the idealistic schoolboys of Eric Maria Remarque's *All Quiet on the Western Front* go into the mincing machine of the Somme as volunteers who believe in their country's cause; those who survive the initial encounters become cynical, angry and believe only in survival and the pleasures of the flesh; eventually, they all die. Nevertheless, it still appeals to millions of us, despite – or perhaps because of – the fact that today our fighting is done for us by other people, and at a great remove. How else to explain the success of *Bravo Two Zero*, Andy McNab's chronicle of a disastrous SAS mission behind enemy lines during the 1991 Gulf War, which has sold over 1.5 million copies in the UK since its publication in 1994?

Most of those 1.5 million readers were male, and one of the reasons they bought the book was that they felt war to be the ultimate test of what it is to be a man. But the good war book does more than allow readers to experience vicariously the moral tests and physical miseries of combat; it also acts as a barometer for a society's prevailing concerns and attitudes. It is not always immediately apparent which attitudes, however. *Bravo Two Zero* may appear to be a gung-ho adventure story, but it can also be read as a bleak morality tale propelled by the tension between the British propensity to cock up – the SAS squad at its centre has the wrong radio frequencies and cannot call in an air pick-up when their mission goes awry – and the inappropriateness of a small European nation attempting to muscle in on other people's oil fields.

So the war book can also be a commentary on a nation's status and its citizens' doubts about that status. Sales of *Bravo Two Zero* picked up when the British government launched its second war against Saddam Hussein in 2003, while *Catch-22*, Joseph Heller's coruscating attack on the very idea of America waging war, just or otherwise, found its massive 1960s audience in those millions of Americans who were profoundly discomforted by the US military intervention in Vietnam. In the other seminal 1960s World War II text, *Slaughterhouse Five*, Kurt Vonnegut revisited the horrors of the Allied firebombing of Dresden in 1945, just as USAF B52s were beginning their saturation bombing of north Vietnamese cities.

But does the war book have to be about actual fighting? *War and Peace*, Leo Tolstoy's unnervingly long examination of the consequences of Napoleon's invasion for the Russian upper classes, may feature several battle scenes, but its focus is the psychological and romantic traumas of a group of aristocrats. Conversely, Jaroslav Hasek's Rabelaisian World War I farce, *The Good Soldier Svejk*, perhaps the funniest book ever written about war or anything else, features no battles at all. Its cast of characters, mainly Czechs serving in the Austro-Hungarian army on its way to fight Russia, don't find redemption and personal change in the cataclysmic deluge

The **Vietnam War**: fertile ground for fact and fiction.

The best guides to enjoying London life

(but don't just take our word for it)

'More than 700 places where you can eat out for less than £20 a head… a mass of useful information in a geuinely pocket–sized guide'

Mail on Sunday

'Armed with a tube map and this guide there is no excuse to find yourself in a duff bar again'

Evening Standard

'I'm always asked how I up to date with shopping and services in a city as as London. This guide is the answer'

Red Magazine

'Get the inside track on the capital's neighbourhoods'

Independent on Sunday

'A treasure trove of treats that lists the best the capital has to offer'

The People

Rated 'Best Restaurant Guide

Sunday Times

Available at all good bookshops and timeout.com/shop from £6.99

100% Independ

of an artillery bombardment, but in their attempts to avoid work and eat as much as they possibly can.

Hasek died just before Svejk could be delivered to near-certain death or injury on the Eastern Front. The last sentence in the book is spoken by the portentous and idiotic Lieutenant Dub: "'Patriotism, fidelity to duty, victory over oneself, these are the weapons that matter in warfare." I am reminded of that especially today when our troops will in foreseeable time be crossing the frontier.'

By this point we have realised that 'victory over oneself' will prove difficult. One soldier, Baloun, eats everything he sees, including officers' food, and goes through paroxysms of shame and guilt afterwards, only to do exactly the same thing again at the first opportunity. Patriotism, the Marxist Hasek makes clear, is a nonsense, and Svejk's desire to fight for an empire on the edge of collapse earns him nothing more than the distrust of his Austrian officers, who are never sure if he is subtly mocking them or not. After all, what sane Czech would enthusiastically demand to fight his fellow Slavs? Such absurdist destabilising of authority would later make Svejk one of the founding texts of Czech nationalism, which is partly why – despite 50 years of Communism – it remained one of Europe's national movements.

Does it matter if a war book is fact or fiction? Not really, for who is to say which is which? Andy McNab, for instance, has been accused of inventing passages in Bravo Two Zero, and Stephan Crane was obliged to imagine the battle scenes in The Red Badge of Courage, published as it was in 1895, 30 years after the American Civil War ended. In Slaughterhouse Five, by contrast, Kurt Vonnegut uses his personal experience as a prisoner of war during the Allied firebombing of Dresden in February 1945 as the basis for an absurdist war novel.

Does it matter which war it is? Sometimes. Both The Red Badge of Courage and Ernest Hemingway's For Whom the Bell Tolls offer personal struggles positioned within wider conflicts with a strong moral dimension. The American Civil War was, after all, in part a war to end slavery, while resisting Franco's nationalists was a self-evidently worthy fight.

The war to end Nazism ostensibly had a similarly moral purpose, but nearly all good

'Those characters in English fiction who believe in the war's essential rightness are either naïve or archaic and out of place.'

American World War II fiction sees that conflict through a fog of cynicism and anti-authoritarian anger. Norman Mailer's The Naked and the Dead, a howl of rage and a superlative study of men at war, remains Mailer's most readable and coherent work. However, it still offers the possibility of individual redemption through combat and doesn't claim that the war itself is insane.

But by the time Catch-22 was published in 1961, the war against Hitler had lost its moral veneer: the only enemy combatants we encounter are German pilots flying missions for an American entrepreneur. In Slaughterhouse Five, Vonnegut replaces cynicism with a profound fatalism. Unable to find a useful explanation for what America does to Dresden, he can only offer the repeated refrain of 'so it goes' as the city and its inhabitants burn to death. To try to make sense of a world that makes no sense, Vonnegut uses the furniture of science fiction: time travel and aliens. War is neither good nor bad – it is just what happens, so is it best to do as the alien Tramalfadorians do and ignore it, or can the individual resist the collective madness?

Aside from the war memoirs of Spike Milligan, the British literary reaction to the war avoided surrealism and embraced cynicism. Those characters in English fiction who believe in the war's essential rightness are either naïve, like Guy Pringle, the non-combatant lecturer in Olivia Manning's Fortunes of War, or archaic and out of place like Guy Crouchback, the bewildered hero of Evelyn Waugh's Sword of Honour trilogy.

The latter thinks he is fighting against the beastliness of modern tyranny, but when he

Norman Mailer.

finds himself on the same side as the Soviet Union, the war is rendered meaningless for him. The retreat from Crete, one of the most cack-handed British failures of World War II, becomes a metaphor for the end of England, Empire and honour. Officers are cowardly or incompetent; the men drink themselves into oblivion, and as the ties of obedience snap and order collapses, the Germans need only advance steadily through the rabble.

Crouchback, as Waugh himself did in Crete, watches with a mixture of horror and detachment as everything he had previously held to be inviolate about England crumbles in front of his eyes. When the retreating troops reach the beach, instead of the mythologised Dunkirk of troops queuing in orderly fashion for boats while Stukas drop bombs, we see chaos, fear and, worst of all for Waugh, an officer threatening the very essence of Englishness itself by leaving his men behind.

The officer, Ivor Claire, is upper class, so he is sent to India rather than being shot for cowardice. Indeed, it is surprising how often Waugh, a very right-wing writer, portrays upper-class characters as shambolic, dishonest and ridiculous. The bloodthirsty Colonel Ritchie Hook is presented as an idiot throughout, and ridiculed as a representative of an outdated martial England. His desire to 'biff' the enemy was useful when all that was required was the destruction of spear-wielding natives with machine guns and aeroplanes, but it is no longer appropriate in the age of Blitzkrieg and total war, like his ongoing battle of wills with Captain Apthorpe over the latter's portable toilet (known as the 'thunderbox'). This obsession is a key motif, and the thunderbox's progress is mirrored by the picaresque travels of Trimmer – an arriviste and social impostor on whom Waugh unloads his considerable reserves of class hatred. Trimmer is the real horror of war, a déclassé sign of the times. In the future, honour, selflessness and religious faith will all be well and truly trimmed.

In Manning's *Fortunes of War*, Guy Pringle embodies the same looming post-war world. Manning's heroine, Guy's wife Harriet, accepts this future – it may be shoddy and full of drunks and impostors, but it is better than fascism (Waugh, one suspects, wasn't so sure). In any case, she is more interested in personal relationships than larger social ones – she has an affair with a handsome British officer, a romantic figure for whom there will be no place in Guy's new world.

There is no better book about the English at war, but for all Manning's genius it is snobbish. The poor bloody infantry who actually win battles by putting their bodies in the way of steel and fire are just as much of an unfocused mob in Manning as they are in Waugh. In Alexandria, Harriet encounters a British sergeant in the dark. Drunk, sentimental and culturally ignorant, he horrifies her. One senses, however, that unlike Ivor Claire, he won't run from the Germans when the Eighth Army finally stops their progress through the Middle East.

When I was in that region I saw no one reading Manning, nor Heller, Vonnegut, Mailer or Waugh. The Americans were playing *Doom* on their Xboxes, and though some British squaddies had battered copies of *Bravo Two Zero*, the volume I saw most often, and usually tucked into an officer's kit bag, was one of the most impenetrable and overwritten books of the last century: *The Seven Pillars of Wisdom* by TE Lawrence. The style is late 19th-century public school; florid and wearily heroic, it is in debt to Burton's translation of *The 1001 Nights*, the *Rubaiyat* of Omar Kayyam, Mallory's *Morte d'Arthur* and Gibbon's *The Decline and Fall of the Roman Empire* (only without the gags). David Lean's 1962 film *Lawrence of Arabia* has left the impression of a tale of derring-do, though the book is more about moral agonies than action. Lawrence takes to fighting with comparative ease; it is his obligation to lie to the Arabs he fights alongside that is the real test of his character, an examination that torments him. 'Instead of being proud of what we did together, I was continually and bitterly ashamed.'

The lie Lawrence told his comrades in arms was that revolt against the Turks would mean the creation of an Arab state; in fact, the British and French governments were planning to install themselves as the colonial rulers in the region once the Turks had been defeated. It is ironic that such a florid and old-fashioned book should speak so clearly to the here and now, but *The Seven Pillars of Wisdom*'s illustration of the dishonesty and frailty of British imperial ambitions in the Middle East ensures that it remains the most important war book of the last 100 years.

ADULTHOOD

Men at war in 20 books

The Assassin's Gate: America in Iraq by George Packer

An unflinching exploration of the causes and effects of the war waged in Iraq, examining both American and Iraqi perspectives. The author is *New Yorker* journalist George Packer – initially a staunch supporter of the invasion.

Atonement by Ian McEwan

By becoming a nurse and dealing with the horrific casualties of World War II, can Briony Tallis make amends for the tragedy that she set in motion as a child? For Robbie, the man she wrongly accused of rape, the horror of Dunkirk casts a new perspective on her 'crime': 'What was guilt these days? It was cheap. Everyone was guilty, and no one was.'

Birdsong by Sebastian Faulks

Stephen Wraysford's world is torn asunder by a failed affair with the beautiful Isabelle, shortly before Europe is itself ruptured by World War I. Lost and heartbroken, he enlists with the British Army to fight in France. The internal misery he faced after his lover's disappearance are soon matched by the external horrors of trench warfare.

Company K by William March

Written by a former US Marine, decorated for his bravery in World War I, the despairing, desolate *Company K* is made up of 123 accounts of the war, each written from a different soldier's perspective. Graham Greene was one of March's foremost admirers, declaring: 'His book has the force of a mob-protest; an outcry from anonymous throats.'

Dispatches by Michael Herr

As a correspondent for *Esquire*, Herr witnessed the horrors of the war in Vietnam first-hand. His account, like the war it describes, is fast-paced, violent and chaotic, mixing his own anecdotes, thoughts and impressions with those of the soldiers he meets. Herr would later collaborate on the screenplays for two of the most visceral films made about the conflict, *Apocalypse Now* and *Full Metal Jacket*.

Goodbye to All That by Robert Graves

Published in 1929, Graves's memoirs draw a vivid picture of life in the trenches in World War I, and its traumatic, psychological after-effects. 'Shells used to come bursting on my bed at midnight, even though Nancy shared it with me; strangers in daytime would assume the faces of friends who had been killed.'

Henry V by William Shakespeare

It's easy to be swept along by the thrilling rhetoric of Henry's famous rallying cry ('Once more unto the breach'), and inspired, impassioned speeches to his men. But to read the play as a celebration of war sits uneasily with the looting, greed and cowardice it depicts; Henry's sudden, brusque order to kill all the French prisoners is also far from glorious.

If I Die in a Combat Zone by Tim O'Brien

The combat zone in question is Vietnam, and O'Brien's powerful, fractured account of his experiences and uncertainties over what he and his fellow soldiers are fighting for makes for compulsive reading.

The Iliad by Homer

Gruesome battlefield deaths are recounted with forensic precision and considerable relish in Homer's epic. Consider the unfortunate Oenomaus, speared in his stomach: 'his bowels came gushing out and he clutched the earth in the palms of his hands as he fell sprawling in the dust.' Peisander is possibly even more unlucky. Hit 'just at the rise of his nose; the bones cracked and his two gore-bedrabbled eyes fell by his feet in the dust.'

The Last Post by Max Arthur

Published in 2005, Arthur's interviews with 21 surviving World War I veterans makes for poignant reading – in light of his subjects' age as well as their compelling, deeply moving accounts of the war.

Life and Fate by Vasily Grossman

Centering on the bloody siege of Stalingrad, Grossman's weighty novel was considered anti-Soviet thanks to the parallels it draws between Nazism and Stalinism. The book was banned for years; by the time it was finally published in Russia in 1988, Grossman had been dead for 24 years.

The Machine Gunners by Robert Westall

When a German plane crashes over Tyneside, 14-year-old Chas McGill salvages its machine gun; with his friends, and a German pilot they capture, he uses it to try to create a semblance of security and protection as imminent invasion looms.

On the Natural History of Destruction by WG Sebald

Sebald's impassioned study examines why the Allied bombing campaign in the latter stages of World War II, which killed some 600,000 civilians, became a taboo subject for the German people, who quietly buried the dead, rebuilt their cities and retreated into a kind of mass amnesia and 'self-imposed silence'. Sebald excavates these buried memories by recounting the untold stories of the Allied raids.

The Quiet American by Graham Greene

As war rages between the French and Communist forces in 1950s Vietnam, a deadly love triangle is played out. And as Thomas Fowler discovers, his

ADULTHOOD

Wilfred Owen, among many others, wrote movingly – and angrily – about **World War I**.

rival in love, the 'quiet American' of the title, Alden Pyle, has his own motives for coming to Saigon.

Regeneration by Pat Barker
A fictional account of Siegfried Sassoon's stay in a Scottish psychiatric hospital for soldiers – where he met Wilfred Owen. Sassoon is put into the care of Dr Rivers, whose patients have witnessed events beyond imagination: one man cannot eat, because a shell blew him face-first into the bloated stomach of a dead German. Gradually, Rivers starts to feel a deep unease about his own role, 'curing' his patients only to send them back to war.

Three Soldiers by John Dos Passos
Focusing on the stories of three very different US army privates who fought in World War I, Dos Passos's novel is a vivid portrayal – and searing indictment – of the psychological impact of military life and war on the individual. Sartre was a great admirer of the Portuguese-American novelist's work, describing him as 'the greatest writer of our time'.

The Tin Drum by Günter Grass
Grass's surrealist masterpiece is narrated by the diminutive Oskar Matzerath, from the confines of the lunatic asylum where is is being held on suspicion of murder. A depiction of German society from the 1930s to the '50s, the book is set against the turbulent backdrop of World War I, the rise of Hitler in the years that followed, and finally the post-war period.

Under Fire by Henri Barbusse
Published in 1916, *Under Fire* is an agonising account of the wartime experiences of a battalion of exhausted, disillusioned French soldiers. It vividly evokes the nightmarish world of the trenches, where the rotting bodies of the dead block the 'wide, twisting, and muddy furrow that the living must still defend'.

The War Poems by Wilfred Owen
Stunned and sickened by the horror meted out to a generation of young men, Owen forces the reader to stare unblinking at individual deaths – at the 'blood… gargling from the froth-corrupted lungs' of a man caught in a gas attack – in order to shatter the 'old Lie' that death in battle is 'proper' or 'valiant'.

The Wind-up Bird Chronicle by Haruki Murakami
Graphic, disturbing flashbacks to atrocities committed during World War II punctuate Murakami's sprawling, ambitious novel. The more faint-hearted might prefer to skip the description of a man being skinned alive.

History rewritten?

The best military histories have the power to change the way we think about war, says **Tim Newark**.

ADULTHOOD

Bogged down in the quagmire of Vietnam… Lions led by donkeys to their death on the Western Front… Two nightmare visions of war that are repeated daily on news bulletins as metaphors for campaigns gone wrong – but how true are they? Military history has the power to unnerve politicians and give ammunition to journalists, but if it is wrong history, it encourages wrong decisions. Military history can kill and it can save lives.

So what is good military history? What is the military history that can change your mind on something you once felt certain about? I once believed I knew everything about World War I – the tragedy of the first day of the Somme, the grinding hell of trench warfare, the incompetence of out-of-date British generals who believed cavalry were better than tanks. But then I started reading a new generation of military historians committed to uncovering the truth about World War I, however much it might clash with our national myths.

In *The Unquiet Western Front*, Brian Bond, Professor of Military History at King's College London, the leading academic centre for war and peace studies, contends that we have got it all wrong about World War I. The depiction of it as a pointless and wasteful conflict is the construct of post-war literature, especially the work of the War Poets and fiction such as *All Quiet on the Western Front* and *Journey's End*; even TV comedy like *Blackadder Goes Forth*. Instead, he shows that at the time, despite the high human cost in casualties, the war was considered necessary and just to halt German imperialism. That this was so

is proved by vivid, if less literary, memoirs of life on the Western Front.

Twelve Days on the Somme by Sidney Rogerson was written by a soldier caught up in the mud and misery of the most infamous of British battles. When he first published his memoirs in 1933, Rogerson was angry at the growing misrepresentation of the war. 'Recently there has been the war of the Sewers,' he said of the myth-makers, 'in which no one ever laughed, those who were not melancholy mad were alcoholically mad…' In reality, he wrote, 'Life in the trenches was not all ghastliness. It was a compound of many things; fright and boredom, humour, comradeship, tragedy, weariness, courage, and despair.'

When wartime prime minister Lloyd George wrote his memoirs in the 1930s, he managed to shift the blame for the conduct of World War I from the politicians to the generals, condemning Field Marshal Haig and his generals as incompetent commanders whose narrow-minded views contributed to unnecessary losses. That this was a great slander is exposed in *Forgotten Victory* by Gary Sheffield, a book that brilliantly shatters many myths of World War I. Contrary to received opinion, the British high command had been the first to warn that war against Germany would be no easy task and to expect heavy casualties. They embraced new technology and devised new tactics, turning a small colonial expeditionary force into an effective modern continental army that won a very definite victory in 1918. So much for lions led by donkeys. The tactical and technological learning curve successfully negotiated by the

World War II: the best-documented conflict of all.

The Japanese march into Nanking, 1937.

British Army is explained by Paddy Griffith in *Battle Tactics of the Western Front*.

Does all this matter? Surely, war is war and always horrible? That is true. But, it has been argued, it was the growing myth of World War I as a pointless war badly fought that encouraged British politicians in the 1930s to appease Adolf Hitler until it was too late and a second, even more destructive, conflict was inevitable.

The same process of military myth-making is true of the conflict in Vietnam. I thought I knew all about that war from watching movies like *Apocalypse Now*. Stoned American soldiers bring death and destruction down on peaceful Vietnamese, who end up chasing them out of their country with US tails between their legs. It is the greatest cautionary tale of American intervention. But then I read *Unheralded Victory* by Mark W Woodruff, a US Marine who served in Vietnam 1967-8.

Woodruff wrote his book because much of the myth of Vietnam just didn't accord with his own experience of the war. He discovered that drug-taking was not widespread among US soldiers. In fact, in 1971, only four per cent of service personnel tested positive for drug use. The Tet Offensive was not a victory for North Vietnam but a calamity for its army, with thousands killed by competent US forces – yet the Western media insisted on portraying it as a defeat, handing a propaganda victory to the Communist north. My Lai was a horrible massacre, but Vietnamese Communists committed many more atrocious crimes against their own people. At Hue, for example, the Viet Cong executed nearly 3,000 South Vietnamese civilians, but this was never reported around the world with the sense of outrage aroused by My Lai. I didn't know any of this until I read Woodruff's remarkable book, which should be required reading for any journalist tempted to abuse Vietnam as a metaphor for contemporary conflict.

World War II is the war we know most about, thanks to hours of documentary footage and movies, but even here, good military history can surprise us. In *Why the Allies*

Won, Richard Overy superbly analyses the economy and management of war, explaining exactly how it was that the Allies overcame their enemies.

Victory was not preordained, says Overy. It was Hitler's managerial incompetence that proved decisive: he encouraged destructive competition between his subordinates; he failed to make the most of the materials he captured; and even though the Nazis could produce rockets and jet fighters at the end of the war, they failed to provide enough trucks and jeeps to shift an army that was still largely dependent on horses for transport in 1944.

The Battle of Britain is our most celebrated victory of World War II, but the popular image of plucky little England beating off the overwhelming military might of Germany is far from the truth. In Stephen Bungay's *The Most Dangerous Enemy*, we learn that it was the Germans who took on more than they could chew. It was the superior technology and professionalism of Britain's fighter pilots that proved too much for the Germans, who had invested too much time and money in developing the wrong kinds of aircraft. The book also reveals that there was little camaraderie among RAF fighter aces who were determined to keep their elite status, even if it meant not passing on valuable tactical information to their colleagues.

The brutality of war is exposed in *The Rape of Nanking* by Iris Chang. It tells the story of the forgotten holocaust of 1937, when conquering Japanese soldiers ravaged the Chinese city of Nanking. In a few weeks, they raped, tortured and murdered 300,000 Chinese civilians in a frenzy of unrestrained violence. Read this, and you understand the continuing sense of outrage felt by Asian countries towards Japan. Cold War politics partly buried this atrocity, but Chang tells all.

A chilling account of the Nazi Holocaust is *Hitler's Willing Executioners* by Daniel Jonah Goldhagen. It shows how it was not just the Nazi Party that embraced the assault on Jewish people, but also ordinary Germans and neighbouring Eastern Europeans. A little-known tale of the price of German occupation is revealed in *Wine & War* by Don and Petie Kladstrup. It reveals how the Nazis looted the finest wines of France, but also how some Frenchmen risked their lives to preserve their heritage. False walls were built in top restaurants to hide vintage bottles, while cobwebs were gently laid over less desirable wines to give the impression of great age.

Modern military history really began in 1976, with *The Face of Battle* by John Keegan. This revolutionary book demolished the idea of military history as a kind of war game described in words, and replaced it with visceral descriptions of what actually happens to soldiers in battle. When I read this as a student, I was transfixed by the new level of reality in this approach: analysing every aspect of a soldier's experience, from the kind of wounds he might receive from different weapons to the psychological impact of combat. Having read this, nobody could ever write military history in the old way again.

Another equally revolutionary book is *The Western Way of War* by Victor Davis Hanson. It reconstructs ancient Greek warfare, but by doing so shows how the Greeks devised a new kind of confrontational fighting that was enormously brutal and violent, and designed to obtain a quick and decisive victory – in contrast to the Asian style of combat, which favoured never-ending guerrilla warfare.

'The Middle East shows that this distinction between two kinds of warfare still matters. The US can win decisive victories over Asian enemies, but when it comes to occupying their land, it faces unending guerrilla warfare.'

That this kind of warfare was uniquely Western and led to the European powers dominating the rest of the world is further explored by Geoffrey Parker in *The Military Revolution*.

Recent conflicts in the Middle East show that this distinction between two kinds of warfare still matters today. America and its allies can win quick decisive victories over Asian enemies, but when it comes to occupying their land, it faces unending guerrilla warfare. What this can mean for the average soldier is brilliantly captured by Mark Bowden in *Black Hawk Down*. In this heart-thumping account of a battle in Mogadishu in 1993, we see the combat unfold through the eyes of a handful of American troops surrounded by thousands of angry Somalis. It is the Rorke's Drift of the

From book to movie: **Black Hawk Down**.

late 20th century. The political cost of this battle, and the sight of dead US servicemen being dragged through Mogadishu, was the reason why America and other Western nations held back from intervening in the genocidal conflict in Rwanda.

The events of 9/11 changed America's natural tendency towards isolationism and led to the subsequent wars in Afghanistan and Iraq. In *A History of the English-Speaking Peoples Since 1900*, Andrew Roberts argues that this War against Terror, like those against Fascism and Communism, is another phase in the struggle of Anglo-Saxon nations against tyrannical powers. In his revisionist championing of English-speaking democracy, Roberts turns many long-held beliefs on their head. The Suez Crisis in 1956 was an error not

ADULTHOOD

for Britain but for America, which should have supported a strike against a Middle Eastern dictator – Gamal Nasser was the model for Saddam Hussein, after all.

A masterful book that savages the dangerous misconceptions of some Westerners towards totalitarian threats is *Reflections on a Ravaged Century* by Robert Conquest. It demonstrates how many intelligent observers in the 1920s and '30s allowed their desire for idealism to overlook the actual crimes of both Fascism and Communism. Conquest goes on to lampoon the way such misguided idealism managed to survive even World War II, continuing to see only good things in the Soviet Union. How Westerners could be so blind to the infiltration of enemy agents in the Cold War is brilliantly exposed by Anthony Glees in *The Stasi Files*, an amazing account of Communist access to the British establishment.

One of the best books to come out of the recent conflict in the Middle East is *We Were One* by Patrick K O'Donnell. This military historian put his life on the line to join a unit of US Marines in the battle for Fallujah in Iraq. Riveting and frightening, his book describes house-to-house fighting against Islamist insurgents, some veterans of the Chechen mujahideen, high on adrenalin jabs. Many of the Marines O'Donnell introduces us to lose their lives. 'We don't do this for freedom, apple pie,' says one of the soldiers at the end of the battle, 'but for the man to the left and right.' This has always been so. Lofty ideals mean little in battle. 'We worked side by side to destroy the enemy who was trying to destroy us.' There can be no 'ethical' way of fighting a war. It is best to understand this truth and forget the myth-making. That is what good military history does.

A book that changed my life

Will Napier

Where I'm Calling From: Selected Stories by Raymond Carver

It's the conversational tone of the narrative that got me. Still gets me. The simplicity of the stories and the way they are told are what make Raymond Carver's fiction stand out. There is a lot to be said for simplicity. There is a lot said with simplicity.

I didn't find Carver until I got to college. I was writing – almost exclusively horror stories back then – but there wasn't anything that made me re-evaluate what it was I was producing. An assigned reading scheduled for an American Literature class changed that.

'A Small, Good Thing' was my first taste of Carver. One of his longer

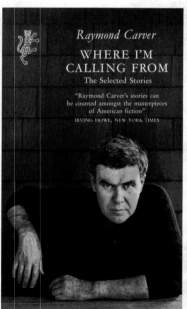

Raymond Carver
WHERE I'M CALLING FROM
The Selected Stories

"Raymond Carver's stories can be counted amongst the masterpieces of American fiction"
IRVING HOWE, NEW YORK TIMES

stories. The pace of his writing took hold. With short sentences, the eyes run on. If you eat small meals you eat more of them. You eat them without knowing. I went to find more of his works. 'The Third Thing that Killed My Father off', 'So Much Water So Close to Home', 'Bicycles, Muscles, Cigarettes' and other stories in his collections. Immediately engaging. Fulfilling, yet leaving you hungry for more.

Short-story writing became my passion. Maybe trying to emulate Carver. Maybe because short fiction fit with my life as it had with his. Producing stories when life gave me the time.

Will Napier's most recent novel is Summer of the Cicada *(Jonathan Cape).*

Working title

Theoretically, 'work', whether it consists of the most rudimentary kind of manual labour or sitting behind a Treasury desk for eight hours a day, ought to be a subject of consuming interest to the novelist. Not only – a few rentier exquisites excepted – is it a universal human experience, it is also one of the great venues for social interaction. Even the members of a chain gang can be guaranteed to speak to each other now and again. Higher up the mercantile ladder, the alliances and animosities of the average office corridor, the conferences over the photocopier and the nigglings by the coffee machine can be conducted with an almost Proustian subtlety. Work, in short, ought to occupy the writerly imagination as much as sex, or money, or power – it is intimately connected to at least two of these literary obsessions – and yet for the most part the Anglo-American novel has spent at least half of the first two or three centuries of its development resolutely denying the fact of its existence.

There were several reasons for this unwillingness to admit that the greater part of most waking lives is taken up by the routine obligation to earn a living. The most obvious has to do with social class. The 19th-century novelist, if not a gentleman by birth, invariably had gentlemanly aspirations: the idea that someone might support his family by breaking stones in a ditch or selling Manchester goods from behind a draper's counter would have seemed vaguely disgraceful. On the one hand, he approved of work's material rewards, and in particular the enhanced social status that proficiency at work allowed. On the other, the vital topic of how a man's salary was earned

scarcely interested him at all. In the entire canon of Dickens's novels, for example, hardly a single character is actually shown working. Mr Dombey in *Dombey and Son* is represented as a great merchant, a titan of the export market and all-round capitalist prince, but what exactly are the goods in which he deals, and where does he send them? Dickens never says. In much the same way, Doyce in *Little Dorrit* is trying to patent an invention that will revolutionise the engineering process, and yet Dickens nowhere tells us what his invention does.

This habitual vagueness over the way in which people earn their salaries infects Victorian fiction like a distemper. Nineteenth-century novels are awash with clerks, lawyers, engineers, medical men and parliamentarians whose whole professional lives exist off the page. When Trollope in *The Claverings* apprentices his hero Harry Clavering to a firm of engineers, he assumes from the outset that his readers will simply yawn over what duties the apprenticeship might entail: the real subject of the novel is Harry's relationship with his employee's daughter, Florence. The only contemporary trade in which Trollope can be got to take a sustained interest – his own professional calling, significantly enough – is the postal service: hence the almost neurotic concern, in the six novels of the *Barsetshire Chronicles*, as to how letters from one character to another make their way around the country.

Towards the end of the Victorian age, a faint democratising element began to declare itself. Jude Fawley in Hardy's *Jude the Obscure* is a stonemason, a trade with which Hardy, professionally trained as an architect, had a

ADULTHOOD

Working life is invisible in most of **Charles Dickens**' novels.

nodding familiarity. George Moore's *Esther Waters* is one of the first English novels to show country house life from the inside; that is, from the angle of the servant class drudging behind the scenes. HG Wells's early novels, notably *Kipps* and *The History of Mr Polly*, are rooted in the world of the late-Victorian drapery trade, where Wells had served his own teenage apprenticeship. But the real interest in work as a subject worth exploring on its own terms comes almost exclusively from American novelists.

Jack London's short story 'The Apostate', for example, is a pioneering attempt to examine the psychological effects of repetitive, long-term manual labour on the people compelled to undertake it. Johnny, its half-starved hero, is a teenage factory operative who has worked since early childhood to support his mother and his younger siblings. Eventually he falls ill: such is his reputation for hard work, though, that an admiring foreman promises to keep the job open for him. Then, on the day he is expected back at his loom, he refuses to get out of bed. His justification, as he tells his sorrowing mother, is that "'I've ben movin' ever since I was born.'" During his illness, he explains, he has made an extraordinary computation: the number of movements clocked up in a decade's hard labour: "'Twenty-five million moves a year, an' it seems to me I've been a movin' that way almost a million years.'" The piece ends with him bidding farewell to his mother (thereby, it is implied, condemning the family to penury) and wandering out of town to begin a vagrant, hobo's life on the freight trains.

This almost forensic interest in the practical processes of work is something new in fiction, but its trail can be followed all over the early 20th-century American bookshelf. This, after all, was the beginning of the US 'machine age', when cities doubled in size almost from one year to the next, and emigrants flooded west from central Europe to fill the millions of manual jobs created in their wake. There is no contemporary English version of, say, Theodore Dreiser's *The Titan*, in which the fortune racked up by its financier hero Frank Cowperwood is calculated almost from one stock-exchange transaction to the next, and hardly anything in the same category as Upton Sinclair's *The Jungle*, an exposé of the Chicago meat-packing plants so scarifying

that the laws were changed within a year. The nearest equivalent would be a novel like Robert Tressell's *The Ragged-Trousered Philanthropists*, which records, in punitive detail, the exploitation of a gang of spectacularly downtrodden Edwardian house-painters.

Tressell (the pseudonym of Robert P Noonan) had worked in the trade himself, at a time when the number of genuine proletarian novelists could be counted on the fingers of one hand. American writers, alternatively, tended to be more humbly born, to have first-hand experience of the kind of low-grade callings introduced into their work, and above all to be interested in putting these kinds of employment to fictional use. Clyde Griffiths, the doomed anti-hero of Dreiser's masterpiece *An American Tragedy*, is seen variously as a soda jerk, a hotel bell-hop and a departmental manager in his rich uncle's collar-making concern. Like Tressell's ground-down cast, Studs Lonigan in James T Farrell's *Studs Lonigan Trilogy* works as a painter and decorator for his father's firm ('His arm was tired. He wasn't at all interested in the damn work. He liked to look at it when it was finished, and see that it was a good job, and he always took pains to do a good job because he couldn't stand to slop on paint and leave it any old way. But goddamn it, he hated to think of going on, painting walls day after day after day…'). Work, or rather its absence, finally does for Studs: he dies of pneumonia, contracted after a day's fruitless job-hunting in Depression-era Chicago.

Studs's grim demise, leaving a pregnant fiancé and a three-act tragedy just waiting to be played out, gestures at one of the paradoxes of English fiction from the same period: the novels that purport to be about work and working people are generally about work's absence, the search for it and the disabling psychological consequences of its being withheld. What became known as the 'working-class novel' was well afloat as a genre by the 1930s, and yet its most characteristic products – novels such as Walter Greenwood's *Love on the Dole* or Harry Heslop's *Last Cage Down* – are actually about unemployment. Significantly, when Greenwood produced a novel in which 'work' plays a more than incidental part – *His Worship The Mayor*, in which a small shopkeeper inherits an opportune legacy – he

Critics' choice
Offices

All the President's Men
by Bob Woodward & Carl Bernstein

With the help of their source, 'Deep Throat', Woodward and Bernstein follow the trail from an innocuous-seeming burglary at the Watergate apartment complex in Washington DC all the way to the Oval Office, where Richard Nixon is in the habit of recording his conversations.

The Brainstorm by Jenny Turner

Lorna works on the 'brainy section' of a national newspaper now marooned in Docklands. The inmates of this corner of the newsroom, wittily described as 'The Pathetic Fallacy Made Flesh', include a statuesque bully named Julie and an intern with an advanced degree in philosophy.

The Castle by Franz Kafka

If Weber is the great theorist of bureaucracy, then Kafka is its poet laureate. The story of the surveyor K. is one of administrative error; the castle is a gigantic bureaucracy that continually rebuffs him.

Economy and Society by Max Weber

Bureaucracy literally means rule from a desk or office, and Weber is its first and greatest analyst; its essence, he argues, is elaborate, rule-governed hierarchy. The key to prospering in such a hierarchy? 'Pliancy towards the apparatus' and being at the 'convenience' of your superior.

A Far Cry from Kensington by Muriel Spark

Mrs Hawkins works at the Ullswater Press, an obscure publishing imprint with no future. Here she meets the preposterous Hector Bartlett, a terrible and incontinent hack with whom she enters into a long feud, after memorably describing him as a 'pisseur de copie'.

The Horned Man by James Lasdun

Lawrence Miller is an Englishman teaching at a university outside New York. The previous occupant of his office died, and now someone is spending the nights in there. The small room, with its polystyrene ceiling tiles and four-drawer filing cabinet, becomes the setting for a terse and beautifully controlled Gothic thriller.

Indecision by Benjamin Kunkel

Dwight Wilmerding spends his days sitting in a 'cube farm' at the headquarters of a big pharmaceutical company, 'colluding' in his own mediocrity. Salvation comes in two forms: the writings of a German philosopher, which he reads during his lunch breaks, and Abulinix, a drug designed to cure chronic indecision.

Microserfs by Douglas Coupland

The titular Microserfs are employees of Bill Gates's empire, the setting the Microsoft 'campus'. Narrator Daniel Underwood, whose obsessions are 1970s TV and the history of Apple computers, leaves serfdom in Seattle for a start-up developing a kind of virtual Lego, 'Oop!'.

Mr Phillips by John Lanchester

This remarkable novel records the quiet disintegration of a man after he is kicked out of his office. Mr Phillips has been summarily sacked from his job as an accountant, but still gets up and leaves the house as if he were going to work. He passes the time calculating, among other computations, the average daily probability that he won't have sex.

Perfect Tense by Michael Bracewell

Bracewell attempts a kind of novelistic phenomenology of modern office life, set in a single day and narrated by a fortysomething functionary. He turns his gaze on everything from the commute to the contents of the average desk drawer.

Post Office by Charles Bukowski

We follow Henry Chinaski as he takes a job sorting mail. *Post Office* is perhaps the best known of Bukowski's books, which perch uneasily somewhere between the Beats and pulp fiction.

Then We Came to the End by Joshua Ferris

In his ambitiously polyphonic first novel, set in an under-achieving Chicago-based advertising agency, Ferris tracks the struggles of employees to 'move up a notch chair-wise' as the company haemorrhages business.

Towards the End of Morning
by Michael Frayn

A more or less definitive example of a now defunct sub-genre: the Fleet Street novel. John Dyson is stuck working in the neglected corners of an ailing national newspaper – 'nature notes' and the crossword. Can he ever escape?

had to set it slightly higher up the social scale. At the same time, the almost self-conscious mundanity of much British fiction of the 1930s – a deliberate attempt to get away from the 'party' novel that had dominated the previous decade – found novelists examining career choices that would rarely have been entertained by their predecessors of half a century before.

Gordon Comstock, the put-upon poetry-writing hero of Orwell's *Keep the Aspidistra Flying*, works, as Orwell had done, in a Hampstead bookshop. Bob, Jenny and Ella, the three central characters of Patrick Hamilton's London trilogy, *Twenty Thousand Streets Under the Sky* are, respectively, a pub waiter, a prostitute and a barmaid. Like his creator, Richard Fanshawe in Julian Maclaren-Ross's *Of Love and Hunger* sells vacuum cleaners on the pre-war south coast.

Alongside them rose a tide of novels about business and the professions, in which, following the Victorian template, interest in the comic or tragic possibilities offered up by the activity involved is balanced by an almost complete separation from the work itself. Not the only Dickensian characteristic of JB Priestley's *Angel Pavement*, in which the sinister interloper Mr Golspie systematically defrauds the firm of Twigg & Dersingham, is Priestley's conspicuous lack of interest in the veneers and inlays in which the company deals. An exception, perhaps, is Anthony Powell's *What's Become of Waring* which, drawing on Powell's own experience of labouring for Gerald Duckworth & Co, offers a horribly accurate account of working conditions in a London publishing firm of the Baldwin era.

This tradition persists deep into the post-war landscape: stacks of novels about the burgeoning national bureaucracy, whether practised by the wartime intelligence services (Anthony Powell's *The Military Philosophers*) or in CP Snow's *Corridors of Power*, but very little about the implications of that bureaucracy

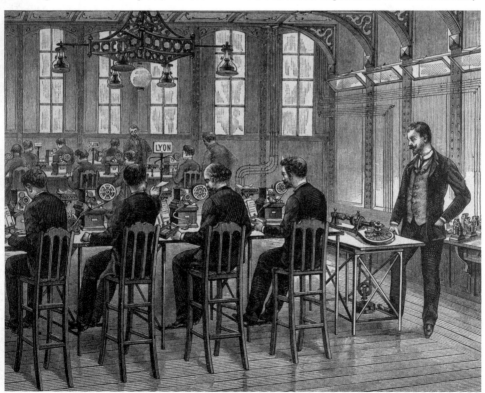

The Victorian office rarely features in Victorian literature.

for the people caught up in it. William Cooper's *The Struggles of Albert Woods* is a typical example of the 'New Man' novel of the 1950s, in which professional life is beginning to be colonised by upwardly mobile grammar school boys, whose lowly social origins would previously have denied them this preferment. Cooper's hero is a brilliant young research chemist who bags an Oxford fellowship, sits on Whitehall committees and eventually synthesises a new kind of nerve gas. From Albert's side of the desk, on the other hand, professional life takes the form of an immensely sophisticated game in which the only real motive is personal advancement, and the work one undertakes merely a means to that end.

A similar displacement can be seen further down the scale in the post-war vogue for gritty social realism from the working-class Midlands and the North. Work, to Arthur Seaton in Alan Sillitoe's *Saturday Night and Sunday Morning* or Arthur Haggerston in Sid Chaplin's *The Day of the Sardine*, has no intrinsic validity or interest: it is there, in Seaton's case at any rate, to provide the funding for a social life that will help the worker to forget the pointlessness of the 9 to 5.

Only in one area of post-war professional life, perhaps, did British novelists dignify 'work' with a moral importance whose implications were worth teasing out. This – all too predictably, given that so many of them came to be involved in it – was the teaching of literature in universities. Usually thought to derive from the upper-brow slapstick of Kingsley Amis's *Lucky Jim*, the 'campus novel' pioneered on this side of the Atlantic by writers such as Malcolm Bradbury and David Lodge invariably disguises a more serious subtext. Taken together, the novels that make up Bradbury's trilogy of campus fiction – *Eating People is Wrong*, *Stepping Westward* and *The History Man* – are nothing less than a defence of liberal humanism against the various ideologies (fashionable Marxism in *The History Man*, for instance) quietly trying to subdue it. As well as being one of the great comic standbys of the post-war novel, the university teacher has another, more subterranean existence, as a symbol of moral and intellectual freedom.

Naturally enough, writers tend to set their fiction in the professional environments with

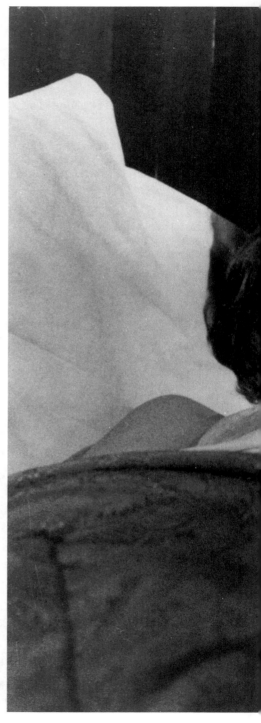

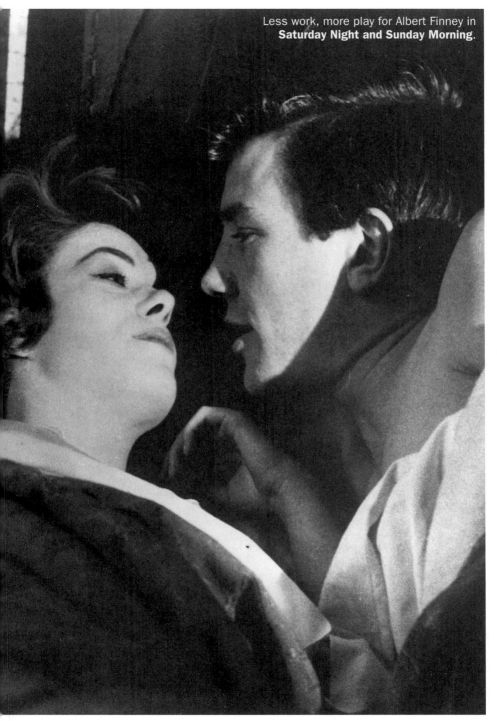
Less work, more play for Albert Finney in **Saturday Night and Sunday Morning**.

ADULTHOOD

The 1981 TV version of **The History Man**.

which they themselves are familiar. Post-war British fiction, consequently, is rife with books set in branches of the media, in advertising agencies, newspaper offices and publishing firms. On the other hand, writers are natural solitaries. Whatever experience they may have gained of 'office life' is usually deeply disillusioning. A novel such as Roy Fuller's *Image of a Society* – Fuller doubled up as a building society lawyer – or, from America, Nicholson Baker's *The Mezzanine*, in which the environment is seen as something more than a charnel house enclosing a band of resentful drones, is a comparative rarity.

As for the really important modern developments in 'work' – globalisation, the rise of the international money markets, the creation of a virtual economic world stratospherically removed from the processes of ordinary life – the number of contemporary writers capable of understanding their complexity, much less

rendering them into fictional form, could be accommodated behind a very small table.

One of the great merits of Justin Cartwright's *Look At It This Way*, set mostly in the City of London at the time of the Lawson boom, or his *In Every Face I Meet*, which examines some of the consequences of the Lawson boom's aftermath, is that Cartwright has done his homework; he can see both the absurdity of running an options desk and the likely effects on the individuals caught up in the high-grade Monopoly game that was late 20th-century capital exchange. If I try very hard, I can just about imagine a 21st-century Dreiser – someone able to write about the financial basis of the modern world at a level beyond the reportage of the average Wall Street thriller. That this panoptic intelligence shows no sign of arriving is perhaps only another mark of the fatal detachment of the modern 'literary' writer from the society that he or she presumes to reflect.

Women in war

Juliet Gardiner finds literary treasure in women's wartime writing.

Invited by Cyril Connolly to review war books for *Horizon* in 1941, Tom Harrison, an ex-ornothologist turned Mass-Observer of the English, found little to commend in what he called 'this conglomeration, chaotic effluvia of a world confused'. And among the producers of this 'effluvia' were the 'lady novelists [who] have reflected the paper war,' including Phyllis Bottome, Daphne du Maurier, Vera Brittain, Storm Jameson, Ursula Bloom, F Tennyson Jesse, Margery Allingham and EM Delafield, but 'hats off to Naomi Mitchison for quietly cultivating harsh lands in the Mull of Kintyre'.

Not that 'lady novelists' confined their wartime writing to novels: Noel Streatfeild – author of *Saplings*, an unsettling book about wartime disruption and disintegration seen from the perspective of four children – noted that she frequently received 'a telephone call asking me to write a fairy story for children in connection with war weapons week'. She also penned regular bulletins for the WVS and kept a 'woman's diary', *London Under Fire* (which her publishers declined to publish until after the war, by which time she had lost interest in it). But when challenged 'about the place of the novelist in the world at war, I stood up for their value as historians of their age.'

Naomi Mitchison might have been 'cultivating harsh lands', but she was also wrestling with her most ambitious novel, *The Bull Calves*, writing poetry and keeping a wartime diary for Mass-Observation, an edited version of which was published some years later as *Among You Taking Notes*, a profoundly intelligent and poignant record of the dilemmas and complexities of wartime life for women of a certain class.

Frances Partridge was not yet a novelist, but she was certainly an embedded chronicler of Bloomsbury at war, and her diaries, *A Pacifist's War*, record its wartime foibles and the angst felt by Partridge and her husband, Ralph, a conscientious objector. But at the centre of Bloomsbury's sensibilities lie Virginia Woolf's magnificent wartime diaries, kept because 'writing is my resistance', as well as *Between the Acts*, her novel about a village community on the eve of war, which was the last book she wrote before she took her own life in March 1941 – and a novel that Harrison appears not to have noticed.

Not all diarists, of course, lived in such a rarefied world. Vere Hodgson, who worked for a charity in Notting Hill, regarded herself as an 'unimportant person', a recorder rather than a writer, but nevertheless she kept a regular diary from 1924 until 1973. Her detailed wartime diaries were published as *Few Eggs and No Oranges*. 'Housewife 41' was the signifier of another 'unimportant person' who kept a regular diary for Mass-Observation. Nella Last was a housewife from Barrow-in-Furness who confessed that 'next to being a mother, I'd have loved to write books'. Published as *Nella Last's War*, her diary has been mined relentlessly ever since by historians avid for small details of quotidian wartime life. The same fate will no doubt befall *Love and War in London*, the recently published diary of another M-O contributor, Olivia Crockett.

In 1941, middle-aged, well-educated Kathleen Church-Bliss and her close friend Elsie Whiteman gave up running a tearoom on the A3, since petrol rationing had severely limited the number of passing motorists. They

ADULTHOOD

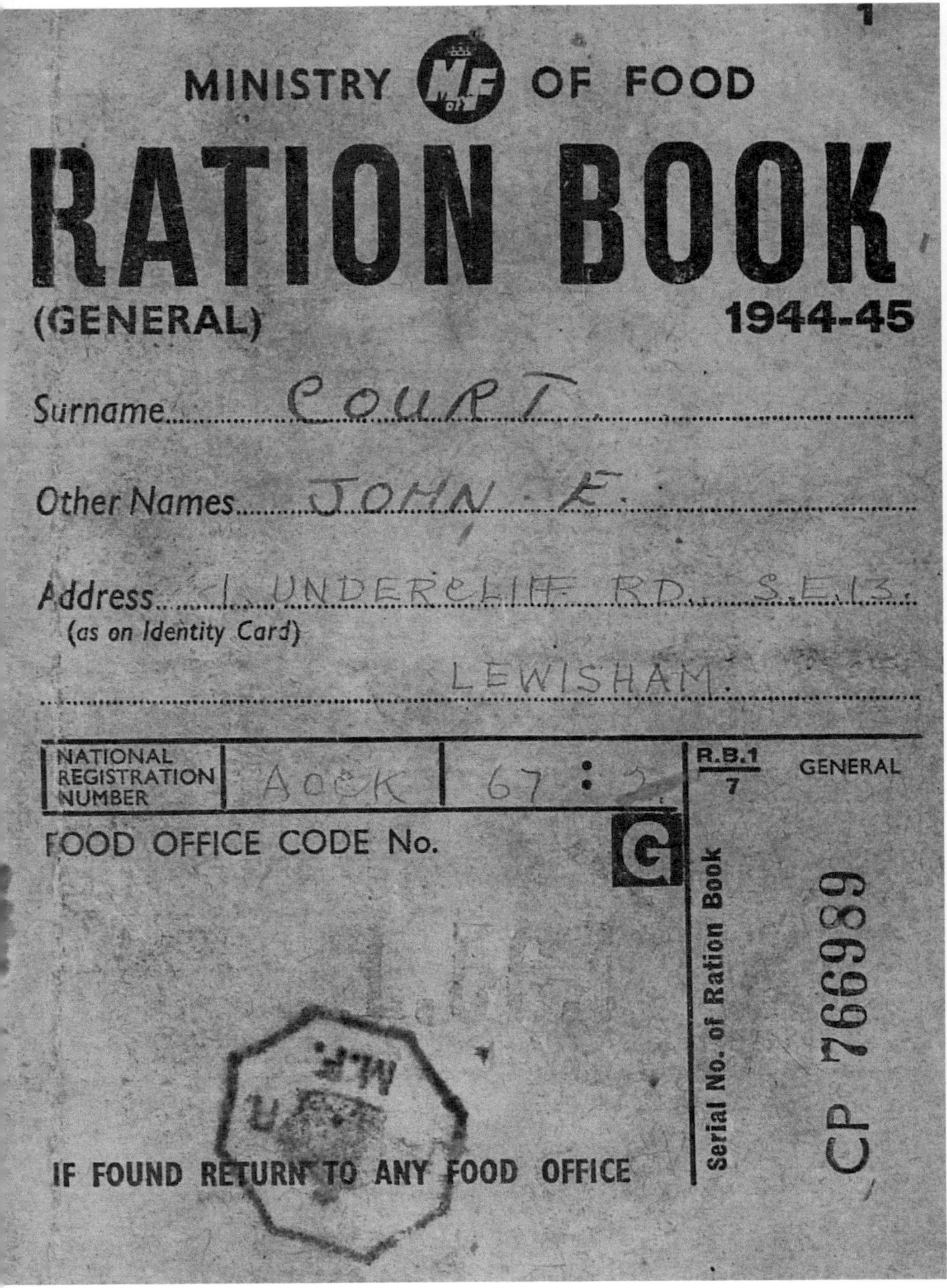

MINISTRY ⟨MF⟩ OF FOOD

RATION BOOK

(GENERAL)　　　　　　　　1944-45

Surname......**COURT**......

Other Names......**JOHN . E .**......

Address......**1. UNDERCLIFF RD. S.E.13.**......
(as on Identity Card)

......**LEWISHAM.**......

| NATIONAL REGISTRATION NUMBER | AOCK | 67 : ? | R.B.1 7 | GENERAL |

FOOD OFFICE CODE No.　　　　　**G**

Serial No. of Ration Book

CP 766989

IF FOUND RETURN TO ANY FOOD OFFICE

volunteered to become one of the three-quarters of a million women working in the aircraft industry. Their co-produced diary, published as *Working for Victory*, provides a sublime insight into the small triumphs, large irritations and perpetual exhaustion of women's war work.

Joan Wyndham could hardly have found a moment to keep a diary, but her breathless fusion of exuberant sexuality with the tough realities of war makes her two volumes of memoirs, *Love Letters* and *Love is Blue* (about her time in the WAAF), an exhilarating adjunct to the usual female preoccupations with rationing and evacuees.

Vera Brittain, whose *Testament of Youth* was the defining text of regret for World War I, published what in effect were three accounts of the next war, as well as several pamphlets, including *Seeds of Chaos*, almost the sole public protest raised against the carpet bombing of German cities. *Testament of Experience* picks up where *Testament of Youth* left off. *Wartime Chronicle* is an edition of her diaries from 1939 to 1945, while *England's Hour* is a 'close-up study' of London during the Blitz that tidies up Brittain's own wartime experience as a campaigning pacifist by eliding events and changing names (her daughter Shirley, now Williams, becomes Hilary for example).

The crime writer Margery Allingham continued to write novels, but also produced a vivid picture of her Essex village's experience of East End evacuees in *The Oaken Heart*, in which she too tactfully veiled identities. Mollie Panter Downes also straddled wartime genres. Her vivid dispatches from a garden shed in Haselmere cabled to the *New Yorker* were published as *London War Notes, 1939-1945*. Downes wrote a near perfect reflection of the hard-won gains of war in *One Fine Day*, and her short stories for the *New Yorker* have recently been collected under the title *Goodnight Mrs Craven*. This is a marvellously bittersweet compilation, redolent of women being brave in gay little hats as their men go off to war.

Short stories came into their own in wartime. This was partly because of the sort of war that it was – with snatched intervals in the shelter during an air raid, on watch as an ARP warden, or on duty at an isolated Ack Ack gun site – and partly because wartime paper quota regulations encouraged collections and anthologies. Elizabeth Bowen, for instance,

found herself incapable of writing a novel during the war. Unable to find a continuous narrative in those fractured years, she produced instead a string of short stories, including the eerie 'Ivy Gripped the Steps'. Her masterpiece *Heat of the Day*, which burns with the ache and treachery of war, was not published until 1949.

But other women writers found themselves able to take as their theme the quiet desperation of so many female lives in wartime. Unlike one of the best-known wartime women, Mrs Miniver (an imaginary character in Jan Struther's weekly column in *The Times*, later published as a book and then released in the US as a hit film), who was preternaturally cheerful about everything from rotting sandbags to the 'singing ropes' of barrage balloons, most women made 'coping' their watchword and 'for the duration' an unspoken subtext.

EM Delafield sent her bestselling *Provincial Lady* to war even though she was 'forced to realise that Cook's gas mask is intrinsically of greater importance than problematic contribution of self to wartime literature'. Elizabeth Taylor's husband served in the RAF, and in her painfully acute first novel, *At Mrs Lippincote's*, Julia Davenant's husband is also in the air force, but on a home posting that his commanding officer hopes will help to repair the couple's unravelling marriage.

Betty Miller's *On The Side of the Angels* evokes the pernicious infection of war, while Marghanita Laski adopted the nom de plume Sarah Russell to write *To Bed with Grand Music*, a cool satire about an serving officer's wife who didn't 'cope' in the accepted way, but instead used the opportunities that war can also bring to women to abandon her family and live a life of scent and fur coats, Polish officers and generous GIs.

'If only I were making munitions, or had joined the Forces,
my grandchildren, I know, would not think I'd fought in vain,
but why on earth I did some of the things I am doing now
Will be terribly tiresome to explain.'

So wrote Virginia Graham in her collection of poems *Consider the Years*, the work of an authentic historian of her age spelling out a 'world confused' by war in all its varied manifestations.

ADULTHOOD

Mightier than the
sword?

What makes a powerful polemic? **Nick Cohen** has his say.

Writers seeking lasting fame are much more likely to find it if they produce romance, children's stories, heist capers, sword-and-sorcery fantasies – any form imaginable, as long as it is not polemic. Nothing brings home the futility of political writing more forcefully than going through an old newspaper and reading the fulminations of 25 years ago. The savaged politicians are retired or dead, the scandals that provoked the writer's scorn forgotten. In the British press, editors praise polemical journalists for producing 'good rants' – a backhanded compliment if ever there was one. Polemicists themselves often agree with their editors and dismiss their craft as the hasty channelling of emotion that would have been better spent elsewhere. In 1944 a weary George Orwell looked back with regret and wrote that 'in a peaceful age I might have written ornate or merely descriptive books, and might have remained almost unaware of my political loyalties. As it is I have been forced into becoming a sort of pamphleteer.'

Yet a few pamphlets live on long after the battles of their age are over – for two reasons, in my view. First, because future generations realise that on one big point, if not every detail, the polemicist was right. Scoring in a debate is not enough, though, if a second condition isn't met: the polemicist must touch on contemporary concerns. However vital they were, no one except historians reads the fights about monetarism in the Thatcher years, but everyone has an interest in the battles of tradition against change, faith against free thought and women's rights against male power, because they define the future as well as the past.

The greatest polemics in English are Edmund Burke's *Reflections on the French Revolution* and Tom Paine's counterblast, *The Rights of Man*. These are great because they define the struggle between conservatism and change. Burke saw how the revolution would lead to a new tyranny and wrote in 1790 that 'the republic of Paris will endeavour, indeed, to complete the debauchery of the army, and illegally to perpetuate the assembly, without resort to its constituents, as the means of continuing its despotism.' That was prescient. The Reign of Terror didn't begin until September 1793.

At the time, Paine replied with a bewilderment shared by many and condemned Burke's 'outrageous abuse on the French Revolution, and the principles of Liberty'. His enemy did not seem so outrageous three years later, when Robespierre ordered Paine's imprisonment. Meanwhile Paine's argument in favour of democratic republics remains the best defence and means of attack against every form of tyrannical government of that time and since. English radicals of the 1790s loved it, but the aristocratic rulers of Britain had never encountered such an articulate assault and tried Paine in absentia for seditious libel.

The history of successful feminist polemics, from Mary Wollstonecraft's *A Vindication of the Rights of Woman* to Germaine Greer's *The Female Eunuch*, is one of abuse – revoltingly violent abuse in Wollstonecraft's case – followed by partial and belated acceptance. George Orwell's condemnations of the indifference of the 1930s Left to the victims of Communism in *The Road to Wigan Pier* and

Late 18th-century caricature of **Thomas Paine**, 'the little American taylor'.

Homage to Catalonia were more unpopular still. Now it is next to impossible to write about the '30s without mentioning him. Christopher Hitchens' comparable attack on modern liberal-Left apologetics for Islamism in *Love, Poverty and War* and other essays has made former friends hate him. I think his work is a modern example of polemic at its best and that it will last, maybe along with Robert Hughes's assault on political correctness in *Culture of Complaint* and Naomi Klein's condemnations of corporate power in *No Logo*.

If I am right, all three will eventually have to convince even those who are politically predisposed to dislike them that they had a case. The great polemicists jump this bar with ease. A modern conservative can read Tom Paine and recognise that he was fighting for the best freedoms of our world, while deploring his belief that it is a simple matter to dispense with the past. Left-wingers have every reason to raise their eyebrows at Burke's saccharine laments for the age of chivalry, but can see that he understood how revolution in the name of

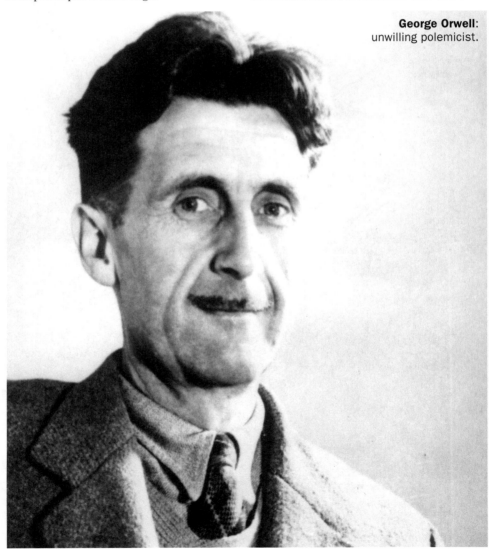

George Orwell: unwilling polemicist.

liberty can beat a path to tyranny that has been trod many times since. By contrast, I can't imagine anyone now choosing to read *What Is to Be Done?* and Lenin's other polemics written before the Russian Revolution. Lenin was a powerful writer, but his ideas about tiny groups of militants seizing power in the name of the working class led to three of the most murderous regimes in history, and among their millions of victims was Lenin's future readership.

Polemicists rarely know if their work will be accepted when they write. The tension between believing you are right and fearing that the world will not listen prompts the anger that fills great as well as dreadful polemics. But it also produces a respect for argument that those who dismiss all polemic as mere ranting fail to see. If you can feel a need to make an unpopular case – and there is no point in being a political writer if you can't – you must use your talent to win over a sceptical audience. You must acknowledge doubts and counter-arguments, and above all, you must write clearly.

For this reason, and despite being intellectuals themselves, the great polemicists of the English tradition from Swift onwards have tended to be anti-academic. Burke loathed the 'sophists, economists and calculators' of the Enlightenment. Robert Hughes denounced the 'kind of wooze, unbolstered by proof or evidence, patched together out of vaguely "radical" apercus,' which poured out of the postmodern cultural studies departments of American universities in the '80s. Whether they are from the Left or Right, good polemicists are the enemies of obscurantism. They crave to be understood, and suspect that those who wilfully place unnecessary obstacles in front of the reader are protecting an established interest from scrutiny.

Is that so terrible? Is that mere raving? It can be. The bluff newspaper writer who comforts rather than confronts his readers' prejudices always claims to be a plain-speaking man of the people. But in better circumstances, polemical clarity isn't philistinism or affectation but a recognition that the unfamiliar is hard to grasp and must be explained in a simple style if readers' assumptions are to be overcome. Great polemicists have a guilty secret. They rant when they have to, but they can also be terribly reasonable people.

A book that changed my life

Jonathan Franzen

The Trial by Franz Kafka

More than any other single book, Kafka's *The Trial* changed my life. There are so many books I feel like plugging, but a particular kind of comedy that I'm suited for and most susceptible to is the comedy of not knowing yourself – of desperately avoiding the news about yourself. *The Trial* was the first book where I really encountered that. It's a giant instance of that comedy! Kenzaburo Oë's *A Personal Matter* is also right up there. Everyone should read that. It's close to perfect. Short, too – you can do it in an evening. I thought Stendhal's *The Charterhouse of Parma* was going to change my life. I briefly thought I would quit writing fiction for a few years and become a political journalist. Then I found out how boring it is to be a political journalist.

Jonathan Franzen's most recent book is The Discomfort Zone: A Personal History *(Fourth Estate).*

Of myths and men

Dave Hill explores the paradoxes of masculinity.

The book has yet to be written that is not in some way about men and masculinity. Even those written by, for and about women are always about the other sex too, precisely because of its exclusion. We talk about the sexes in terms of oppositions, often literally as opposites, sometimes as the two halves of a complementary whole, sometimes as wholly incompatible. It's as though one sex can't be defined except in contrast to the other. My favourite books about masculinity explore the workings of this polarisation, or expose its implications, or do both.

Non-fiction works are the easiest to pick. That's because there have been so depressingly few resisting the seemingly interminable tide of gene-fever tomes proclaiming 'hard-wired', bedrock psychological divides between all men on the one hand and all women on the other, denied at our peril and so on. Denial, though, is not the problem. Routine acceptance of such dreary essentialism is.

Significantly, the wisest feminists have often been best at pointing this out. Lynne Segal's *Slow Motion* has recently been republished, fully revised from its 1990 original. A basic premise of this exhaustive overview of modern male conditions is that there is no absolute masculinity, but many masculinities, all of them always embedded in a culture and constantly shifting according to social context and through time. Y-chromosomes, testosterone and the so-called 'male brain' barely begin to explain the ways men are. Another classic, Australian gender theorist RW Connell's *Masculinities*, comes from the same direction, demolishing conventional models of analysis and making the man-friendly case for a majority of men seeing genuinely progressive feminism as their ally, not their enemy.

A different kind of read coming to similar conclusions is Michael Kimmell's *Manhood in America*, a cultural history tracing how definitions of masculinity have changed as America has changed, and how they've affected the way men go about being alive. It draws on the worlds of work, sport, popular culture and more in order to examine the roots of the 'crisis of masculinity', demonstrating that some of those crying 'crisis' most stridently seek only to reassert those aspects of 'traditional' maleness that generate crises in the first place.

Kimmell, like Connell and Segal, takes apart the 'mytho-poetic' masculinist movement launched by Robert Bly's *Iron John* and Sam Keen's *Fire in the Belly*. Both were huge bestsellers at the start of the 1990s and worth reading for that reason. But, gentleman – beware the call of the fantasy wild. You're better off with a cool girl like Susan Faludi, whose *Stiffed* shows that many men get a raw deal from society not because of 'the feminists' or the 'feminisation' of work, education and everything, but because corporate culture exploits them. *Stiffed* is a companion to Faludi's earlier *Backlash*, which tracked the reaction against women's struggles for equality. 'One of the gross misconceptions about feminism,' she told *Mother Jones* magazine, 'is that it's only about women. But in order for women to live freely, men have to live freely, too.'

Masculinity in its harshest and most neurotic forms cages far more men than it liberates. This truth still attracts ridicule, yet it has always and everywhere been self-evident. Find it in the fragility of men interviewed in Shere

Masculinity and domesticity: a fraught arena.

Critics' choice
Fights

The American by Henry James

'Quite apart from the goodness of the cause in which a duel may be fought, it has a kind of picturesque charm which in this age of vile prose seems to me greatly to recommend it [...] Depend upon it, a duel is never amiss.' But Valentin's duel, fought over the affections of the scheming Noémie Nioche, is to end in tragedy.

Brighton Rock by Graham Greene

Forget the Queensbury Rules and fighting fair: cut-throat razors and sulfuric acid are the weapons of choice by the seaside, in the dark, claustrophobic world of Pinkie and his gang.

David Copperfield by Charles Dickens

Our hero is roundly defeated in his skirmish with the fearsome butcher's boy, and left feeling 'very queer about the head' – but at least Agnes is there to tenderly administer beefsteak and brandy.

Death in the Afternoon by Ernest Hemingway

Hemingway loved the rituals and drama of the corrida (bullfighting). 'I was trying to learn to write, commencing with the simplest things, and one of the simplest things of all and the most fundamental is violent death,' he explains – and he saw plenty in the dusty bullrings of Spain.

The Duel by Anton Chekhov

Ivan Andreich Laevsky, a minor goverment official, lives in a small town with his mistress, Nadezhda Fyodorovna, who has abandoned her husband to be with him. As their relationship sours and both grow increasingly bored and discontent, she embarks on an affair. Enraged by Laevsky's apathy and indecision, another man, Von Koren, challenges him to a duel.

The Fight by Norman Mailer

The Rumble in the Jungle – the historic 1974 heavyweight title clash between Muhammad Ali and George Foreman – is the subject of Mailer's classic piece of sports reporting, notable for its fine, evocative imagery. Foreman's hands, we are told, 'were his instrument, and he kept them in his pockets the way a hunter lays his rifle back into its velvet case.'

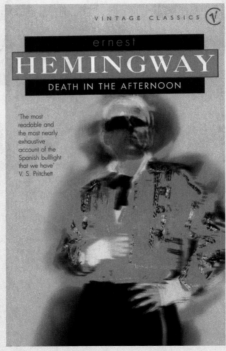

VINTAGE CLASSICS

ernest

HEMINGWAY

DEATH IN THE AFTERNOON

'The most readable and the most nearly exhaustive account of the Spanish bullfight that we have' V. S. Pritchett

Money by Martin Amis

'I live like an animal,' narrator John Self declares. 'Eating and drinking, dumping and sleeping, fucking and fighting – and that's it.' Self is typical of Amis's protagonists, who are forever ready to 'fuck or fight'.

Hamlet by William Shakespeare

Horatio's misgivings about Hamlet's duel with Laertes prove well founded – there's treachery afoot.

Royal Flash by George Macdonald Fraser

GMF pens a terrific final swordfight between his infamous coward-cum-hero Harry Flashman and the villainous Rudi von Starnberg. Unable to plead, flee or (heaven forbid) fight his way out of trouble, Flashy does what he does best: he cheats.

Women in Love by DH Lawrence

The unmistakeably homoerotic scene in which Gerard and Rupert wrestle naked, their bodies 'clinched into oneness', is notorious – partly thanks to Alan Bates and Oliver Reed's spirited (and full-frontal) onscreen re-enactment.

ADULTHOOD

Hite's *Report on Male Sexuality*; in the escapist, obsessive and homosocial compensations football provided for Nick Hornby as described in *Fever Pitch*; the forgotten history of hands-on fatherhood disinterred by Adrienne Burgess in the course of *Fatherhood Reclaimed*; the psychotherapeutic findings of Anthony Clare in *On Men*; the transvestite wanderings of *The Naked Civil Servant*, Quentin Crisp in the dim streets of interwar Pimlico.

In all these we meet men negotiating mismatches between the forms of maleness they're asked to strive towards and the more delicate flowers – the nuanced human beings – they actually are. That is not to say that some Real Man archetypes and aspirations don't appeal. They do; ask a bloke. And in fiction they may beguile. Raymond Chandler's Philip Marlowe often sees the worst in girls but makes a virtue of sardonic solitude, while his anti-heroic incorruptibility speaks to a male ideal of honour without reward or frills. Find it in *Farewell My Lovely*, *The Long Goodbye* and other classic private-eye pulp.

Ernest Hemingway, of course, is the scribe most routinely – and tellingly – named the man's man of writers, elaborating what's been dubbed a 'philosophy of manhood' in all his work. His 1952 novella *The Old Man and the Sea* expounds this with touching and terrible simplicity: an unequal struggle with ageing and with nature to which his wrinkled fisherman is drawn nonetheless. For Hemingway, to duel with death is true manhood's almost divine destiny. Has fishing ever been less relaxing?

Others, more contemporary, address suburban maleness and its discontents. Joseph Heller is more famous for his legendary war satire *Catch-22*, itself a guy-stuff tale. But its successor, *Something Happened*, captures a certain postwar, white-collar masculinity brilliantly, its hero Bob Slocum enduring slow spiritual death by office politics, paternal helplessness and loveless domesticity. It identifies emotional isolation as a disabling state of manhood more than a decade before its general recognition. Something similar assails Richard Ford's creation, Frank Bascombe, in *The Sportswriter*, adrift in the 'dreaminess' with which he lags himself against the grief of losing a child to death, a wife to divorce and a life to easy options. We meet him again in *Independence Day*, selling real estate. Say no more.

'Masculinity in its harshest and most neurotic forms cages far more men than it liberates.'

Bascombe represents the kind of problem to which Chuck Palahniuk's *Fight Club* proposes a solution. It's the Bly diagnosis in a different form: time to get back to challenge, brotherhood, pain. The book is brilliant and funny. How is its diagnosis, though? Depends on the man. They vary, hadn't you heard? And they are full of paradox. Is Jack Kerouac's beat icon Sal Paradise, narrator of *On the Road*, man as adventurer or man as closet gay melancholic, fixated on his own hero, Dean Moriarty? A less celebrated yet equally beautiful novel is William Maxwell's *The Folded Leaf*, first published in 1945, about a college friendship between a young scholar and a young athlete. The nerd worships the warrior; even as it fulfils him, the relationship is doomed.

What's missing from this survey? Only almost everything. You're thinking Updike, Mailer. But most and least obviously, what's missing is women novelists writing of men. Ira Morgan, loving, infuriating, forbearing husband of Maggie is the lovely creation of Anne Tyler in *Breathing Lessons*, her portrait of a marriage in transit through its own past. Another lady on lads' lives and loves? Annie Proulx with *Brokeback Mountain*.

To end, two lauded modern works by modern men. *The Line of Beauty*, Alan Hollinghurst's prize-winner, is called a gay novel, but that makes it a guy novel too. Its central player, Nick Guest, is accepted into a circle where heterosexual marriage is hailed as a quintessential building block. As such, his welcome could only be conditional. He's ambitious, on a personal quest, but he's doing masculinity all wrong. He's also writing a thesis on Henry James. Colm Toibin's *The Master* is a fictional account of four years in Henry James's life: four years in which James sacrificed emotional intimacy in order to concentrate on his work. Typical man?

Poetry
in motion

Jason Cowley picks the big hitters in sports literature.

ADULTHOOD

Richard Ford's *The Sportswriter* has one of the most arresting openings of any contemporary American novel: 'My name is Frank Bascombe. I am a sportswriter.' In the sentences that follow, Ford establishes an idiom and a style for what is a book less about sport and journalism than early middle-age male drift and disappointment: Bascombe is divorced from a wife he still loves, his son has died and his career as a writer of fiction faltered after just one promising collection of stories. The novel that he began many years before remains unfinished in a desk drawer. He won't be picking that up again.

Bascombe works for an unnamed sports magazine in New York and specialises in events away from the field of play, in hard-luck and where-are-they-now stories. He understands, as Ford naturally does, how central sport is to the American psyche, how absorbing yet also irrational fandom can be, and how so many of us live vicariously through the experiences of others, through those who act on the field of play rather than watch. He understands how sport offers the sense of continuity and narrative definition so often absent from life itself. It provides good stories and significant human drama, played out in public and often in vast supercharged stadiums and auditoriums, and it's often through fandom that many of us find our own sense of identity.

This was certainly the subject of *Fever Pitch*, Nick Hornby's memoir about his life as an Arsenal fan, which remains one of the most influential books of the past two decades. It was not that Hornby invented a new way of writing about sport – Fred Exley had already written about obsessive fandom and self-

discovery in the late 1960s, in *A Fan's Notes*. It was more that he showed how, as the American journalist and author Adam Gopnik has written, 'our [sporting] connection with our heroes is through an act of imagination, and the act of imagination, not the connection, is what is worth savouring and saving.'

Why aren't there more great works of fiction about sport? One of the first books I read as a restless teenager, more interested in sport than in sitting down to concentrate on anything remotely demanding, was Alan Sillitoe's *The Loneliness of the Long Distance Runner*. It's about a rebellious youth who is sent to reform school, where he discovers he has a remarkable talent for running. My English teacher gave it to me to read because he knew that I spent most of my time either thinking about or playing sport, and that in those days I read little more than the Tintin books and the *Victor* comic. I was excited to read Sillitoe's portrait of adolescent alienation: here at last was a book, written for the most part in an engaging, wised-up vernacular, that spoke directly to my own sense of adolescent yearning.

Sillitoe's novel, and others like it, such as David Storey's *This Sporting Life*, which is about the adventures of a rugby-league professional in the north of England, were characteristic of the novels being written during the late 1950s and early '60s. This was when the educated working classes were beginning to emerge from the grammar schools and the new universities, and wanted to write about the subjects that defined their own cultural experiences.

Yet as good as these books are, there is no canon of literature about sport in this country to rival the American tradition, where John Updike (in the *Rabbit* tetralogy the eponymous hero dies playing basketball with a group of kids on a public court), Norman Mailer, Ernest Hemingway, Bernard Malamud (notably *The Natural*, about baseball), Philip Roth (*The Great American Novel* and *The Human Stain*, among others) and Don DeLillo have written well about sport in their novels. One thinks, most obviously, of the long opening section of DeLillo's *Underworld*, in which he vividly recreates the National League play-off between the New York Giants and the Brooklyn Dodgers in 1951. Bobby Thomson's winning strike, which was hit high and far into the crowd, became known as the 'shot that was

The village cricket match, a key moment in LP Hartley's **The Go-Between**.

Muhammad Ali, 'King of the World'.

heard around the world'. DeLillo imagines what might have happened to the ball after it disappeared into the crowd, how it was passed through different hands and down the generations, so that, in the end, it becomes less a baseball than a metaphor for the disturbed and complicated postwar history of America itself.

There is often sport of a violent kind in Hemingway's novels and stories, notably those about bullfighters, fishermen and other restless solitaries. Death is never far away for Hemingway Man. I especially like Hemingway's two-part story, 'The Big Two-Hearted River'.

Nick Adams, recently returned from World War I, and someone we've encountered in earlier stories, sets off on a fishing expedition to Seney, a once-thriving lumber town that now resembles nothing so much as a burnt-out battlefield. Nick is seeking solace in nature. He sets up camp and then early the next morning wades out into the river in search of trout. The prose is spare and precise; this is a story of exclusion, of what is being left out and unsaid – such as what Nick experienced in wartime.

Is fishing a sport or a pastime? I can't really say, since I've been fishing only once. All I know is that Hemingway's story captures

Carraway, is a young golf professional called Jordan Baker. Nick learns that, in a competition, she once moved her ball into a more favourable position. Later in the book, when Jordan lies to him, Nick remembers this story as he begins to understand just how dishonest and careless his girlfriend can be.

Beyond fiction, I aadmire Mailer's *The Fight*, a high-energy account of the famous 'Rumble in the Jungle', the 1974 heavyweight-title fight between George Foreman and Muhammad Ali in Kinshasa, Zaire. I also like David Remnick's *King of the World*, a book about Ali that is also a study of America and race in the 1960s; John Updike's writings on golf, collected in *Golf Dreams*; Laura Hillenbrand's book about the champion racehorse of the American Depression years, *Seabiscuit*, and former Arsenal and England captain Tony Adams's *Addicted*, in which Adams writes of his struggles with alcoholism and of how, in his early thirties, he decided to change his life and become the person he always wanted to be.

Another favourite is Yasunari Kawabata's *The Master of Go*, which is about the oriental board game of Go, as well as being an elegy for an older, more ritualised imperial Japan that is inexorably being overwhelmed by change.

More recently, some of our best British writers have delighted in featuring marginal sports in their novels. Martin Amis, for instance, wrote amusingly about darts in *London Fields*, and there is a long, fastidiously described account of a squash match in Ian McEwan's *Saturday*. My favourite sporting scene in literature, however, remains the gentlemen and players village cricket match in LP Hartley's novel of thwarted love and class divisions, *The Go-Between*. The match was vividly recreated in the 1970 film of the book, starring Julie Christie at her loveliest and Alan Bates.

And the most influential sports book of recent times? That has to be Michael Lewis's *Moneyball*, an investigation into sports management which tells of how one of the least wealthy teams in baseball, the Oakland Athletics, became one of the most successful, winning an improbable number of games. It's a book that has inspired several English Premiership football coaches as they look for ways of beating the wealthy superpowers of the game.

something of the magic of being alone early in the morning on a river in an isolated setting when it must seem as if nothing else matters beyond the task in hand, not even the memory of war. (George Orwell also wrote well about fishing, in his novel about a suburban clerk's longing for escape from imprisoning adult routine, the war-shadowed *Coming up for Air*.)

I like, too, the way F Scott Fitzgerald uses golf in *The Great Gatsby* and in some of his stories (notably 'Winter Dreams', whose central character is a caddy) to reveal important moral truths about his characters. The girlfriend of the narrator of *The Great Gatsby*, Nick

Middle Age

'And then the justice,
In fair round belly with
good capon lin'd
With eyes severe and
beard of formal cut,
Full of wise saws and
modern instances;
And so he plays his part.'

A moveable feast

From classic cookbooks to 'kitchen fiction', **Lesley Chamberlain** samples some culinary delights.

Jean-Anthelme Brillat-Savarin's *The Physiology of Taste* is the mother of all modern food books. Neither the original French title faithfully translated, nor *The Philosopher in the Kitchen*, which was the long-standing name of the English version, capture the unique mixture of social wisdom, gastronomic know-how, amateur science and sheer sensual appreciation that this versatile French lawyer set down for posterity. As the first restaurants were opening in Paris, courtesy of the liberty and equality enjoyed by the French after the revolution, Brillat articulated the emerging middle class's new preoccupation with gastronomy.

His bitty masterpiece has been compared to a groaning Louis XIV table on which all the dishes are served at once. You need to know where to dip in. The aphorisms and anecdotes make a great introduction to the naturally careful French way with food. And Brillat is

better still on the art of living in general: men who don't know how to eat, he says, are like lovers oblivious to tenderness. Here is a 'food writer' who understands tiredness, deplores haste and loves good conversation. Brillat is the father of the dinner party and restaurant meal alike, and his gastronomic attitude has made the world a more congenial place.

After Brillat's death, gastronomy was the province of gentlemen travellers rarely his equal, but in the 20th century gifted female writers put their own spin on his civilising mission. Michigan-born MFK Fisher wrote numerous books that were funny, discerning, idiosyncratic and packed with anecdotes and simple recipes. 'I know a man who gave up what could be called an enviable life in central Nevada because he refused to eat any sea fish more than a day old.' The chapter on fish in *With Bold Knife and Fork* sees Fisher on top form, a connoisseur of the ideal state

An arbiter of good taste: **Elizabeth David**.

'Everything is commodified in our ultra-free market society – including honest chefs and reliable cookbooks.'

of gastronomic affairs, but also a clever cook and host who knows how to cut corners. 'I can still fake a lot, thank God.' Elsewhere she's busy hating dips, getting drunk on tea and not fussing about germs. Her recipes have a decided 1960s feel, but she was also fighting debasing tendencies that continue to beset food and cooking today.

Fisher occupies in the US the hallowed ground that Elizabeth David does in Britain. This waspish daughter of the manor, who trained in fine art, lived in France and ran away with the wrong kind of men, spent an eventful World War II marooned in various Mediterranean safe havens. When she got back to England, she turned to writing, in the certain knowledge that the French, the Italians, the Greeks and the Turks cooked better than the British did. Her first five books – written before the writer in her succumbed to the historian – were the best, led perhaps by *French Provincial Cooking*, with its *daube de boeuf provençale*, *rillettes de porc*, cassoulet and so on. David shows what honest food is and how rarely it's found. Read her to find out how she set succeeding generations on the right track. She's a justified snob, who hates the Anglo-Saxon way of complicating everything. 'Does a Paris milliner put lace trimmings on a fur hat?' In David's day, both cooks and milliners conformed to an unshakeable canon of good taste.

Honest food as an important part of a decent way of life is something the Canadian Margaret Visser appreciated. In *Much Depends on Dinner* she reminded the next generation that 'food is never just something to eat'. Visser made a wonderfully readable book out of her investigation into the main ingredients of a simple meal: 'Corn with salt and butter/Chicken with Rice/Lettuce with Olive Oil and Lemon Juice/Ice Cream.' She knew as well as Brillat did that 'a meal is an artistic social construct, ordering the foodstuffs which comprise it into a complex dramatic whole, as a play.'

Her books, which understand the high art of the table, also mark the moment when we first woke up to the need actively to combat the convenience-food industry. Food has to be real, but keeping it that way is a costly struggle – and what the media put our way, marketing dressed up as information, often doesn't help.

As the food industry grows new tentacles, one of Visser's targets becomes the 'bandwagon cookbook'. Everything is commodified in our ultra-free market society, including honest chefs and reliable cookbooks. So learn true discernment from the likes of Fisher, David, Visser, and one other classic, Patience Gray. Her *Honey from a Weed* features food from southern Italy, Mallorca and the Cyclades islands. Showing what you can conjure up out of not much more than bread, water and a few herbs, Gray's championing of a lifestyle of 'aesthetic poverty' is the real thing.

If Brillat and his successors fire our pleasure at being alive, the best modern encyclopedias, like Alan Davidson's *Oxford Companion to Food* or the updated *Larousse Gastronomique*, are unrivalled sources of factual knowledge for those seeking a more scholarly approach to gastronomy. Davidson's witty entries include 'salmonella' and 'washing-up' but also identify the most esoteric ingredients and place food practices in their cultural context. The prose in the *Larousse* is deadpan, but the book does have the merit of being packed with recipes and superb colour illustrations showing you how to tell a dwarf bean from a kidney bean, how to truffle a chicken or gut a fish. The French bias explains culinary terms and celebrates the careers of French chefs like Paul Bocuse and the brothers Troigros.

Complementing these doorstop guides is a new genre in food writing, the product of historians' fascination over the past quarter-century with material culture. In his *Food A History*, Felipe Fernández-Armesto treats food as a 'theme in world history, inseparable from all the other interactions of human beings with each other and the rest of nature'.

Why did agriculture begin? Fernández-Armesto suggests we are hard-wired to scratch the soil and plant seeds. But his sophisticated

Allegory of Taste by Breughel the Elder.

analysis indicates human beings have always put an overriding cultural and political value on food. The desire to add value to life has changed our food more readily than material forces. Food is a class act, with the gastronomically privileged always wanting to show off.

If this competitive, acquisitive element is omnipresent through the ages of food, it is nevertheless economic factors that drive farming and supermarkets in the short and medium term. Mark Kurlansky's *Cod: A Biography of the Fish That Changed the World* not only pioneered a fashion for biographies of single ingredients, but was also an expert story grippingly told. You sit with Kurlansky in a fishing boat tossing on the Atlantic swell and twitch a baited line, waiting for the cod to snap while their fresh, sweet, white flesh fries beside you for breakfast. Kurlansky tells how men from the Basque country to Canada, via Greenland and Iceland, France and Britain, have been chasing cod for 1,000 years, bringing health and prosperity to their communities. Only now has the world's appetite for cod exhausted what nature can offer.

In a quite different style, Sri Owen and Thao Soun Vannithorne's *The Rice Book* also tells the story of a single commodity on which the underdeveloped world has relied for centuries. Owen and Vannithorne's magisterial 100-page introduction to their favourite subject, coupled with a global compendium of recipes, gives the reader two good books in one.

Nicola Humble's *Culinary Pleasures* really ought to have been called by its subtitle, *Cookbooks and the Transformation of British Food*. Endlessly intelligent and astute, it entertainingly decodes what modern food writing is about and rescues a few discarded reputations, like that of *The Constance Spry Cookery Book* for instance. Spry recorded the culinary practices of middle-class Edwardian England, showing them poised between a fashion for foreign tastes and a timorous stay-at-home formality. Her designs for cocktail party fodder are historically informative and seem set for a playful revival one day.

A significant development in post-war British food writing has been the laying of the ghost of Isabella Beeton, to whose *Book of Household Management* Humble has also written an enlightening introduction. Beeton was the journalist who, several generations before Spry and her co-author Rosemary Hume, codified the culinary practices of mid-Victorian England. Beeton entrenched the habit of boiling vegetables soft and counselled against anything 'foreign'. The role of her dashing husband and publisher Sam, and the myth that substituted for the real Mrs Beeton who died aged 28, are compellingly recounted in Kathryn Hughes's *The Short Life and Long Times of Mrs Beeton*.

A chef whose recipes Beeton didn't hesitate to plunder, and who was another extraordinary Victorian personality in his own right, was Alexis Soyer. His life, stretching from London's Reform Club to running soup kitchens in a starving Ireland and feeding the army in the Crimean War, is told with panache by Rosemary Cowen in *Relish*.

Publishers queue up these days to print the reminiscences of contemporary chefs. Nigel Slater's *Toast*, however, is several notches above the usual level of idle chatter. It's a charming and affecting portrait of family life told through the eyes of a boy sensitive to what turns up on the table, not to mention the travails of his hapless mum. He reminds us that real food doesn't have to be precious. Anthony Bourdain's *Kitchen Confidential*, meanwhile, replaces childhood tenderness with freewheeling sensuality and lust for success, but his confession is an equally compelling read. Bourdain dishes the dirt on expensive restaurants, while remaining loyal to the ideal of good food. A tough-minded high-flyer in the New York restaurant business, he has also pioneered highly readable fiction fuelled by sex and drugs in the kitchen.

'Kitchen fiction' works better than other food fiction, partly because kitchens are already social stories in themselves. But that hasn't stopped a wave of fiction featuring food over the last quarter-century. One of the highlights is Laura Esquivel's combination of magical realism and recipes in *Like Water for Chocolate*. If food and romance appeal, give it a try; otherwise, male detectives solving their cases as the digestive juices flow make for a better story. Georges Simenon's Maigret shares his Paris-inspired gastronomic passion with the Catalan writer Manuel Vázquez Montalbán's Pepe Calvinho, who bases himself in Barcelona's tapas bars. Both writers know many things, not least that good meals concentrate the mind.

The eroticism of food, the sociability, creativity and raciness, as well as the biological and chemical facts, are the reasons it finds its way into so many aspects of our lives. When we pick up the latest recipe book, it's not just kitchen instruction we're being sold, but also the chance to dodge social pitfalls, reap a sexual kick or realise a lifestyle dream – one more often than not related these days to a television programme or a famous restaurant. A few years ago, Nigella Lawson caught the public imagination by playing on the eroticism of food. It seemed we couldn't get enough of seeing Nigella fellate a strawberry. On the screen she was gastroporn lusciously incarnate, though none of this stopped *How to Eat* being full of sound advice about real food. Lawson can be greedy, but she is a clever writer, who knows how to manipulate her audience.

Most serious cookbooks pretend to good manners and gastronomic discernment, but a rather different history of food and books on food could be written tracing the joys and horrors of excess. It would start with two classics of the French Renaissance, François Rabelais's *Gargantua* and *Pantagruel*. The former gave us the word 'gargantuan' for those supersized burgers that are now driving the so-called developed world to mass obesity. Rabelais's giants, with their heaving appetites and their love of local produce, managed better. They defeated the puritanical tradition of the medieval church in a wild and fantastical *tournée* of sensual imagination. But this was literature, an exploration of possibilities, not a document of grunting life as it is taking shape in 21st-century London.

The thing about gross behaviour and obesity is that they used to be confined to the margins of what we were willing to talk about in mainstream discourse, including cookbooks. They cropped up in medical literature, or fairgrounds, or in fantasies for children. Billy Bunter, the fat boy star of a series of children's stories written between 1908 and 1940 by the pseudonymous Frank Richards, is, as George Orwell noted, one of the great characters of English literature; but we don't hear much about him today, perhaps because obesity is a tricky subject for a politically correct age to handle.

Fat is not always a tragic affliction, however, and there are lots of greedy, out-of-control eaters around. William Leith's *The Hungry*

French gastronomist **Jean-Anthelme Brillat-Savarin** – the original foodie?

Years confirms that fat people discriminate against themselves, even if they hate you to discriminate against them. His book is a highly engaging, landmark confession of what it's like to be a male compulsive eater; it also taps into the awkward social silence surrounding the issue of fat.

From food as pathology to food as art is not a great step, but it takes a subtler touch than much present-day writing offers. For a notion of food as art that goes beyond the ravishing photos in today's recipe books, and also a chance to see where restaurateurs like Ferran Adrià and Heston Blumenthal might have derived their freaky ideas, consult FT Marinetti's *The Futurist Cookbook*. Marinetti, the poet and inventor of Italian Futurism, had violent mannerisms and unattractive political views. But he was a pioneer of food's expressive potential and devised recipes that were like abstract paintings, and gastronomic charades that anticipated today's lifestyle ads in a remarkable way.

There's so much going on in and around food because it is language as well as nourishment. You can say, do and sell almost anything with it, and this is what popular culture has discovered in the last 50 years. If you're really interested in making good food to eat, however, you need to concentrate on a few good writers and titles. Any recipes written by Elisabeth Luard (*European Peasant Cookery: The Rich Tradition*), Tamasin Day-Lewis, Clarissa Hyman (*Cucina Siciliana*) and Anna del Conte on Italian food are likely to work. These are real food writers.

Simon Hopkinson's *Roast Chicken and Other Stories* likewise introduces a collection of sound recipes in a deliberate attempt to hark back to an age before all the hype. Yet the way Hopkinson rushes to reassure the average punter that food needn't be scary makes one realise that the publishing industry has found a new market in all those unadventurous wimps who are actually afraid of the food cooked by glamorous chefs and famous restaurants. Nicola Humble wittily calls it *cuisine-mère*.

Real practice is one way to sort out the 'bandwagon' books from the genuine thing. If you're a Brit and sufficiently motivated, for heaven's sake go and live in a country where real food is still the habit, and bring your knowledge back home. That's what many food writers have

done. The grass isn't greener in every way, and certainly few countries in the world publish the range of food books that Britain does. But it's hard to disagree with Joanna Blythman, who argues in *Bad Food Britain* that confusion and exploitation underlie this country's cult of posh nosh. Andrew Whitley has the details of how our daily staple has been ruined, and what you can do about it, in *Bread Matters*.

Food & feasts in 20 books

Babette's Feast by Isak Dinesen
Fleeing the Paris Commune of 1871, Babette is taken in by two elderly sisters who live in a remote Lutherian community in Denmark. When, 14 years later, a letter from France reveals she has won the state lottery, she decides to spend the entire sum on the ingredients for a magnificent thank-you dinner. The deeply religious villagers decide they must eat her sumptuous feast without enjoying it – but will their resolve falter in the face of champagne, stuffed quail and rum baba?

The Belly of Paris by Emile Zola
The city's 'belly' is Les Halles, the gargantuan food market founded in the 1850s. Seen through the eyes of Zola's young hero, the half-starved prison escapee Florent, it is both enticing and repellent. With its sensuous, richly evocative descriptions of food, this is a tale to avoid if you're feeling peckish.

Charlie and the Chocolate Factory by Roald Dahl
Charlie Bucket's golden ticket unlocks the gates to confectionary nirvana: Willy Wonka's marvellous factory. After reading about its chocolate waterfall, fudge mine and mouth-wateringly inventive creations, from sugar eggs that hatch into chirruping chocolate birds to edible marshmallow pillows, a simple bar of Dairy Milk seems dreadfully inadequate.

Chocolat by Joanne Harris
Vianne Rocher arrives in the rural town of Lansquenet-sous-Tannes at the beginning of Lent, with plans to open a chocolate shop. Her magical confections bring new happiness to the townspeople, but win her the bitter enmity of the parish priest, Francis Reynaud, who suspects there is devilry afoot.

Dead Souls by Nikolai Gogol
Food and 'the Russian stomach' is a recurrent theme for Gogol in *Dead Souls*. The pretentious St Petersburg elite nibble at exotic delicacies ('oysters and crabs and a quantity of other monsters'), much to the horror of the earthy provincial types. 'Sugar a frog as much as you like, but never shall it pass MY lips,' declares one.

The Debt to Pleasure by John Lanchester

Narrator Tarquin Winot is a gourmand and a snob. En route from Norfolk to Provence, Tarquin shares his gastronomic wisdom with the reader. Here's a taste: 'Every act of civilisation is also an act of barbarism: a fact of which the potato reminds us.'

The Epicurean by Charles Ranhofer

An exhaustive – and exhausting – late 19th-century treatise on the culinary arts, written by New York chef Charles Ranhofer. Within its pages are a wealth of recipes and helpful tips. Some are still handy, others less so ('bear's meat when young can be broiled and after it is cooked has much the same flavour as beef').

Farmer Boy by Laura Ingalls Wilder

Wilder's tales of frontier life may be a touch too saccharine for modern tastes, but her descriptions of food remain mouth-wateringly good. 'Almanzo ate the sweet, mellow baked beans. He ate the bit of salt pork that melted like cream in his mouth. He ate mealy-boiled potatoes, with brown ham-gravy. He ate the ham. He bit deep into velvety bread spread with sleek butter, and he ate the crisp, golden crust.'

Fast Food Nation by Eric Schlosser

This stomach-turning piece of investigative journalism serves up some unpalatable truths about America's fast-food industry – including the economic (and hence political) power it wields.

Feast by Roy Strong

A scholarly study of the history of grand eating, from Ancient Greece to the present, Feast looks at the social and symbolic significance of formal meals, as well as cataloguing some truly opulent spreads. Though honey-dipped dormice are possibly an acquired taste.

Feeding Frenzy by Will Self

This collection of Self's non-fiction work includes his no-holds-barred restaurant reviews. Written for the Observer in the 1990s, his missives from the culinary frontline furthered his reputation as enfant terrible of the English literary scene.

Five on a Hike Together by Enid Blyton

The Five, always partial to a good picnic, are positively piggish here, demanding a princely eight sandwiches apiece. Nor are they the sort of children to skimp on breakfast, feasting on 'a steaming tureen of porridge, a bowl of golden syrup, a jug of very thick cream, and a dish of bacon and eggs, all piled high on crisp brown toast. Little mushrooms were on the same dish.'

Heat by Bill Buford

A middle-aged man quits his day job as a high-flying hack (former fiction editor of the New Yorker, no less) to volunteer as a low-ranking minion in the kitchens of New York superchef Mario Batali. Such is the premise of Buford's excellent memoir, which sees him rising from despised ignoramus to… well, a pretty decent cook.

The Life of Hunger by Amelie Nothomb

Food is an endlessly resurfacing obsession in the Belgian novelist's 'fictional memoir' of an unsettled, peripatetic childhood. God, she decides, 'isn't chocolate, he's the encounter between chocolate and a palate capable of appreciating it'. At 13 she becomes anorexic, hungry for hunger itself, and transfers her voracious appetite to books. 'Because there was no more food, I decided to devour every word in existence.'

The Life of Pi by Yann Martel

Adrift at sea for 227 days, our hero keeps starvation at bay with turtle innards; 'a chopped-up mixture of heart, lungs, liver, flesh and cleaned-out intestines sprinkled with fish parts […] made an unsurpassable, finger-licking thali.' In the background is the threat that Pi himself will be consumed by the Bengal tiger who shares his cramped quarters. Or does he…?

The Man Who Ate Everything by Jeffrey Steingarten

There's no doubting the Vogue food critic's devotion to his calling – this is a man prepared to import tubs of horse fat in order to create the perfect French fry. His concerns range from finding the best ketchup to unmasking salad as 'a silent killer' – in delightfully pedantic and uproarously funny fashion.

Nose to Tail Eating by Fergus Henderson

The intrepid Fergus Henderson is famed for creating culinary masterpieces from the most unpromising of ingredients – namely offal and other unlikely bits of beast. His cookbook includes the recipe for his most famous dish, Roast Bone Marrow and Parsley Salad.

The Pedant in the Kitchen by Julian Barnes

Barnes is both a gastronome and a francophile, and he indulges both of these proclivities in this witty collection of his kitchen-based columns, originally published in the Guardian.

Symposium by Plato

Socrates and his friends gather round the dinner table to discuss the nature of love and friendship – and the perils of drinking with a hangover.

The Wind in the Willows by Kenneth Grahame

Has any picnic hamper contained as many goodies as Rat's 'fat, wicker luncheon-basket'? 'There's cold chicken inside it,' replied the Rat briefly, 'coldtongue coldhamcoldbeefpickledgherkinssaladfrenchrollscress sandwichespottedmeatgingerbeerlemonadesodawater.' 'O stop, stop,' cried the Mole in ecstacies: 'This is too much!'

Words of
wisdom

Jonathan Derbyshire discovers that great philosophy can make great literature too.

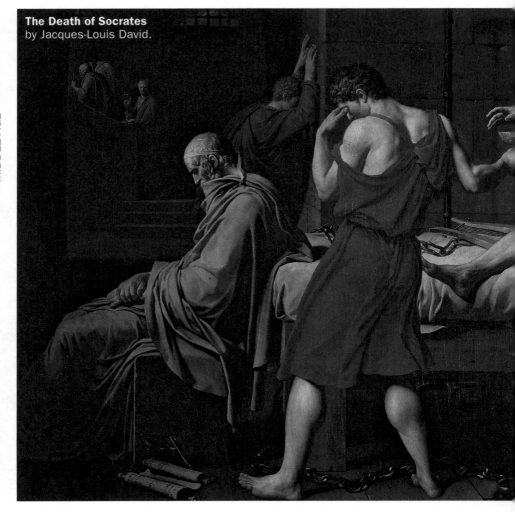

The Death of Socrates
by Jacques-Louis David.

In 1996, the journal *Philosophy and Literature* invited entries to its first 'Bad Writing Contest'. The idea was for bemused readers to submit the most obscure pieces of writing they could find in the work of contemporary philosophers and cultural theorists. The editors received so many submissions of such extravagant unintelligibility that they ran the competition twice more – evidence, if it were needed, that the tide of 'turgid academic prose' wasn't about to recede.

Although the barbarous jargon in which many of the entries were couched was new, complaints about the way thinkers and philosophers write are not. For example, in the *Defence of Poesy*, first published in 1595, Sir Philip Sidney contrasts the philosopher with the poet – much to the philosopher's disadvantage. For all his subtle wrangling with virtue and the nature of the good life, the philosopher's 'wordish descriptions', says Sidney, compare unfavourably with the imaginative power of the poet. The philosopher teaches by precept, but so obscurely that only those who are already learned can understand him.

Sidney isn't just mocking the shortcomings of most philosophical prose, however. He also wants to know how the philosopher might fulfil his true vocation and 'plant goodness in the secret cabinet of our souls'. (This is an

Philosophy meets fiction in the novels of **Jean-Paul Sartre**.

understanding of the authentic task of philosophy, incidentally, that Sidney shares with his near contemporary Montaigne, who wrote in the *Essays* of the author's duty to compose character rather than just books.)

Sidney thinks the answer lies not in 'thorny argument' and the use of the tools of logic and dialectic, but in the 'fashioned image' of poetry. For when it comes to engaging the reader's emotions and moving him, as opposed merely to instructing him, the poet is without equal. Consequently, if philosophy is to have practical as well as theoretical significance, as one of the greatest of the ancient Greek philosophers, Aristotle, said it should, then it ought to 'borrow the masking raiment of Poesy'.

In fact, Sidney takes one his main arguments from Aristotle. In the *Poetics*, Aristotle says

that poetry is 'more philosophical' than, for instance, history. History tells us what has actually happened, whereas poetry (Aristotle is thinking principally of Greek tragedy) shows us the kinds of thing that might happen to human beings. And where history deals with particular matters of fact, poetry is concerned with 'universal truths' about the sorts of things certain kinds of people might get up to.

So when Sidney says that the poet can be considered the 'right popular philosopher', he is leaning heavily on Aristotle. However, Sidney doesn't use Aristotle to illustrate his case any further. Instead, he refers to Plato. This is perhaps because Aristotle, for all his greatness as a philosopher, was not a great writer. Plato was. If the substance of Plato's work is philosophy, Sidney writes, 'the skin as it were and beauty depended most of poetry.'

Sidney mentions the tale of the Ring of Gyges, told by Glaucon to Socrates in the *Republic*. Glaucon describes how Gyges, a Lydian shepherd, discovers a ring with a singular property: when the collet of the ring is turned inwards towards the hand, the wearer becomes invisible. Taking advantage of this, Gyges seduces the king's wife and then, with her help, kills him and seizes his kingdom. Now imagine, Glaucon goes on, that there are two such rings, and that one is given to a virtuous man, the other to an unvirtuous one. No man, however good and just, could resist the temptation to make himself invisible and steal from, sleep with and slaughter whoever he liked. Virtue, Glaucon concludes, is therefore nothing more than the inability to do wrong.

The Ring of Gyges is far from the only memorable image in Plato: there is the famous allegory, also in the *Republic*, in which the situation of ordinary human beings is compared with the predicament of prisoners chained and condemned forever to watch the play of shadows on the wall of a cave; or the demiurge in the *Timaeus*, a divine craftsman who fashions order out of chaos.

Anticipating a point that Nietzsche would make nearly 300 years later in *The Birth of Tragedy*, Sidney observes that there is something paradoxical about Plato's way with a memorable image and his preference for using the ludic and ironic form of the dialogue. The paradox is that Plato took an apparently dim view of poets and indeed 'banished them from his commonwealth'. Sidney is referring to what Plato says is an 'old quarrel between philosophy and poetry', and also to the famous passage in the *Republic* that recommends that any poet daring to visit the ideal state be covered in myrrh, crowned with fillets of wool and sent packing to another city.

Why is Plato so suspicious of poetry? Because it tempts the rational part of the soul to 'relax its guard over the plaintive part', which is irrational. Plato thinks all art, including poetry, is imitative – it takes sensory experience for granted and simply copies it, rather than trying, as philosophy does, to get at the reality that lies beyond appearances.

It would be tempting to conclude from this that literary form for Plato is merely decorative,

> '*True philosophy is as much about storytelling and the weaving of persuasive spells as it is about the working out of structured arguments.*'

a desirable but not essential add-on. Yet some of the dialogues, particularly the earlier ones, suggest a rather different understanding of the relationship between philosophy and literature – one in which the way a philosopher chooses to write is itself philosophically significant.

Perhaps the best example of this is the *Phaedo*. In this dialogue, Phaedo, a pupil of Socrates, movingly describes to a group of friends the final hours of his teacher's life. We see Socrates in his cell awaiting execution, having been found guilty by a court in Athens of corrupting the minds of the young. Phaedo tells his friend Echecrates that on that last day, he had turned up at the prison as normal with several others and that what took place was one of 'our usual philosophical discussions'.

That such a discussion should have taken place in these circumstances is extraordinary enough; but most extraordinary of all, says Phaedo, were his own feelings: 'It never occurred to me to feel sorry for [Socrates] … The master seemed quite happy [and] met his death so fearlessly and nobly.' This portrayal of Socrates' equanimity on the edge of oblivion prepares the reader (or listener) for the claim he makes during a discussion of the immortality of the soul to the effect that 'true philosophers make dying their profession'. A philosopher who reconciles himself to the idea that the body is but a temporary home for the soul will naturally look forward to the moment at which he can escape the 'unwelcome' associations of mortality.

Socrates offers a number of logical proofs for this doctrine, but recognises that several of his interlocutors are still not convinced. Cebes and Simmias, for example, are unable to banish 'childish terror' at the thought that the soul would not survive being detached from the body on a windy day; they're afraid that the wind 'may really puff it away and scatter it'. Socrates's response is not to provide a further proof, but to tell them a story about what happens in the after-life. If Socrates is intended by Plato to exemplify the authentic (dying) philosopher, then this suggests that true philosophy is as much about storytelling and the weaving of persuasive spells as it is about the working out of structured arguments.

The *Phaedo* ends with Socrates drinking the hemlock that will kill him. As the poison works its way through his body, Socrates turns to his friend Crito and says: 'We ought to offer a cock to Asclepius. See to it, and don't forget.' These are the philosopher's last words, and far from being idle talk, as some commentators have maintained, they in fact amount to a final insight into his condition: for Asclepius was the god of healing to whom it was customary to offer a cock in thanks for a cure.

David Hume offered no such thanks on his deathbed. But he did leave behind a last testament, written in the spring of 1776 as he awaited death from a 'disorder' in his bowels. *My Own Life* is a brief, lapidary summary of his career and an autobiography that doubles as an obituary, written as if from the beyond the grave, with Hume correcting his tenses ('I am, or rather was …') as though the 'speedy dissolution' he anticipates had already happened.

This dense little text is famous, or infamous, principally for two things: Hume's account of the disastrous reception met by his first philosophical masterpiece, the *Treatise on Human Nature*, published when he was only 26; and his candid admission that throughout his life 'love of literary fame' had been his 'ruling passion'.

The *Treatise*, Hume's attempt to do for human nature what Newton had done for inanimate nature, was received with perfect indifference when it came out in 1738. He writes that it fell '*dead-born from the press*, without reaching such distinction as even to excite a murmur among the zealots' (the

italicised words flatter Hume's readers' erudition, as well as advertising his own good taste, by quoting from Pope's 'Epilogue to the Satires'). This is a very clear-eyed appraisal, if one wholly uncomprehending review from 1740 is anything to go by: 'I should have taken no notice of what he has wrote if I had not thought this book, in several parts, so very abstruse and perplex'd, that, I am convinced, no man can comprehend what he means.'

One reason for such mystified responses is the note of apparently destructive scepticism that Hume strikes at the end of Book I of the *Treatise*. He surveys and finds wanting the available rational proofs for a number of our most fundamental beliefs, including that in the existence of the world itself. Hume declares his mind so 'heated' by the contradictions and imperfections of these proofs that he is 'ready to reject all belief and reasoning, and can look upon no opinion even as more probable or likely than another'.

Some more unforgiving commentators have seen evidence in this passage of Hume's unseemly obsession with notoriety. It was his lust for 'literary fame', they argue, that led him to draw such extreme conclusions from the empiricism of his illustrious predecessors, Berkeley and Locke.

On this reading, Hume appears as an unscrupulous careerist with an eye for the main chance. There are at least two problems with it, however. First, it's clear from *My Own Life* that when he says he was 'seized very early by a passion for literature', he is referring to philosophy as well as belles lettres; second, it is misleading to say that Hume is presenting those sceptical conclusions at the end of Book I as straightforwardly true. Rather, he is using the tropes of ancient Greek scepticism in order to dramatise a dilemma that confronts us when we see that reason is incapable of supplying a proof for our belief in the existence of the external world. The right conclusion to draw, he thinks, is not that we ought to suspend judgement on the world's existence, but rather that we should come to see that our belief in it – which isn't optional, after all – is not rationally grounded, but is instead a brute fact about human beings. Hume's scepticism, therefore, is less a counsel of despair than the *via negativa* to a brand new experimental science of human nature.

Friedrich Nietzsche – self-proclaimed master of aphorism.

Hume thought the failure of the *Treatise* had to do with its 'manner rather than the matter'. Accordingly, he set about rewriting it in a more digestible way. The result was the *Enquiry Concerning Human Understanding*, published in 1748.

At the beginning of the *Enquiry*, Hume draws a distinction between two species of philosopher, the 'easy' and the 'abstruse'. The easy philosopher treats men primarily as creatures of 'taste and sentiment' and consequently takes all the help he can get from 'poetry and eloquence'. The abstruse philosopher, by contrast, sees man as an essentially rational being. And since he seeks esoteric truths, it's of no consequence to

Pause for thought: novelist and philosopher **Iris Murdoch**.

him if his work turns out to be 'unintelligible to common readers'.

Hume's aim in the *Enquiry* is not to sacrifice abstruseness for the charms of ease; rather, he wants to fuse the best of both modes. He identifies one of the great 'defects' of his age as the separation of the 'learned' and 'conversible' worlds. Hume imagines himself not as an emigrant from the world of the learned and the abstruse, chasing the promise of literary renown, but as 'ambassador from the dominions of learning to those of conversation'.

It is a measure of Hume's achievement in the *Enquiry* that he should have received the approbation of his most notable successor, Immanuel Kant. 'Few writers,' Kant wrote with some justification, 'are gifted with the subtlety and, at the same time, the grace of David Hume.' Kant regretted that his own prose style was no match for Hume's, especially as he too had been forced to become his own expositor, after the *Critique of Pure Reason* attracted a stream of wrong-headed reviews following its publication in 1781. Faced with some serious misconceptions about the import of his doctrine of 'transcendental idealism', Kant wrote a much shorter, and supposedly more pithy, digest of his views, the *Prolegomena to Any Future Metaphysics*. Anyone finding that hard-going, he said a little grumpily, probably lacks a flair for metaphysics and should apply his talents elsewhere.

Aside from a compelling account of how the human mind makes sense of the world, Kant bequeathed to the 19th century an enduring preoccupation with the question of the literary forms most appropriate to the articulation of genuine philosophical thought. This is particularly noticeable in the work of Søren Kierkegaard and Friedrich Nietzsche. Several of Nietzsche's books, notably *Beyond Good and Evil* and *The Antichrist*, are composed as collections of aphorisms, couched in prose of dazzling and epigrammatic brilliance that survives translation from German into English.

Kierkegaard went even further, and wrote several works under pseudonyms, including *Either/Or* ('Victor Eremita') and *Fear and Trembling* ('Johannes de Silentio'). His use of pseudonyms and other literary devices might seem gratuitous or simply quixotic – particularly to anyone brought up to expect 'thorny arguments' rather than alluring images from a philosopher. But in a book helpfully entitled *The Point of View of My Work as an Author*, Kierkegaard explains why he chose an 'aesthetic' mode of presentation.

The formal properties of a work like *Fear and Trembling* reflect a particular conception of philosophical difficulty, according to which it is the task of philosophy not to convey doctrine but, obliquely and indirectly, to deliver the reader from illusion. Kierkegaard was concerned specifically with illusions about the relationship between ethics and religious faith. The aim of pseudonymous works is to loosen the grip that certain pictures or outlooks have on us. And they function, Kierkegaard thought, in much the same way that Socrates intended his pedagogy to work on his pupils. He interprets the Socratic doctrine of *maieusis*, or teaching, not, as Plato does, as involving the 'recollection' of truths lying dormant in the soul, but rather as a means of persuading the pupil to acknowledge an error.

Among the errors Kierkegaard aimed to lay bare was the assumption that ethics is a matter of disinterested deliberation on the part of perfectly rational agents. For him, ethics is about particular human beings making choices in concrete situations. This is an idea that had a profound influence on the existentialism of Jean-Paul Sartre, who actually went as far as to present his theories in a novel. In *Nausea*, Sartre uses the reflections of the narrator Roquentin to explore the themes of individual freedom and bad faith.

Iris Murdoch, herself a novelist as well as a philosopher, described *Nausea* as the 'instructive overture to Sartre's work', albeit one that stands as a work of art quite independently of the theories it is designed to illustrate. In fact, Murdoch was deeply preoccupied with the relationship between philosophy and literature, and in a 1961 essay entitled 'Against Dryness' (later collected in *Existentialists and Mystics*), she argued that a remedy for the superficiality and barrenness of much analytical moral philosophy could be found in the novel. By presenting us with believable characters, novels furnish us with pictures of human goodness and freedom. In doing so, literature takes over many of the tasks 'formerly performed by philosophy'. Sir Philip Sidney, you suspect, would have approved.

A book that changed my life

Geoff Dyer

Culture and Society by Raymond Williams

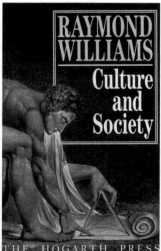

I read English at Oxford, ploughing through everything from *Beowulf* to Beckett. When I left, in 1980, my conception of literary history was a succession of authors, coming one after another. After leaving university I expanded my reading geographically to take in the Russians and French, but I read them in exactly the same narrow way. Then, in 1982, I read *Culture and Society* by Raymond Williams, and everything changed. Here, broadly speaking, was the curriculum I was familiar with (or part of it, anyway), but presented and understood in a different, larger way. Literature became connected with a broader historical movement, culture became a contested record of 'the changed conditions of our common life'.

Hard to believe, now, that my education should, up to that point, have been so blinkered. Before then, I had always thought of writers in terms of novels, fiction, poetry. *Culture and Society* opened up a difficult new world of reading, thinking and writing. I read everything by Williams after that. Through him, more than anyone else, I began, retrospectively, to understand that the process I had gone through – working-class family, exams, Oxbridge – was a question not just of autobiography, but of politics.

Goff Dyer's books include Yoga For People Who Can't Be Bothered To Do It and The Ongoing Moment (Abacus).

Metropolis

Nicholas Royle finds his way around the city in literature.

Writers adapt and remake the city in many different ways. Kim Stanley Robinson turns it white in his story 'Zürich', while in 'Ultima Thule' Gareth Evans makes London disappear. For Jonathan Raban, the city is always 'soft'. Angelica Jacob, meanwhile, represents cities as cheeses, both hard and soft. Shelley Jackson reimagines London menstruating, blood bubbling through pipes and pressing at 'lady hole' covers. For Paul Auster, New York's grid system is a piece of graph paper on which he plots the arcane geometries of *The New York Trilogy*.

There's no denying the intellectual fun and games to be had with Auster's best-known work, though its reputation has somewhat overshadowed texts by a number of very interesting writers working the same territory. In 1970, for instance, Alain Robbe-Grillet, the leading exponent of the French *nouveau roman*, wrote a novel entitled *Project for a Revolution in New York* in which the myriad possibilities of narrative are reflected in the routes and by-ways of street geography. The narrator attends a demonstration in which models act out rape, arson and murder, while another character confuses a locksmith peering voyeuristically through her door by holding a book cover illustration up to the keyhole.

Indeed, the voyeur is a mainstay of urban literature. In David Knowles's novel *The Third Eye*, Jefferson sublets his Manhattan apartment to a series of handpicked young women whom he then secretly photographs from his studio across the street. Similarly, Lisa Natalie Pearson's short story 'Stage Fright' begins: 'I watched their television because I didn't have one. It was almost always on: a blue

cycloptic giant. Their apartment is just across a narrow one-way side street from mine. We are three stories high and the width of two bedsheets apart.' The two apartments may only be a few yards apart, but because of the open curtains that hang like theatre drapes, the narrator continues watching without embarrassment, while her neighbours grow into their roles as performers.

Pearson's narrator is complicit in the fantasy. The fantastical event in Kim Stanley Robinson's 'Zürich' is more symbolic, however. An American SF writer, Robinson lived in the Swiss city during the 1980s. This short story, collected in *Remaking History*, concerns the narrator's efforts to clean his apartment before a routine inspection by the Federal Institute of Technology. Already knowing what to expect, the narrator spends days scrubbing and polishing. Almost done, he allows some bleach to touch his finger. Not only does the bleach turn his finger white, but the same thing happens in turn to anything he touches.

The narrator walks around Zurich for one last time and everything he touches turns white; everything except the colourful robes of a South American busker who boards his white tram, upsetting the Swiss passengers as he twangs his guitar.

By turning his city white against a backdrop of snowy mountains, Robinson almost makes it disappear. Gareth Evans does exactly that in his story 'Ultima Thule' (published in *The Time Out Book of London Short Stories Volume 2*). Evans's London is a vast model of the city made from paper and card and stored in an abandoned warehouse, where it is discovered by a gang of street kids. Coming

MIDDLE AGE

across the corpse of the model's maker – a pale, Christ-like figure – they apply boot to bone. The destruction of the model follows, and when they step back outside the warehouse, London has vanished. There is nothing to see or hear. 'Not even the sound of their hearts, building in them like a long runner, or their rubbing of eyes in doubt...'

In Evans's model, the Thames is the only detail not made of paper: 'It is glassy, a fixed flow of need, at permanent high, layered in sheets to give an idyll hue and shifting glint to its way.' The river offers a way into many London fictions. In Russell Celyn Jones's novel *Ten Seconds from the Sun*, the river is essential not only to an understanding of the city, but also to readerly sympathy with the narrator, Ray Greenland, a Thames river pilot with a hidden past. Vulnerable on land, Ray feels untouchable when on the water. His mother-in-law observes that 'the river is something you can never quite describe', yet Ray's verbal snapshots are convincing: 'a seminally unchanging mass with subliminal internal movements and minor disturbances.'

The river is also central to Iain Sinclair's second novel, *Downriver*. The rest of his oeuvre, meanwhile, embodies Jonathan Raban's idea of the 'soft city', set out in a non-fiction book of the same name. The soft city is one that you mould and make your own. 'Inside one's private city, one builds a grid of reference points, each enshrining a personal attribution of meaning.' The pattern of private reference points becomes as important as the Tube map. 'It is precisely because the city is too large and formless to be held in the mind as an imaginative whole that we make recourse to irrational short-cuts and simplifications.'

While Sinclair's investigations into patterns and energies – Hawksmoor, ley lines, the Ripper murders – are now well known, his London is also the stage for an ever-expanding cast of colourful characters. Robin Cook, Chris Petit, Brian Catling, Michael Moorcock, Stewart Home and many others come and go, each with his own capital obsession.

Sinclair's third novel, *Radon Daughters*, probably best nails his relationship with London. In it, the London Hospital meshes with the very fabric of the city, its basements gouged out of the clay and hidden from view. The same hospital appears in Angelica Jacob's

The **Manhattan** skyline looms large in literature.

Critics' choice
Midlife crises

Back When We Were Grownups
by Anne Tyler

'Once upon a time, there was a woman who discovered she had turned into the wrong person.' The cynical subversion of a fairy tale beginning sets the tone for Tyler's sharply observed novel, which explores the sudden unravelling of its protagonist, 53-year-old Beck. 'How on earth did I get like this? How?,' she asks in despair, proving that the midlife crisis is far from exclusively male terrain.

Bliss by Peter Carey

One of life's good guys (despite being an advertising executive), Harry Joy is perfectly content with his lot. Until, that is, he has a heart attack on his front lawn. After lying dead for nine minutes, Harry comes round – to discover that life suddenly looks considerably less rosy.

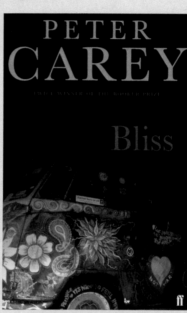

PETER CAREY

TWICE WINNER OF THE BOOKER PRIZE

Bliss

Disgrace by JM Coetzee

An eminent South African professor, David Lurie, is forced to leave his post in disgrace, after an ill-fated affair with a student ends in an allegation of sexual harassment. Refusing to co-operate in what he sees as a witch hunt, the 52-year-old retreats to his daughter Lucy's rural, isolated smallholding. It's here that the real 'disgrace' occurs, in shockingly violent fashion.

The Ice Storm by Rick Moody

Parental midlife crises overlap with adolescent angst in Moody's magnificent study of suburbia and its discontents, set in 1970s Connecticut. As the grown-ups engage in disastrous affairs and joyless swinging parties, their children turn to sexual experimentation of their own. As the ice storm rages, events reach crisis point.

The Information by Martin Amis

Richard Tull is a bitter man. Utterly unsuccessful as a writer, in the firm grip of a midlife crisis and unreasonably jealous of his friend and fellow author Gwyn Barry, he commits himself to a bizarre scheme: he will ruin Gwyn's reputation – he's going to 'fuck him up'. Set in the usual Amis terrain of a grimy, shit-smeared, overpopulated London, this exploration of male inadequacy and frustrated ambition is very angry and very funny.

Intimacy
by Hanif Kureishi

A brutal, unsparing account of a middle-aged man's decision to leave his wife and two young sons for a younger woman. The novel caused a storm of controversy when it was released – as did Patrice Chereau's film adaptation, thanks to its uncensored oral sex scene.

Operation Shylock
by Philip Roth

A novelist named Philip Roth suffers a breakdown as the result of excessive use of sleeping pills. While he convalesces, he learns that in Jerusalem, someone is passing himself off as 'Philip Roth' and urging Jews to abandon Israel for the diaspora – while at the same time attending the trial of the Treblinka guard John Demjanjuk. The real Roth flies to Israel, where he meets the real novelist Aharon Appelfeld. 'What swell ideas I have. Going to make lots of new pals for me in the Zionist homeland.'

Oxygen by Andrew Miller

Two brothers return home to see their elderly mother as she lies dying of cancer. Alec Valentine is a translator, working on a play by a Hungarian writer, entitled 'Oxygene'. He regards his brother Larry as the family success story. But Larry has problems of his own: his acting career is sliding irreversibly into decline – auditions for a seedy porn director called T Bone do not bode well.

short story 'Reverse Evolution', in which London steadily falls apart around the narrator's ears after her partner leaves her. The images of putrefaction and decay that dominate the story recall Jacob's novel *Fermentation*, in which striking refuse collectors and a heatwave combine to create a stifling atmosphere in an unnamed European city (probably Paris). The narrator and her boyfriend recall a story about Salvador Dalí describing US cities as cheeses (New York was a gothic roquefort, San Francisco a romantic camembert). They play the same game with European cities, casting Dublin as 'a virgin mozzarella', Copenhagen as 'a melancholic Comte' and Prague as either 'a hedonistic feta' or 'sybaritic Port Salut'.

London itself, with its Underground and various other tunnel systems, could be an ancient emmenthal. Conrad Williams sets much of his novel *London Revenant* underground. His narrator is lured beneath the city where a hidden tribe of otherworldly tunnel-dwellers offers the ragged hand of friendship. Or do they?

Geoff Ryman set his experimental novel *253* entirely below the surface, on the Bakerloo line between Embankment and Elephant & Castle, whereas Christopher Fowler's first novel, *Roofworld*, was set on London's rooftops. In a later book, *Soho Black*, the action is concentrated in a square half-mile.

Chris Petit focuses on the same district in *Robinson*, his first novel. 'My horizons shrank until it became hard to leave the area. It felt as though I would be breaking a spell.' Soho becomes an idealised place, like Alain-Fournier's lost domain or M John Harrison's Egnaro; indeed, it has its own 'border post', the archway at the end of Manette Street, where the narrator and Robinson first met and at which 'all obligation could be left behind'.

Geoff Nicholson shoots through a wider lens. In his novel *Bleeding London*, Mick Wilton visits the Smoke and falls in with a woman who had conducted walking tours for a man called Stuart London. But it is she herself who personifies the capital: 'My veins throb as though with the passage of underground trains. My digestive tract is sometimes clogged. There are security alerts. There's congestion, bottlenecks.' Stuart conceives the idea of

> *"It is because the city is too large and formless to be held in the mind as an imaginative whole that we make recourse to irrational short-cuts and simplifications."*

walking down every street in London, scoring them through in his *A-Z* as he goes.

Ghostwriter José Costa, in Chico Buarque's novel *Budapest*, has a different way of engaging with a new city: 'It took me a long time to learn that to know a city it is better to shut yourself away in a room within it than ride around it in a double-decker bus.' Married with a family in Rio, José becomes seduced by Budapest during a stopover there. He falls in love with Kriska and tells us he can understand Kriska's language before he knows any of the words. It's as if he has Hungarian blood running in his veins.

In American writer Shelley Jackson's story 'Blood', which appears in her collection *The Melancholy of Anatomy*, the streets of London conceal pipes and tunnels filled with blood. It is the job of blood-larks, using sanitary towels and cotton balls, to staunch the monthly flow.

From an extraordinary vision of the whole of London to one back garden in 'Islington'. In his short story of that name, which appears in *Here is Where We Meet*, John Berger writes about recovered memories and the effects of passing time on people, their houses and gardens: 'The density of the foliage was not like that of a jungle, but like the density of a closed book, which had to be read page by page.'

As Paul Buck has shown in his guide, *Lisbon: A Cultural and Literary Companion*,

MIDDLE AGE

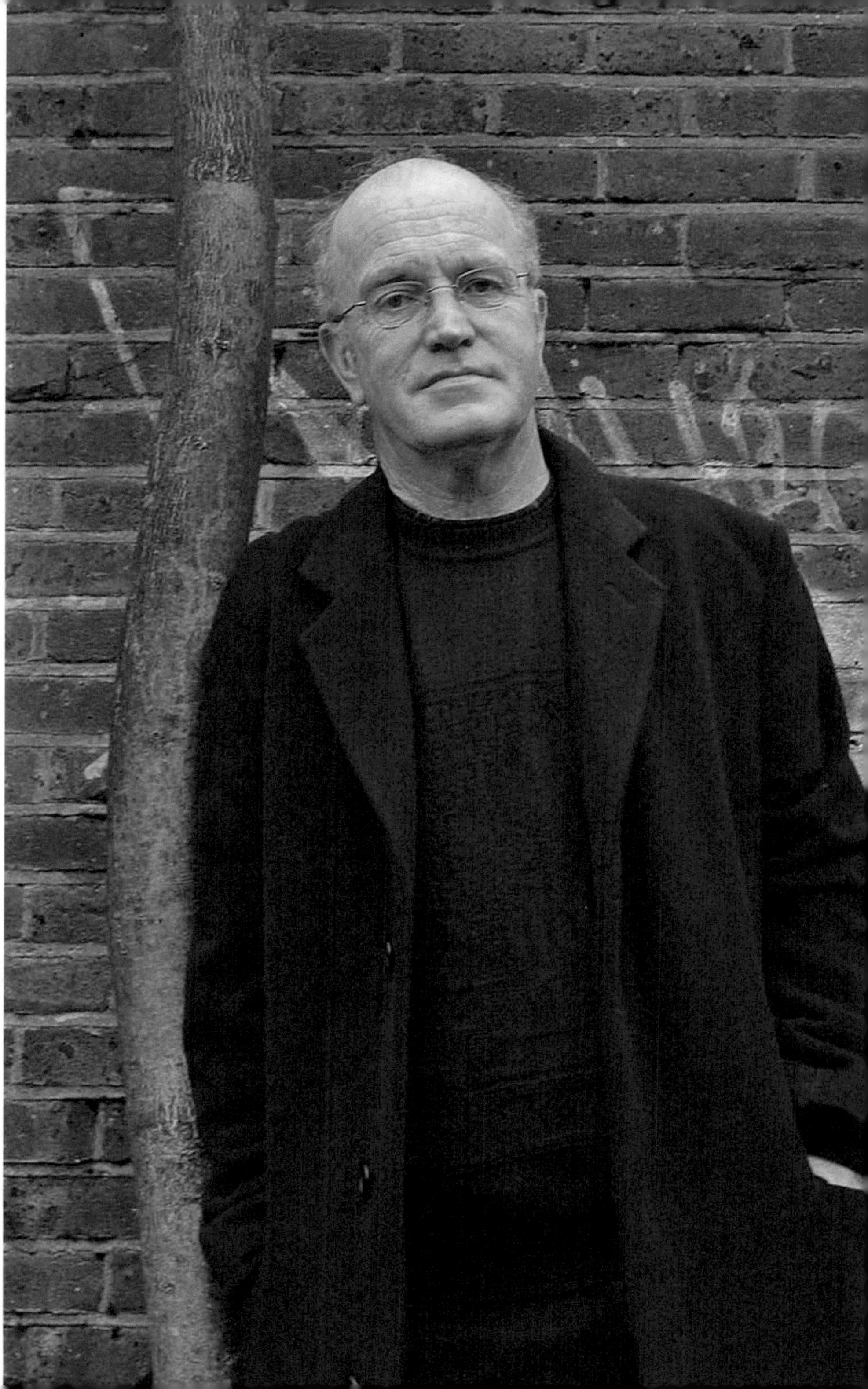

London flâneur **Iain Sinclair**.

the Portuguese capital has inspired many oustanding works of art. If Alain Tanner's haunting *In the White City* is one of the best Lisbon films, John Berger's 'Lisboa', which opens *Here is Where We Meet*, is one of the city's great stories. On a hot day at the end of May in Lisbon, John sees an old woman walking across the park. He recognises her walk as that of his mother, who has been dead 15 years. 'The dead don't stay where they are buried,' she tells him. 'Lisboa' is a magical evocation of the White City, with its seven hills, labyrinthine streets and endless steps. The trams pass so close to people's homes, he writes, that you could reach out an arm and give a birdcage a gentle push. 'Perhaps Lisboa is a special stopover for the dead,' thinks John, 'perhaps here the dead show themselves off more than in any other city.'

What's different about Lisbon are the trams. 'It's not any place, John, it's a meeting place,' his late mother tells him. 'There aren't many cities left with trams, are there?' Berger then remembers the tram they took when he was a boy growing up in Croydon, the number 194. 'We took it every day from East to South Croydon and back.' Trams shuttle memories back and forth in Michael Moorcock's short story 'London Blood', as well as in his masterpiece, the novel *Mother London*. As a boy, David Mummery prefers trams to buses: 'A tram's stairs are outside, unprotected from wind or rain, and a boy can stand with his back to the curved metal, pretending to be aboard some more romantic vessel.'

Cultural geographer Stephen Barber, author of *Extreme Europe*, a study of peripheral urban landscapes, has written widely on cities. A forthcoming 'theoretical fiction', *Forgotten Cities*, explores what might happen in the aftermath of a global digital crash. 'The world itself had been near-erased by that disaster, since those technologies had become inseparably integral to its urban fabric and to the corporeal life of its inhabitants.' Nevertheless, optimism springs from the narrator's discovery of a fragment of a book about 'the devices of a human technology known as "cinema"'. Following a further discovery, images on celluloid will be projected on to digital screens so that the cities of the world can start to reclaim their lost memories.

MIDDLE AGE

Corridors
of power

Political diaries show that the powerful are human too, says **Iain Dale**.

Political autobiography is normally defined as a work of fiction by the author, about the author. Rarely do we find examples of 'good autobiography'. Indeed, it would be easier to draw up a list of Top Ten Worst Political Memoirs.

The late Alan Clark, Conservative MP for Plymouth Sutton and latterly Kensington & Chelsea, is, without doubt, the best right-of-centre diarist of recent years. Deliciously indiscreet and sexually rampaging, his diaries offer insight, gossip and smut – an unbeatable combination. Clark's *Diaries* are published in three volumes and span the years 1972-99.

Another great diarist is the raconteur, star of *Countdown* and occasional wearer of woolly jumpers Gyles Brandreth. His diary of his five-year sojourn in the House of Commons during John Major's government still serves as the best record of that awful, tired administration. *Breaking the Code* is the title of the diary, and the book revolves around the fact that, as a former Government whip, Brandreth has broken the whips' code by writing about his work. He is indiscreet about everyone and everything, and the diaries read like a novel at times.

But the granddaddy of political diaries is the prolific left-wing firebrand Tony Benn. Benn retired from Parliament in 2001 to, as he puts it, go back into politics. He has written close on two million words of diaries, stretching back to the 1940s. They have been lovingly edited by Ruth Winstone into seven volumes. Benn's *Diaries* are a complete, if somewhat biased, history of post-war Labour politics, but actually they reveal far more than that. His story of ideology getting the better of his ambition is

a fascinating one. Benn is also not afraid to show emotion, and must surely count as the most prolific 'crier' in British politics.

Although they are not strictly political diaries, Jeffrey Archer's three-volume *Prison Diaries* are a must-read for anyone wanting to understand the futility of our prison system. Cast aside your preconceptions of Archer and read the first volume, *Hell*. I guarantee you'll then want to read the other two.

Edwina Currie's *Diaries* received so much attention in the newspapers that they barely sold a fraction of what the publishers had expected. But that doesn't make them bad. Indeed, they are highly readable and reveal a woman who was quite clearly emotionally dependent. Despite the appearance of self-confidence, Currie just wanted to be loved. The diaries are not dominated by her affair with John Major, and the rest of the book should serve as a warning to all those who think that politicians have the ultimate power.

A successful political diary or memoir will help you discover something you didn't know about the author or their career. Too often, unfortunately, political memoirs fail on that score. Norman Tebbit's *Upwardly Mobile* and the memoirs of William Whitelaw are examples of volumes by towering politicians that failed to live up to their billing.

In fact, memoirs from the Thatcher government are almost too numerous to mention. To get a proper perspective of her administration from the inside, Margaret Thatcher's own memoirs are an obvious must. They come in two volumes, *The Path to Power* and *Downing Street Years*. The latter is somewhat drier than the former, but both

Critics' choice
Diaries & letters

Clarissa by Samuel Richardson

The trials and tribulations of the beautiful and spotlessly virtuous Clarissa Harlowe are enumerated in Richardson's monumental epistolary novel. His admiration for Clarissa led Henry Fielding to pen a letter of his own to his literary rival, fulsomely praising the book – it moved him, he says, to grief, terror and 'Raptures of Admiration and Astonishment'.

The Diaries of Kenneth Williams

Published posthumously, Williams's diaries are by turns mischievous, acidly malicious and heartbreakingly sad. Spanning 40 years of his life, the entries paint a vivid picture of a complicated, often tormented man; egotistical but full of self-doubt, intensely private but an inveterate show-off. As he himself admits; 'It is extraordinary that I'm so liked because I'm invariably rude & tetchy.'

The Diaries of Samuel Pepys

Pepys lived through some of London's most formative events – including the Great Fire and plague, and the Restoration of Charles II – and led a colourful life drinking, womanising and working hard. But it is his relation of day-to-day life in the 17th century that affords the most fascinating insights: 'The fanatics do say that the end of the world is at hand, and that next Tuesday is to be the day.'

The Diary of Anne Frank

School and boys occupy the early pages of the diary of Annelies Marie Frank, a 13-year-old schoolgirl living in Nazi-occupied Amsterdam. More and more references to the increasing oppression against Jews begin to creep in, however, and eventually Anne and her family are forced to go into hiding. Her final entry is dated 1 August 1944; three days later, the military police burst in, and Anne was deported to the concentration camp where, aged 15, she died.

Dracula by Bram Stoker

A chilling blend of barely repressed sexual desire and good old-fashioned monster-chasing, Dracula begins with letters from lawyer Jonathan Harker to his fiancée Mina, as he travels through Transylvania to meet his new 'client'. What follows is a dire warning about mankind's abandonment of religious values, and tolerance of female sexuality – plus plenty of bloodsucking, decapitation and other such gory delights.

Evelina by Fanny Burney

A runaway success on its publication in 1778, Burney's novel unfolds in a series of letters composed by its eponymous heroine. These chart her entry into fashionable London society, and the journey from innocent ingénue to polished – and marriageable – young lady.

Julie, or the New Heloise by Jean-Jacques Rousseau

Based on the story of Abélard and Héloïse, Rousseau's 18th-century bestseller depicts the passionate – and ultimately tragic – love affair between a tutor, Saint-Preux, and his pupil Julie. This is not just a love story, however, but also a *roman à thèse* in which Rousseau rehearses some of his most important philosophical themes.

The Letters of Kingsley Amis

Amis *père* was a magnificently dyspeptic and enthusiastic letter-writer. Here he is on the success of his novelist son Martin: 'Last year he earned £38,000. Little shit. 29, he is. Little shit.' At the heart of this collection are Amis's letters to Philip Larkin, with whom he corresponded faithfully, hilariously and sometimes really rather movingly for many years. Following one of Larkin's poetical successes, Amis wrote: 'I am beside myself with anger and grief and envy, and am really very pleased for your sake, you lucky bastard.'

The Screwtape Letters by CS Lewis

Lewis's epistolary novel is subtitled 'Letters from a Senior to a Junior Devil'. The two satanic emissaries are Screwtape, a high-up functionary in the Infernal Civil Service, and Wormwood, a 'very junior Tempter'. Lewis attempts to impart a Christian message in reverse, by having his devils show how easy it is to find oneself on the 'gentle, sliding slope of habitual small sins'.

A Writer's Diary by Virginia Woolf

Virginia Woolf was not an obsessive diary-writer – there are sometimes week-long gaps here – but she was an unsparing and honest one, who recognises that her writerly impressions are not always an 'infallible guide' to the truth.

MIDDLE AGE

volumes show Thatcher in a more human light than most would expect. Nigel Lawson's *View from Number 11* and Geoffrey Howe's *Conflict of Loyalty* are both detailed yet human accounts of life in government at the highest level. They reveal the conflicts that politicians at the highest level are constantly wrestling with. The other excellent memoir from the Thatcher period is John Nott's *Here Today*

Gone Tomorrow (Nott was defence secretary at the time of the Falklands War). Like so many political memoirs, some of the best passages relate to his childhood and career before entering Parliament. Few expected much of John Major's *Autobiography*. They assumed that a lacklustre prime minister would produce a lacklustre book. Wrong. They forgot about the scores he had to settle. Major's

Inimitable diarist, legendary lothario: the late, great **Alan Clark**.

'*Deliciously indiscreet and sexually rampaging, Clark's diaries offer insight, gossip and smut – an unbeatable combination.*'

avuncular personality outside politics, which he used to good effect in writing his books. Roy Jenkins's *A Life at the Centre* is, as one might expect, a rather grand and elegant, if personally unrevealing, memoir. Jenkins dominated centre-left politics in the late 1960s and '70s before leaving the Labour Party to form the SDP in 1981 and become its first leader. His memoirs demonstrate why he never quite reached the top – like so many politicians, he lacked the killer instinct.

Bill Clinton's *My Life* is so long and detailed that it's a bit daunting for the casual reader. It's also very self-serving, although that is not unusual in political memoirs. But for all that, it reveals a weak man who recognises his own failings. Another weak man who became US president and was involved in sleaze was Richard Nixon. His *Memoirs* rank as my favourite political memoirs of all time. He is the finest political writer of his generation, but because of Watergate he is reviled and disrespected in both the political and literary worlds. It's understandable, but prejudice has no place in literature.

The publishing of political memoirs and diaries is on the decline. That's partly because publishers think no one is interested in politics; but it is also because of commercial reality. Few big publishers will take on a book that they don't believe will sell 10,000 copies, and there are few political books that fall into that category. Can you really see yourself forking out £18.99 to read the memoirs of Alastair Darling, Jack Straw or Patricia Hewitt? Thought not.

autobiography is perhaps the best (and bitchiest) Conservative memoir of modern times.

The finest recent Labour memoir is *Time of My Life* by Denis Healey, chancellor during the beleagured 1974-9 Labour government. Healey is one of the few politicians with a hinterland beyond Westminster. Although universally hated by left and right when he was chancellor, he quickly developed an

Crime
and punishment

Maxim Jakubowski explores the literary underworld.

Why is crime and mystery fiction so popular? In addition to the important fact that, unlike much of what one would term as mainstream or normal fiction, it invariably tells a story with a beginning and an end, it's a literary genre that appeals to all ages, genders and tastes.

On the one hand, in the grand old tradition of Edgar Allan Poe and Conan Doyle's illustrious Sherlock Holmes, it offers the great satisfaction of puzzle-solving, while on the other, taking a leaf from, say, Charles Dickens and, indirectly, the gothic novel and its downmarket successors the 'penny dreadfuls', it can also deliver social comment and psychological depth. Add to this potent cocktail the fact that mystery fiction is also a great opportunity for larger-than-life characters, be they goodies or sinister villains, to strut their stuff in the theatre of the imagination, and you have a lethal and attractive combination that keeps readers relentlessly turning the pages, and creates a sense of wonder, involvement and even fear that few other forms can match.

Over the years, crime and mystery fiction has, very roughly, been divided into two camps: on the one hand, the so-called 'cosy' tradition exemplified by Agatha Christie and her literary heirs, in which the puzzle and the investigation are paramount; and, on the other, the hard-boiled school typified by Raymond Chandler, in which darkness, a sense of place and oblique social commentary take precedence and in which the characters are often more important than the actual plot. Today, however, these boundaries are much less clear-cut, as practitioners travel with ease back and forth across the genre frontier.

Trends in crime and mystery fiction come and go, but when it comes to straightforward detective tales, all you need is a body (or more than one), clues, a mystery, red herrings galore and an investigation – as Sherlock Holmes, Hercule Poirot and Miss Marple have so ably demonstrated over the years (novels like *The Sign of Four*, *The Mysterious Affair at Styles* and *They Do It With Mirrors* are perfect starting points at which to meet these immortal characters). A more modern incarnation, made hugely popular by TV, has been Colin Dexter's Inspector Morse (possibly at his best in *Last Bus to Woodstock*), with the genial Lewis as the obligatory sidekick, following in the hallowed footsteps of Holmes's Doctor Watson. Another sleuthing duo of note are the indomitable Northern cops Dalziel and Pascoe, created by Reginald Hill. Fat Andy and his bright but eternally frustrated sidekick are not only determined and resourceful investigators but also striking characters, very much of flesh and blood and myriad contradictions. And like all good fictional detectives, it's not just their qualities but also their defects that endear them to the reading public (see, for example, *Exit Lines* or *A Clubbable Woman*).

The hard-boiled stream has its origins in the American pulp magazines where Raymond Chandler, Dashiell Hammett and an entire regiment of crime writers of a darker hue (David Goodis, Cornell Woolrich, Erle Stanley Gardner, John D MacDonald, to name only a few) took their first steps. Here, the private investigator or cop faces reality and a school of hard knocks much closer to everyday life than the often remote world of middle-England charted by Christie and co. It must be said that

Corrupt cops and murder most horrid in **LA Confidential**.

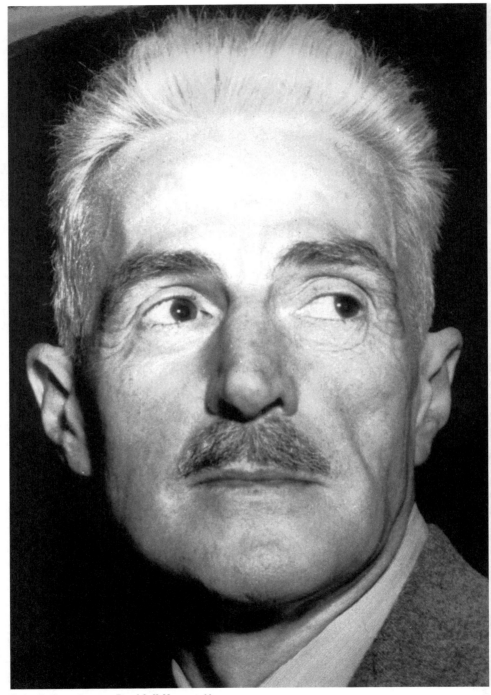

Pulp fiction pioneer **Dashiell Hammett**.

their books have dated better than their cosy counterparts, and Chandler's *The Long Goodbye* or *The Big Sleep* and Hammett's *Red Harvest* or *The Continental* still have an insidious power to excite and thrill today. The mean-streets ethos continues to thrive unabated to the present day, and is best exemplified by James Ellroy (*LA Confidential, The Black Dahlia*), James Lee Burke (*Neon Rain, A Morning for Flamingos*) and Ed McBain (any book in the *87th Precinct* series, which openly inspired *Hill Street Blues*). A more recent phenomenon has been the absorption of this hard-boiled current into the mainstream of British crime fiction, with remarkable home-grown results: John Harvey, Mark Timlin, Mark Billingham, Mo Hayder, Ian Rankin and Val McDermid, among others.

In the thriller, crime is not always necessarily at the heart of the plot, even if along the way many a death intervenes and the body count is often even higher than in the mystery. Thomas Harris's saga of Hannibal Lecter, the serial killer and cannibal, saw its apotheosis in *The Silence of the Lambs* and has influenced, for better or worse, a new generation of psycho-thriller authors such as Dean Koontz, John Sandford, Lee Child, Patricia Cornwell and others, who have colonised a disproportionate chunk of the crime and mystery field over the past, somewhat bloodthirsty, decade.

In addition to the underlying mystery in the plot and the memorable characters, another necessary ingredient of crime and mystery writing is a strong sense of place. Holmes had Victorian London, Chandler's Philip Marlowe had Los Angeles. Today, Janet Evanovich has New Jersey, Morse has Oxford and Sara Paretsky's VI Warshawski moves through the mean streets of Chicago. A striking example of the way new territories and timelines are being annexed as stamping grounds for strong characters and plots is the unexpected success of Alexander McCall Smith's gentle adventures of Mama Ramotswe, which are set in Botswana and are a reminder that crime fiction is able to integrate humour and irony with ease (Donald Westlake, Christopher Brookmyre and Carl Hiaasen are other prominent examples of this). Just like real life!

With such a diverse range of situations, unforgettable characters, devious stories and fascinating places, it's no wonder readers never tire of crime and mystery fiction.

A book that changed my life

Nigella Lawson

David Copperfield by Charles Dickens

I don't know how it's possible to choose one book, one book alone, but if there's a novel I had to read and reread, again and again, without ever tiring of it, I think it would be *David Copperfield*. I came to Dickens late, resisted him for too long as a child and adolescent. Perhaps that's best: he's got such savagery and unbearable honesty that there's no point reading him before you're ready to notice that. Yes, of course, he's funny; yes, of course, the names are peerlessly coined; yes, of course, he has a genius for plot: but he is also heartbreaking to read.

David Copperfield seems to me to be about as complete a story of what it is to be human as it could be possible to read – or write. I'm not surprised that it was Freud's favourite book.

Nigella Lawson's most recent book is Feast: Food That Celebrates Life *(Chatto & Windus).*

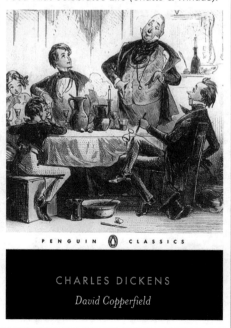

PENGUIN CLASSICS

CHARLES DICKENS
David Copperfield

Middle youth

Amanda Craig looks at books that bridge the generation gap.

Crossover books – novels that appeal to adults as much as they do to children – are the publishing phenomenon of the past decade. JK Rowling, Philip Pullman, Lian Hearn and Mark Haddon are all stars of a genre loved by child and adult alike, often published with two different covers but successful in both markets.

There has always been a fruitful exchange between the worlds of child and adult literature. The authors of *Sleeping Beauty*, the *Arabian Nights* and *Grimms' Fairy Tales* did not have infants in mind when those stories were originally collected or composed. Equally, many children's classics, such as *Gulliver's Travels*, were originally intended for adults, while children were expected to understand and enjoy novels by Dickens and Robert Louis Stevenson.

Children's literature became a special genre in the early 19th century, but Tolkien's *Lord of the Rings*, or Ursula le Guin's *Earthsea* trilogy, the earliest modern crossover books, have many familiar features. On the one hand, they used the tropes of fairy tales (magic wands, fabled creatures and prophecies); on the other, their heroes were more experienced and less innocent than those of a children's novel. Tolkien's is a world in which torture, genetic experiment, dismemberment and wanton cruelty are rife. Even if good triumphs at the end, it involves sacrifices from which the protagonists (including the child-like hobbits) will never recover.

Ursula le Guin's hero is equally poised between the child and the adult. Ged is 'mageborn', a proud, wilful boy with a great gift that he abuses. Prone to envy and anger, he unleashes a Shadow on his world from the Land of the Dead, which hunts him until he realises that he can defeat it only by speaking its true name. The name, inevitably, is his own. Many, though not all, crossover novels feature magic, the popularity of which may be due to the realisation that magic realism, so popular in the 1980s, was far sillier than outright fantasy.

Crossover fiction usually features protagonists who are on the cusp between childhood and maturity, inhabiting both worlds. Harry Potter starts off as an 11-year-old about to go to secondary school, but grows a year older (and wiser) in each book, which is correspondingly darker. Philip Pullman's Will and Lyra, as the new Adam and Eve, ultimately fall in love and lose their virginity to each other. Mark Haddon's Christopher in *The Curious Incident of the Dog in the Night-time* is unusually intelligent but handicapped by autism. In *How I Live Now*, Meg Rosoff's teenaged Daisy swaps anorexia for incest, while Lian Hearn's Japanese hero Takeo, bent on avenging his murdered mother, falls passionately in love with the exquisite Kaede, the murderer's bride, whom he must rescue in *Across the Nightingale Floor*.

The advent of sex into children's books may seem like a loss of innocence (and typically presages the loss of magic), but is done with tact and skill in many crossover novels. It has always been around (see Rumer Godden's *The*

Watch out, Harry – Philip Pullman's **The Golden Compass** hits the big screen.

MIDDLE AGE

WINNER OF THE WHITBREAD
BOOK OF THE YEAR

MARK HADDON

The CURIOUS INCIDENT

of THE DOG
IN THE NIGHT-TIME

'OUTSTANDING...A stunningly
good read' INDEPENDENT

VINTAGE

Peacock Spring, Dodie Smith's *I Capture the Castle*) as an essential ingredient, but modern versions acknowledge sex as a source of joy as well as irrevocable change. It reminds adults of the strength and purity of first love, and informs children of its potential for pain. Crossover books allow readers a double insight – into the past for adults, and into the future for children. They give adults the consolations of children's literature, but also give children a taste of the gravity and responsibility of adulthood.

Crossover books can, like Rowling's, be largely comfort-reads, but others, such as Pullman's *His Dark Materials*, are far more intellectually challenging. Like le Guin, Haddon and Hearn, Pullman writes with an exceptional beauty of style. He uses theories about quantum physics, and probably introduced many adults to the concept of dark matter and the multiverse (though the latter had already been explored by children's authors such as Diana Wynne-Jones). Mark Haddon's hero understands complex mathematics better than human emotion. Lyra's parents experience complex passions for each other that adult readers enjoy and children feel flattered in gaining some apprehension of.

Of course, most adults don't read crossover books to find out about sex – they have quite enough of this in their own fiction – or science, but to recapture the vigour and enchantment of a world in which the fantastic is given equal weight with the real. Rowling captured the sheer fertility of a child's informed imagination just as Nesbit, Dahl and CS Lewis did before her, by thinking about what logical consequences magic and mythical creatures would entail. The typical children's novel cuts them off from adults; Rowling's children are involved with them. Mark Haddon's narrator responds differently to adults because of his disability, and therefore achieves things an ordinary child would not. Making the magical mundane and the mundane magical is crucial to this new genre.

It is the power of storytelling, however, that lies at the heart of the rise of the crossover novel. For most of the past century, the narrative grasp of literary novelists has been lost in social minutiae, an obsession with sex and the elevation of literary style as the hallmark of substance. In other words, literature became dull. Good children's literature is, by definition, well written, for the attention span of children does not allow

A book that changed my life

Ian Sansom

Selected Poems by WH Auden

In the early 1990s I was working in Foyle's bookshop, on the Charing Cross Road in London. I liked working in Foyle's: I liked opening up the big boxes of books; I liked the tea trolley that came round in the morning and again in the afternoon; I liked hiding from the customers and pretending I was busy. Also, I earned more money working in Foyle's than I ever had before, and than I ever have since.

But all good things must come to an end. I left Foyle's and somehow ended up studying for a PhD. My subject was the poetry of WH Auden. On my last day at Foyle's, I used my staff discount to buy a copy of the *Selected Poems*.

I spent three years reading and writing about Auden. Was it worth it? Go into a bookshop – Foyle's is still there, I believe, though gussied up now and made to look pretty – and find a copy of the *Selected Poems*. Read 'Hearing of Harvests Rotting in the Valleys', and 'In Praise of Limestone' and 'The Fall of Rome'. I think it was probably worth it. I don't know. What do you think?

Ian Sansom is the author of the Mobile Library *series of detective novels (Harper Collins).*

MIDDLE AGE

for authorial self-indulgence, but it has also stayed true to the need to grip and entertain.

Crossover fiction allows a much bigger, broader canvas for friendship, courage, self-sacrifice, evil and loyalty to come into violent conflict, much as they do in children's literature. What it risks is the subtler rewards of more demanding, less plot-driven fiction becoming palatable to the next generation of readers. The experience of reading, say, Tolstoy or Henry James is qualitatively different from reading about Hogwarts, Middle Earth or medieval Japan. Feeding the proliferating fantasy life of adults has possibly endangered this kind of writing (and reading). Then again, it may be reviving it from the bottom up. Only time will tell.

Class
acts

John Lewis traces the lineage of the upper-class twit in literature.

There's a scene in Oscar Wilde's *The Importance of Being Earnest* in which the truculent Lady Bracknell is cross-examining Jack Worthing as a potential suitor for her daughter. 'I have always been of the opinion that a man who desires to get married should know everything or nothing,' she announces. 'Which do you know?' Jack pauses for some time before replying. 'I know nothing, Lady Bracknell.' 'I am pleased to hear it,' she says. 'I do not approve of anything that tampers with natural ignorance. Ignorance is like a delicate fruit; touch it and the bloom is gone.'

It's an exchange that explicitly lays down the blueprint for an enduring archetype of English literature – the upper-class twit. He is a figure who takes many improbable monickers. Most famously, in the novels of PG Wodehouse, he is Bertie Wooster, or Psmith, or Ukridge, or Lord Emsworth. In the short stories of Hector Hugh Monro, aka Saki, he is Reginald, or Clovis Sangrail, or Comus Bassington; in the crime novels of Dorothy L Sayers he is Lord Peter Wimsey; in AA Milne's *Once on a Time* he is Prince Udo; in Baroness Orczy's 1905 novel he is *The Scarlet Pimpernel*, the dashing counter-revolutionary who poses to all the world as a superficial idiot.

The posh twit is independently wealthy. He is expensively educated but proudly philistine. He is suspicious of high culture and intellect, even though he often narrates his stories with the simple elegance of a literary master. He is profoundly lazy (with a nod to Jerome K Jerome's *Idle Thoughts of an Idle Fellow*) but keeps a fanatically busy social schedule. He is proudly apolitical in a way that only the most instinctively reactionary

men can ever hope to be. Oscar Wilde's Jack Worthing is just one of his literary ancestors. The upper-class twit also shares his DNA with the foolish fops and dandies who turn up on the fringes of Shakespeare or Sheridan plays, as well as the moronic aristocrats of Dickens's *The Pickwick Papers*. His comic grammar was forged by George Grossmith's Charles Pooter, the lower-middle-class suburban drone who serves as the endearingly pompous protagonist of 1892's *Diary of a Nobody*.

The twit truly reached his apotheosis in the first two decades of the 20th century, when the likes of Wodehouse, Chesterton, Saki, Stephen Leacock and Jerome K Jerome shifted Pooter a few notches up the class spectrum, divested him of trifling duties like a regular job, but retained his naïvety, vanity, pomposity, snobbery and gaucheness. The posh twit can occasionally be a dandy and a cad, like Peter Wimsey, but more often he is not only baffled by the opposite sex but asexual to the point of neuter. 'The attitude of fellows towards finding girls in their bedroom shortly after midnight varies,' says Bertie Wooster in 1934's *Thank You, Jeeves*. 'Some like it. I didn't.'

It's echoed by Saki's 'Tea', where the 34-year-old bachelor James Cushat-Prinkly is described thus: 'He liked and admired a great many women collectively and dispassionately without singling out one for especial matrimonial consideration, just as one might admire the Alps without feeling that one wanted any particular peak as one's own private property.'

Wilde's social satires were written from a militantly left-wing perspective, one where the upper classes unselfconsciously expose

Critics' choice
Class struggle

Animal Farm by George Orwell

Orwell's allegory is about the betrayal of revolutionary class politics. The farm animals rise up against their master, led by the pigs, pre-eminent among whom is Napoleon, a 'rather fierce-looking Berkshire boar'. Before long, Napoleon is interpreting the 'spirit of Animalism' in ways the other beasts could never have imagined.

Capital by Karl Marx

Marx's magnum opus is best read not as prophecy, but as a handbook for socialist advocacy. Capitalism hasn't bred its own gravediggers, as he predicted. But his depiction of injustice and the 'phantom-like objectivity' of commodification is still compelling.

The Making of the English Working Class by EP Thompson

A self-styled 'rebellious humanist', historian Thompson rescues the early industrial working class – the Luddite croppers and 'utopian' artisans – from the 'enormous condescension of posterity'. At times, the story he tells reads like a 'history of civil war'.

Mary Barton by Elizabeth Gaskell

'It's the masters as has wrought this woe; it's the masters as should pay for it.' A 'condition of England' novel, Mary Barton is set in industrial Manchester in the first half of the 19th century. Mary's loyalties are torn when her father John Barton, an out-of-work mill operative turned trade union official, becomes involved in a plot to murder the local factory owner.

Nickel and Dimed by Barbara Ehrenreich

Journalist Ehrenreich spends a year with the American poor, working for starvation wages as a waitress, cleaner and checkout clerk.

Noblesse Oblige by Nancy Mitford

The centrepiece of Mitford's enquiry into the 'identifying characteristics' of the English uppper classes is her infamous and imperishable essay 'The English Aristocracy'. In it, Mitford refines the distinction between 'U' and 'non-U' English usage, originally devised by the linguist Alan Ross. 'Napkin' is U, 'serviette' non-U. 'Lavatory' or 'loo' pass muster; 'toilet' does not.

Reflections on the Revolution in France by Edmund Burke

MODERN CLASSICS

George Orwell
Animal Farm

Burke's reflections on the events of 1789 drew a furious response from Tom Paine in *The Rights of Man*. Paine thought his opponent was heaping 'outrageous abuse on the principles of Liberty'. Burke, however, claimed to be defending not reaction but an older notion of liberty against the tyranny he predicted the revolution would unleash.

Sybil by Benjamin Disraeli

Part-time novelist Disraeli invented 'One Nation' Toryism in *Sybil*. The heroine describes two nations 'between whom there is no intercourse and no sympathy'.

The Tortilla Curtain by T Coraghessan Boyle

In Boyle's novel, the 'Tortilla Curtain' separates prosperous bourgeois bohemians Delaney and Kyra Mossbacher from the Rincuns, illegal immigrants from Mexico.

To the Finland Station by Edmund Wilson

Wilson traces the emergence of the idea of socialist revolution – from the Paris Commune to the October Revolution, and from Fourier to Trotsky. He may have lacked a grasp of the dialectic, but was still genius enough to read Marx's *Capital* as a kind of Gothic novel.

MIDDLE AGE

their bigotry and idiocy. His detailed subtext slyly reveals a world beyond the drawing room (poverty, slavery, rioting, crime) that pulls the rug from under the characters. But usually the satirical function of the upper-class twit is more gentle. In classical terms, writers like Wodehouse, Leacock and Saki belong to the Horatian rather than the Juvenalian school of satire; their role being to mock folly gently rather than to attack evil.

However, in the hands of Catholic moralists such as GK Chesterton or Evelyn Waugh, the posh twit becomes a symbol of all that is rotten about society. In *Club of Queer Trades*, Chesterton's short comic novel about a club of people who have invented their professions, we are asked to side with the swindlers who extract money from the idle rich. They include the 'Organiser of Repartee', who is paid to visit rich people's dinner parties and feed comic lines to ensure that the host gets the laughs. 'This fat old gentleman strikes you, as I have no doubt, as very stupid and very rich,' says Basil Grant, the sleuth investigating the Club. 'Let me clear his character. He is, like ourselves, very clever and very poor… He is a swindler, and a swindler of a perfectly delightful and novel kind.'

Waugh goes further along the Juvenalian route. His upper-class twits are not harmless and genial buffoons, but thuggish and irresponsible children of privilege. The opening page of *Decline And Fall* describes a party at Oxford that concludes with a caged fox being brought in and stoned to death with champagne bottles ('What an evening that had been!'), and catalogues how the posh twits conspire to ruin the highly moral protagonist Paul Pennyfeather. In its 1930 sequel *Vile Bodies*, Waugh appears to positively drip with contempt for the feckless, grotesquely drawn Bright Young Things.

Perhaps Waugh's contempt was generational. The upper-class twit flourished within a brief window in British history – somewhere towards the end of Queen Victoria's reign and before the start of World War I. In the introduction to the 1967 edition of *The Complete Saki*, Noël Coward writes of Saki that: 'His satire was based primarily on the assumption of a fixed social status quo which, although at the time he was writing may have been wobbling a bit, outwardly at least, betrayed few signs of

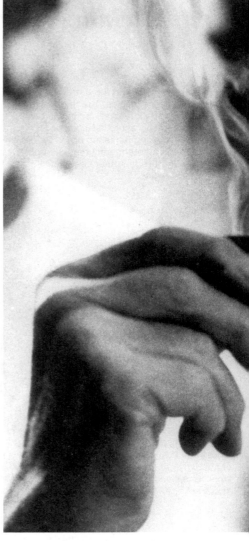

its imminent collapse.' He could be describing every upper-class twit when he says that Saki's 'effete young heroes, with their gaily irreverent persiflage and their preoccupation with oysters, caviar and personal adornment, finally disappeared in the gunsmoke of 1914.'

The ruling classes are ambivalent about the upper-class twit. When Wodehouse was recommended for an honour in 1967, Sir Patrick Dean, British ambassador in Washington, argued that it 'would give currency to a Bertie Wooster image of the British character, which

MIDDLE AGE

we are doing our best to eradicate'. Yet the twit's relentless simpleness also serves to humanise the aristocracy. The Queen Mother is said to have been so keen for Wodehouse to be knighted that she offered to perform the service herself. In his recent study *On Royalty*, Jeremy Paxman recounts a weekend spent at Sandringham at the invitation of the Prince of Wales. He discovers a bookshelf containing highbrow philosophy textbooks and Wodehouse novels – the philosophy tomes turned out to be fake bookends; the

Wodehouses were extremely well thumbed. He concludes that this Wodehousian philistinism gives the Royals 'much in common with their people, who tend to consider intellectuals in much the same way as they regard people who claim they can levitate'.

Just as wealthy patrons at St James's Theatre in the 1890s would roar with laughter as Wilde's social satires mercilessly mocked them, it seems that there are still plenty of posh twits who like nothing better than to be reminded how stupid they are.

Old Age

'The sixth age shifts
Into the lean and
slippered pantaloon,
With spectacles on nose
and pouch on side.'

Decline
and fall

Michael Bywater takes the pulse of the grumpy old man in literature.

Infant, schoolboy, lover, soldier, justice…
Shakespeare's cherry-stoning of the ages
of man takes a sudden dive when we come
to our sixth age, which

'…shifts
Into the lean and slipper'd pantaloon,
With spectacles on nose and pouch on side,
His youthful hose, well saved,
a world too wide
For his shrunk shank; and his big manly voice,
Turning again toward childish treble, pipes
And whistles in his sound.'

Before the sheer oblivion of Shakespeare's
last act, the great change has already happened:
the schoolboy, lover, soldier, justice, even the
mewling, puking infant: all had something to
do. But not our character. He is nothing but
a shrivelled frame and a wizened voice. He no
longer acts in the world. He is reduced to the
visual and aural: a fluting whistle, a scrawny
crooked scribble in the margins of life, which
goes on around him.

Sometimes he is fitfully reanimated, as in
the *Satyricon* of Petronius, where the old fool
Eumolpius enlists his slave Corax to lie under
the mattress heaving upwards in rhythm with
the reverse cowgirl downstrokes of Eumolpius's
popsy (foisted on him by her venal ma), giving
the impression of a vigorous virility that, in
reality, he lacks. The old sod saddled with a
young wife is a staple of fiction from the ancients
onwards, his near-impotence and confirmed
bachelordom exposed and disrupted by a
younger woman. Sir John Brute in Vanbrugh's
The Provok'd Wife, speaks for the lot of them
when he first appears:

'What a cloying meat is love, when
matrimony's the sauce to it! Two years'
marriage has debauched my five senses.
Everything I see, everything I hear, everything
I feel, everything I smell, and everything I
taste, methinks, has wife in't.'

Brute still has his senses (stripped from him
in the last scene of all, the senescence of 'mere

'A very foolish fond old man';
Laurence Olivier as **King Lear**.

oblivion/Sans teeth, sans eyes, sans taste, sans everything'), but they turn upon him. Just as Pantalone in the Italian commedia dell'arte schemes to grow rich by exploiting another, only to be thwarted by his slaves, so Brute, attempting another sort of (bodily) exploitation is betrayed and buggered up by the servants of his own physical existence, his senses.

But the John Brutes are rarer than Shakespeare's knackered, enfeebled old shags. *They* abound.

Dickens, in particular, loves them, and gives them life in various disguises. Sometimes he can do nothing with them at all, as in the case of Curious Old Chuffey in *Martin Chuzzlewit*,

hovering around pointlessly like a vaguely benign spring onion lightly coated in unction. At other times he reanimates them, like Mr Pickwick in *The Pickwick Papers*, who, despite his ability to get about the place in top boots and tall hat, is still an easy gull for the predatory Mrs Bardell, still flutes and pipes and flutters his hands and, instead of going into battle, goes for appeasement at every turn. Pickwick is the prototype of the Dickensian character whom George Orwell called 'the good rich man… a superhumanly kind-hearted old gentleman who "trots" to and fro, raising his employees' wages, patting children on the head, getting debtors out of jail and in general, acting

the fairy godmother.' But this, too, is a form of impotence: appeasement rather than combat, the tyranny of the weak – and the fate of the Good Old Man is to end up in some terrible cottage somewhere, with his descendants around him and no worries, and everything lovely in that particularly Dickensian way which comes down to the certainty that nothing whatsoever can ever happen again.

His occasional monsters are better: Tony Weller (Senior), gullible pugnacious father to the wery saintly Sam, Mr Pickwick's servant; the abominable retired Major Joe Blagstock in *Dombey and Son*; the majestic, neologizing piss-artist Mrs (Sairy) Gamp (*Martin Chuzzlewit* again), with her imaginary friend Mrs Harris and her teapot full of gin (the two being not unconnected). But the greatest of Dickens's old monsters is unquestionably Ebenezer Scrooge in *A Christmas Carol*, a short book that, despite its message of Redemption through Niceness, manages mostly to steer clear of Victorian Christian sententiousness (Dickens being, in his soul, not an early Victorian but a late Georgian) and to achieve so miraculous a cinematic compression of language and signification that you find yourself wondering just how the hell he pulled it off.

But *A Christmas Carol* leads us to another question: just how old are these sixth-agers? How old, for example, is Scrooge? Dickens's chronologies are contradictory, but Scrooge – drawn by Cruickshank as a withered old man

A book that changed my life

Benjamin Markovits

What Maisie Knew by Henry James

One of the questions writers can struggle with, as they try to build their characters out of, among other things, a careful observation of themselves, is this: what do you do with your own literary ambition? How do you feel your way imaginatively into people who don't share it? This is one reason, I think, that so many characters in books come across as vaguely childish: they have been talked down to. In stripping them of literary ambition, their authors have stripped them of the human faculties that serve it: penetration, subtlety, detachment. Sometimes, writers try to imagine what they think of vaguely as an 'equivalent' trade for their heroes to pursue: Woody Allen might figure his protagonist as a sportswriter, instead of a filmmaker; Wordsworth writes about farmers rather than nature poets. I didn't get around to late James until my twenties, but what struck me, with the force almost of revelation, was the intelligence he granted so many of his characters. There was no talking down; they were equal, really, to the subtlety of the narrator himself – and equality, in its moral sense, was the impression one took from them.

His characters are grown-ups. They hold a great deal in reserve; and even when they express their deepest feelings, they tend to preserve that quantity. It is a commonplace of good writing that a novel should suggest in every detail its author's intentions, without ever giving them away; the lesson James teaches is to apply the same standard to his characters. There is no need to expose even children to the reader's completest sympathies. What Maisie Knew, for example, is not only the title of his wonderful novel, but a question that should remain, up to the end, partly unanswered. The last thing people (writers included) like to give away is everything they know.

Benjamin Markovits's latest novel is Imposture *(Faber).*

with Pantalone's hooked nose, spindle shanks and a bald head – seems somewhere between late forties and mid fifties, with my own best guess putting him at 53. Or, looking elsewhere, how old is Shakespeare's own King Lear? Middle fifties at the latest, and perhaps just a little older than Sir John Falstaff when Prince Hal, come into his kingdom, rounds on his one-time drinking buddy: 'I know thee not, old man. Fall to thy prayers.'

Oedipus at Colonus, written by Sophocles some 2,400 years ago, shows the sometime king of Thebes as a physically ruined man on the point of death; but it seems unlikely that Oedipus was, in the play's 'reality', more than in his late forties. We might think that life was shorter then, and forty was old; but once you survived babyhood and the childhood illnesses and got through military service alive, your chances of a ripe old age were good. And let's not forget that Sophocles himself was in his late eighties when he wrote the play; old men do not habitually defame themselves by writing old characters as doddering on the grave's brink.

We can continue – the withered and self-deluding academic Casaubon (literary father to many a desiccated don) in George Eliot's *Middlemarch* is probably no more than 42; King Gilgamesh, in the Sumerian *Epic of Gilgamesh*, written over 4,500 years ago, would seem to have been in his mid thirties when he was presented as a wise old king, ripe in years and soon to die, building the walls of Uruk as his final gift, on which his story was to be inscribed. And Ulysses, the founding father of western mythology – and

still a dominant force in Hollywood storytelling, whether explicit (as in *Oh Brother Where Art Thou?*) or beneath the surface (*The Lion King*, for example) – would have been, according to the chronology in Homer's *Odyssey*, no more than 38 when he returned to Ithaka and his faithful Penelope.

We might think of 'old', therefore, more as a condition of being – an acted character, if you like – than a function of age; and where age is explicit, the writer seems more often than not to be at pains to point out his character's (whether fictional or his own) vigour.

Anthony Burgess's *Earthly Powers* – the lead character being based, some say, on W Somerset Maugham; others, on a hopeful self-projection of Burgess himself (then 63), turned gay for the fictional hell of it – could hardly be more explicit on both counts in its magnificent opening sentence, one of the most memorable in all fiction: 'It was the afternoon of my eighty-first birthday, and I was in bed with my catamite when Ali announced that the archbishop had come to see me.'

The same thing, if less in-your-face, applies to Jean-Jacques Rousseau's *Confessions* – one of the literary seeds of Romanticism, remade by William Boyd in *The New Confessions*. The author strides about the place picking quarrels, getting into trouble, shagging, boasting, scheming, getting rich, getting poor again, getting paranoid but invariably with an almost intolerable vigour and combative virility – if not physical, then always mental. Same, too, for Casanova's memoirs and for Edward Gibbon's *Memoirs of My Life*, and for the great encylopedist Pliny the Elder, who died in the eruption of Vesuvius in 79 AD, and whose *Natural History* is filled with digressions and denunciations and tongue- or pen-lashings against anything that arouses his ire (mostly Greeks and luxury).

The fragile antiquary John Aubrey presents himself, in his fragmented *Brief Lives*, as a far more vigorous and endlessly curious character than his stage portrayal (by Roy Dotrice, complete with Pantalone wig, spectacles, nose and buggered teeth) would suggest. Returning to fiction, perhaps one of the finest confrontations of age in literature, Gabriel Garcia Marquez's *Love in the Time of Cholera*, depicts its old narrator and his equally ancient beloved as still fired with the passions of youth,

'Old men's acting-in-the-world is almost always confined within strict boundaries. Well outside those boundaries is any hint of sexuality.'

Samuel Beckett paints a mordant picture of old age in *Malone Dies*.

Oedipus at Colonus, 'physically ruined, on the point of death'.

which they finally consummate on a riverboat on the endless Amazon: sex in the face of death. If, as Sophocles wrote, 'Nobody loves life like an old man', then these authors, and many like them, echo his words in their own. Shakespeare's old men may not act, but these old men act, and keep acting.

Their acting-in-the-world, though, is almost always confined within strict boundaries. Well outside those boundaries is any hint of sexuality: one of the saddest things about ageing is the knowledge that, confined within withered flesh, the slightest glimpse of eroticism is simultaneously laughable and disgusting. If there's one thing worse – in literature as in life – than a dirty old man, it's a dirty old woman. The grotesquery of the stout and elderly housekeeper in Elias Canetti's *Auto da Fè* is only matched by the repulsion her employer, a Casaubon-style withered Herr Professor, feels at her advances.

The literary device of the repugnantly old falling for the gold-diggingly young has been a staple for so long that it would be impossible to single out a particular example; the same goes for the predatory widow who's seen a pack of husbands into the grave and hasn't lost her eye for a codpiece. Very, very occasionally – as in 'The Swan', an episode in Ray Bradbury's *Dandelion Wine* – do we get a sympathetic (and moving) portrayal, in this case of the young Bill Forrester falling in love with the 93-year-old Helen Loomis; or, rather, with 'the swan' he sees when imagining who she once was. But it stays within the boundaries: their love is entirely chaste, the old woman retains a respectable sense that time has removed her forever from the arms of Eros, and Bradbury himself justifies the proceedings by hinting that they were meant for each other; there had been an unfortunate timeshift; but one day they would be reincarnated in synchrony and be able to fall in love. And to do something about it.

Bradbury's tale is a rarity. Otherwise, the old are out of it, though allowed to reminisce. The novelist Henry Green – little read now, but a revolutionary stylist in the last century – told his *Paris Review* interviewer in 1958 that he'd got the idea for his novel *Loving* from hearing of an old butler who had been asked what he most loved in the world. 'The reply was "lying in bed on a summer morning, with the window

'We would prefer to consider the old as coeval grotesques, fetching up knackered, struck down and going to their long home among their own kind.'

open, listening to the church bells, eating buttered toast with cunty fingers." I saw the book in a flash.' For the old, sex, like the past it belongs in, is another country. Sometimes authors may survey that country – like Ronald Blyth in *The View in Winter* – by recording the memories of its inhabitants, but usually we do not even want to know. Just as we don't particularly want to know about the home lives of immigrants before they came here, so we prefer – in literature at least – to see the old as asylum seekers. Their backstories would be too disturbing; all we want to know is how they're assimilating. Anything else would be like the old Roman admonition *hodie mihi, cras tibi*: 'Today, me. Tomorrow… you.' TS Eliot picks up the trope in 'Death by Water' from *The Waste Land*:

> '*Gentile or Jew*
> *O you who turn the wheel and look to windward,*
> *Consider Phlebas, who was once handsome and tall as you.*'

Consider Phlebas? We would prefer not to. We would prefer to consider the old as coeval grotesques, fetching up knackered, struck down and going to their long home among their own kind, as in Kingsley Amis's *Ending Up* and *The Old Devils*: hints of a now-lost potency, a withered distinction, even the grotesque odour of sex (dead but lurching beneath the ground like a *vrykolokas*, an Undead) confined within the boundaries of a literary old-folks' home. Life is first boredom, then fear, Philip Larkin wrote:

OLD AGE

*'Whether or not we use it, it goes,
And leaves what something hidden from us chose,
And age, and then the only end of age.'*
(*'Dockery and Son'*)

Frankly, we're more at home with seeing the old as somehow grown into wisdom (as Dumbledore in the *Harry Potter* books, or the waspish Slartibartfast, planetary designer, in Douglas Adams's *Hitchhiker* series); happily barking, like PG Wodehouse's various aunts, or unhappily sinister, like *Doctor Fischer of Geneva* in Graham Greene's novel of the same name. We can relish an entire society of the

old, crock-bound and ritualised, whether grotesquely sinister (the *Gormenghast Trilogy* by Mervyn Peake) or grotesquely comic (the fellows of Porterhouse College in Tom Sharpe's *Porterhouse Blue*). We can have them genteelly religiose, like Lord Brideshead in Evelyn Waugh's *Brideshead Revisited* or Crouchback père in his *Sword of Honour* trilogy, quietly making his soul. Waugh's range of old men is almost as fine as Dickens's, but whether celibate uncle or superannuated soldier, they are, again, out of the action. Life has passed them by, and it is as if they have always been like that. In extremis, they are not only castrated,

but silenced, like the lovers in John Betjeman's 'Late-Flowering Lust': 'The mouth that opens for a kiss/Has got no tongue inside.'

Silenced and erotically maimed: here is one condition of literature's old, the other most common one perhaps being the elegiac regret of the *Nunc Dimittis* ('Lord, now lettest thou thy servant depart in peace') or the not-so-elegiac realisation that the jig's up good and proper, as in Betjeman again, this time his 'Song of a Night-Club Proprietress':

'There was sun enough for lazing
upon beaches,
There was fun enough for far into the night.

But I'm dying now and done for,
What on earth was all the fun for?
For I'm old and ill and terrified and tight.'

That's how we like them: knowing their place. We prefer Eliot's old man in 'Gerontion' – 'Here I am, an old man in a dry month/Being read to by a boy, waiting for rain' – to his more irascible 'Lines for an Old Man': 'The tiger in the tiger-pit/Is not more irritable than I...'

But despite it all, the Old Man wins over Gerontion and all too often refuses to be contained. The old may be indistinguishable, reduced, like puppets, to a set of characteristics (thin voice, sharp nose, rheumy eye, regrets,

A book that changed my life

M John Harrison

The Flight from the Enchanter
by Iris Murdoch

I first read this book in a college library in 1965. When I got to the end, I turned back to the beginning and read it again. Eighteen-year-old Annette discharges herself from school the way you might discharge yourself from hospital; Peter Saward struggles to decipher a vanished language for which he has no referents or historical context; Rosa Keepe is sexually enmired with the unpredictable Lusiewicz brothers. These and other naïve or grotesque characters flutter like moths around the mysterious financier Mischa Fox who, with his charismatic smile, his millions and his mismatched eyes, seems to have both shaped and ruined their lives. They beg from him, they blame him, they commit suicide to attract his attention, the enchanted pursuing the enchanter, relentlessly constructing his character and motives from whatever flimsily subjective bits of evidence they can find. Dedicated to Elias Canetti, published in the same year as Barthes's *Mythologies*, and received with perplexity, *The Flight from the Enchanter* was Iris Murdoch's second novel. What I enjoyed about it in 1965 was its irresolvability. What I enjoy about it now is its up-to-dateness: Mischa Fox seems like the perfect metaphor, not for a novelist but for a novel.

M John Harrison's latest novel is Nova Swing *(Gollancz).*

crotchety enfeeblement); any old person may be substituted for any other old person without penalty; but one quality appears again and again.

Grumpiness.

The grumpy old man – or woman – is a sort of perpetual opposition to the idea of autumnal resignation. Dylan Thomas may have urged his dying father to 'rage, rage against the dying of the light', but literature has needed no telling.

From the Sibyl, hanging in her bottle (Petronius's *Satyricon* again) who snarls her longing for death at the taunting young to the mercurial ill-temper of King Lear, from the crazed defamatory rantings of Molloy and Malone in Samuel Beckett's trilogy to the monumental grumpiness of the porter Skullion in *Porterhouse Blue*, right back to Cato's demand, 2,000 years ago, that old men should 'not add the disgrace of wickedness to old age, which was accompanied with many other evils'; behind almost every kindly old soul in literature lies a snarling horror, denouncing the young, the times, the manners of the age. The old seldom do what we require of them in books, are not content to act as a foil to the glories of youth and vigour. Write them as we will, they rise up to snarl at us; even, as in Hilary Mantel's *Beyond Black*, refuse to die and, like the first great Gothic novel, Bram Stoker's *Dracula*, come back, agelessly malign, to bugger us up.

Hodie mihi, cras tibi: we know it in our bones and, like the kid in the advertisement for X-ray specs, are horrified to discover that we, too, are walking around with a skeleton inside us. We may want our literary old to display a suitable unsexed resignation, but they refuse (unless clamped up to the neck in Dickensian pink marshmallow) to play along. Where can they get it from? Perhaps, in the western canon, from that grumpiest and oldest of all grumpy old men, the leading character in the great bestseller of all time. You know the one I mean. Older than the ages but refuses to let up, cursing, denouncing, lovey-dovey one minute, recriminatory and implacable the next; emotionally labile, unpredictable, given to tantrums and baroque displays of wrath: truly the grumpiest of the literary grumpy.

God.

Old age in 20 books

And When Did You Last See Your Father?
by Blake Morrison

The author's account of the weeks leading up to his father's death is notable for its unerring, unsparing honesty, as he looks back on their difficult relationship and tries to make sense of his father's life.

Cold Comfort Farm by Stella Gibbons

Matriarchal Ada Doom rules the Starkadder clan with a rod of iron, using an unpleasant but unspecified childhood experience to affirm her authority. Armed with a copy of *Vogue*, Flora finally persuades her 79-year-old aunt to leave for the high life in Paris.

Collected Later Poems by RS Thomas

The Welsh poet and priest fearlessly broached the big issues in his powerful, uncompromising poetry, questioning love, life, death and God. Best of all are his unexpectedly tender meditations on his wife's death.

Embers by Sandor Marai

Two elderly former friends meet in a remote castle 40 years after the events that forced their split. Márai conjures the passions of youth, the turbulence of the end of empire and the dangerous depth of art but most of all, the impotence of age.

Gilead by Marillyne Robinson

Struggling with a weak heart, months from his death, Reverend John Ames writes a letter to his seven-year-old son – one that runs to hundreds of pages and can have only one end. He considers his life in small-town Iowa, the happiness he found in later years with his young wife and child and, finally, terribly, a world in which this beloved family will live on without him.

House Mother Normal by BS Johnson

A series of monologues delivered by the residents of an old people's home. Ever alert to the possibilities of formal invention, Johnson arranges the novel in ten sections of exactly 21 pages each. The occasional blank page registers the slow but inexorable debilitation of senile minds.

The House of the Spirits by Isabel Allende

As the military coup he staunchly supported wreaks a bloody toll on his country and family, 90-year-old Esteban Truba finds himself stripped of power and thrown into confusion. Declaring himself 'just a poor destroyed old man', the stubborn, irascible patriarch finally learns humility, and in it finds redemption.

Indian Summer of a Forsyte
by John Galsworthy

The 1967 BBC adaptation of Galsworthy's three-volume epic on the tangled lives and loves of the Forsyte clan kept the nation gripped for an unprecedented 26 episodes. The poignant Indian Summer describes the final weeks of Old Jolyon's life, and his fierce, unappeased hunger for beauty and life.

Iris by John Bayley

Bayley found himself in the unsettling position of having to cope with the loss of his wife, novelist Iris Murdoch, even before she died – Alzheimer's rendered her the barest shadow of her brilliant former self.

Krapp's Last Tape by Samuel Beckett

'Perhaps my best years are gone. When there was a chance of happiness. But I wouldn't want them back.' In Beckett's dramatic monologue, Krapp, now an old man, listens to tape recordings of his younger self. Harold Pinter recently played Krapp on the London stage – from a wheelchair.

Last Orders by Graham Swift

Four ageing south Londoners drive out to Margate to scatter the ashes of their late friend Jack Dodds, the butcher. Swift's sixth novel is an intricately patterned feat of polyphony, in which several characters take turns in telling the story in their own voices.

The Lemon Table by Julian Barnes

Ageing is a bleak prospect for the protagonists in this sharply drawn collection of stories on old age and its discontents. Two lonely widows breakfast together, in spite of their mutual dislike; an old man sets off for his annual regimental dinner and visit to Babs, an equally elderly prostitute; a dying man finally declares his lifelong love, only to be misunderstood.

Old Goriot by Honoré de Balzac

Goriot is an elderly tenant in a rather flyblown Parisian boarding house. This 'Christ de la paternité' is not the central character in the novel, but rather an admonitory presence at the shoulder of the younger Rastignac, who is trying to insinuate himself into the *beau monde* of early 19th-century Paris.

The Old Man and the Sea
by Ernest Hemingway

'The old man was thin and gaunt with deep wrinkles in the back of his neck.' Santiago, a superannuated Cuban fisherman, wrestles for three days and three nights with an enormous marlin at the end of his line in Hemingway's Pulitzer Prize-winning novella.

Patrimony by Philip Roth

Roth's memoir of his father, which opens by his parents' graves in a New Jersey cemetery, is a kind of autobiographical blueprint for his 2006 novella *Everyman*. Struck down by a brain tumour, Roth senior is left imprisoned 'within a body that had become a terrifying escape-proof enclosure, the holding pen in a slaughterhouse.'

OLD AGE

Prufrock and Other Observations by TS Eliot

Written when Eliot was just 22, *The Love Song of Alfred J Prufrock* captures the creeping despair of a lonely, middle-aged man with painful acuity. As his days ebb by, 'measured out by coffee spoons', Prufrock realises that he has hesitated on life's margins for too long, and old age and death are all that remain.

Remind Me Who I Am Again by Linda Grant

Grant's memoir of her mother is a book about Jewish identity as well as a study of her mother's bewildering slide into dementia. 'Just remind me,' her mother says at one point. 'How am I related to you?'

The Spire by William Golding

Jocelin, the dean of a medieval cathedral, has an all-consuming obsession; the construction of a 400ft spire before he dies. But as the human cost of his visionary project adds up, doubts creep into the reader's mind. Is the spire a 'prayer in stone', or a soaring monument to an elderly man's selfish folly and pride?

Talking Heads by Alan Bennett

The cleanliness-obsessed 75-year-old narrator of *A Cream Cracker Under the Settee*, Doris may not be likeable, but still cuts a pitiful figure as she waits for help to arrive after a fall. The part was memorably played by Thora Hird, before her own death in 2003.

A Voyage Round My Father by John Mortimer

Mortimer's portrait of his irascible, blind barrister father, originally written as a radio play, was famously adapted for television, with Laurence Olivier in the lead role.

Critics' choice
Decay

Being Dead by Jim Crace

The novel opens with the violent murder of a middle-aged couple, before tracing how they met and fell in love. Disturbingly graphic descriptions of their physical decomposition punctuate the narrative, becoming ever more stomach-churning as the days pass.

Death in Venice by Thomas Mann

The crumbling palazzos and piazzas of Venice are the haunting backdrop to the ageing protagonist's obsessive, irresistible pursuit of the beautiful and youthful Tadzio.

Dorian by Will Self

Self skilfully refashions Wilde's famous fable for a new century, transposing it to the 1980s and introducing AIDS, graphic sex scenes and lashings of class A drugs. The telltale portrait, meanwhile, becomes a video installation.

The Five Gates of Hell by Rupert Thomson

Moon Beach is what you might call a 'burial resort' – its main industry is the tidy management of death. And Neville Creed, the local funeral magnate, is one of the great grotesques of recent fiction.

Great Expectations by Charles Dickens

Surrounded by her decaying wedding feast and dressed in the rags of her dress, the jilted Miss Havisham broods on her revenge in the mouldering darkness of Satis House.

To the Lighthouse by Virginia Woolf

Like a speeded-up film, Woolf's crystalline prose charts the decay of the Ramsays' home with unflinching clarity. Characters' deaths are reported in the briefest of bracketed asides and the message is clear: time's march is inexorable; death merely a footnote in history.

Midnight's Children by Salman Rushdie

'Please believe that I am falling apart,' begs Saleem, Rushdie's narrator. He is true to his word, and the book ends with his disintegration, a 'bag of bones falling down down down', as the weight of India's past closes in on him.

The Picture of Dorian Grey by Oscar Wilde

Dorian's portrait becomes a mirror into his soul and an unbearable reminder of his moral decay in Wilde's cautionary tale of fin de siècle decadence and debauchery.

The Radetzky March by Joseph Roth

Roth uses the lives of three generations of the Trotta family to examine the decline of the Hapsburg empire. The novel ends with the emperor's body being entombed in Vienna.

The Stones of Venice by John Ruskin

Ruskin's essays are a reminder that worries about the watery fate awaiting Venice aren't new. Each wave lapping against the stones of Venice, he says, contains a warning.

OLD AGE

In memoriam

Brian Dillon explores the art of the memoir.

'When I was born, they thought I was dead,' writes Tracey Emin in her memoir, *Strangeland*, a book that starts off interestingly unsure who the real 'mad Tracey from Margate' might be, and ends up settling the matter with a lot of new-age fluff about roots and empowerment. In truth, the greatest memoirs always leave the subject of the self as a suggestive ellipsis: their remembered 'I' is a rumour, a ghost, a riddle. Autobiography, at its best, means not so much writing the self as unravelling the thread of who we thought we were.

The ur-memoir is St Augustine's *Confessions*. A book ostensibly all about its author's conversion to Christianity, it swiftly reveals a writer obsessed by whether his past self ever really existed at all. How is it, asks Augustine, that I came to be in the first place, having not been to begin with? And having been born a helpless infant without language or reason, in what sense was I myself in those months, and even years, that I cannot recall? Twin voids – the unknowable nothings of womb and grave – gape either side of his narrow notion of himself, making it all but impossible to tell a coherent story. Predictably, however, Augustine fills the blanks with divine presence; God sees the whole frieze at once, encompassing past, present and future in one picture. The fog of human memory is more than compensated for by the clear vantage point of the ultimate storyteller.

Later autobiographers, lacking Augustine's faith, assert their identity as though it justifies itself. Rousseau, introducing his *Confessions*, declares: 'I am by birth a Genevese', and assumes that that is all the authority he needs

to begin. But his literary descendants soon discover that such origins seem to slip away on close inspection; they remember too little or too much. In *The Confessions of an English Opium Eater*, Thomas De Quincey excavates (a century too soon) something like the Freudian unconscious, and is understandably appalled. Writing of his childhood, he seems unable to forget anything. The tiniest details are inscribed on his mind like the layered letters of a medieval palimpsest; his life is a whispering gallery in which faint echoes of past events are amplified in the present, and torment him incessantly. His drugged brain produces horrid metaphors for the act of autobiography itself: he dreams his whole life in one opiated night. In De Quincey's mind, everything is linked to everything else, and his labyrinthine sentences keep expanding to accommodate the connections.

Style is one way to corral unruly memories and, at the same time, acknowledge that the most interesting thing about them may be that they do not cohere. In the 20th century, Marcel Proust provides the model for this way of writing an autobiography, so that many of the best memoirs read as much like modernist novels as acts of self-revelation. Vladimir Nabokov's *Speak, Memory* is among his most intricately patterned and deceptive books. Its motifs recur with exquisite tact and timing: a particular slant of summer light, a child holding his father's hand in the park. But despite its perfection, the pattern fails to reconcile the author's idyllic Russian childhood and his exiled adult self. Or take Roland Barthes's peculiar critical study of his own life and career, entitled *Roland Barthes*, in which he reflects on

Mnemosyne, Greek goddess of memory.

fragments of his past: family photographs, medical records from his time in a TB sanatorium, lists of his likes and dislikes. 'It must all be considered,' he writes, 'as if spoken by a character in a novel.'

Augustine wondered whether a life story was not actually a sort of list: a chaplet of unconnected instants. 'Memory' is a fluid medium, but 'memories', so we imagine, are discrete entities, and a certain strand of extreme autobiography reduces the whole process to a laconic litany. In 1970, the artist and poet Joe Brainard published *I Remember*, a book entirely composed of sentences that begin with that phrase. Marbles, locker rooms, dirty necks, Lois Lane, Cherry Coke and wet dreams about Montgomery Clift: Brainard's list is half Proustian parody, half Warholian history of post-war America. (He followed it with *I Remember More* and *More I Remember More*.) The book inspired the French novelist Georges Perec to compose his own *Je me souviens*. Perec had already written an autobiographical essay entitled 'I Was Born', in which he found it impossible to advance beyond an opening sentence: 'I was born on 7.3.36.' Instead, he reflects that he is both 'satiated and nauseated' by his own memories.

Which is not to say that a refusal of the normal narrative thrust of memoir need make for bloodless abstraction. (Perec's bald date of birth reminds him, and us, how young he was when he lost his parents to the Nazis a few years later.) In fact, a certain archness, or aesthetic distance from one's own story, seems the very condition for an affecting autobiography. Dave Eggers's *A Heartbreaking Work of Staggering Genius* is on one level a confection of baroque postmodern whimsy: the story of his parents' deaths is hedged about with so much prefatory material and ironic glosses that you would think its emotional content must be crushed; instead, the book pulls intriguingly in two directions at once. And in Joan Didion's *The Year of Magical Thinking*, the writer's account of her husband's sudden death is all the more compelling for Didion's brittle, forensic intelligence.

We're often told nowadays that we live in a confessional age, that we can't help blabbing our once shameful secrets to all and sundry: that we all, lamentably, seem to have a memoir in us somewhere. But confession

A book that changed my life

Jenny Turner

Selected Poems
by William Carlos Williams

We were given the exam paper at the beginning of the summer, and would sit it at the end. The first question quoted, whole, William Carlos Williams's 'The Red Wheelbarrow':

> so much depends
> upon
>
> a red wheel
> barrow
>
> glazed with rain
> water
>
> beside the white
> chickens.

'Why is this a poem?' we were asked, in that haw-hawing university-examination way. Impressed, back then, by this sort of thing, I looked hard at those 16 words for weeks. I bounced my way through the rest of WCW – trees, spring, springtime, 'the poor', 'the faucet of June' – yet also the dolorous flatness of 'Death': 'He's dead/the dog won't have to sleep on his potatoes/any more…' It is from this period, I like to think, that I started reading carefully, humbly, as an adult.

And yet, only the other day I realised that for years and years now, the wheelbarrow in my mind has been green; the softer mass ranged against it has never been wide and fluffy, but something tall and sleek. Though white at least, and with feathers certainly wet from the recent rainfall, for years and years now, the birds I always see when I think about this poem are geese.

Jenny Turner is the author of The Brainstorm *(Jonathan Cape).*

is not just some peristaltic urge; it is a genre with conventions and formal problems of its own. At its worst, it describes narrative arcs that would look sickly in a work of contemporary fiction: chief among them, an Augustinian interest in sin and redemption. At its best, oddly, it is often just one damn thing after another.

Novelist,
heal thyself

Sickness and disease are central to the creative process, says **John O'Connell**.

Trivial or terminal, illness is an injunction never to take for granted the state of fragile equilibrium we call wellness. It's a perpetual background hum, though quieter in this century than in, say, the 17th. 'Variable, and therefore miserable condition of Man!' laments John Donne in his 'Devotions Upon Emergent Occasions', scrawled in a fever daze. 'This minute I was well, and am ill, this minute. I am surpriz'd with a sodaine change, and alteration to worse, and can impute it to no cause, nor call it by any name.'

We have causes now, and names. We know that typhoid is not spread by 'miasma'; that the 'madness' Jonathan Swift believed to be enveloping him was actually Ménière's disease, a degenerative disorder of the inner ear. We no longer conceive of disease as God-given and unavoidable. Donne thought the greatest misery of sickness was solitude – half the time, your doctor would be too scared of infection to see you. Nowadays, illness is a party to which everyone is invited, and the last decade has spawned a mawkish new genre whose virulence we might, were we so inclined, compare to Spanish flu: the sickness memoir.

In John Diamond's *C: Because Cowards Get Cancer Too*, the cancer is his. In Gloria Hunniford's *Next to You*, it's her daughter Caron Keating's. In Dave Eggers's witty deconstruction of the form *A Heartbreaking Work of Staggering Genius*, it's his parents' – both of them, simultaneously. Many of these memoirs are deliberately explicit reactions to perceived taboos about illness. Do we read them to be shocked? Sometimes. To empathise? Inevitably. To make ourselves feel better? Always. This isn't as paradoxical as it sounds.

There's a selfishness in our compulsion to bear witness. We believe, at some level, that reading about illness will prepare us for it, perhaps by alerting us to danger signs we might otherwise miss.

Literary illness often deals in metaphor and analogy, giving rise to expressions like 'the diseased body politic'. Illness denudes man and, in the process, reveals him to himself. The Nobel Prize-winner and former political prisoner Alexander Solzhenitsyn was treated for stomach cancer in Tashkent in the mid 1950s. He took care to stress that the focus of *Cancer Ward*, the novel he wrote out of that experience, was medical rather than political, yet its authorial surrogate Kostoglotov still asks: 'A man sprouts a tumour and dies – how then can a country live that has sprouted camps and exile?' In Albert Camus's *The Plague*, the Algerian city of Oran is reduced to chaos by bubonic plague. Suffering is a tenet of Camus's existentialism, of course; but the book is also an allegory of the French resistance during World War II. (All well and good, but we should be wary of associating particular diseases with particular concepts or attributes, as Susan Sontag points out in her essay 'Illness as Metaphor'.)

Disease can be useful to novelists because it removes characters from what Thomas Mann called the 'flatland' of quotidian life. In Mann's erudite parody of the Bildungsroman, *The Magic Mountain*, Hans Castorp is committed to a sanatorium in the Swiss Alps when a bronchial infection develops into tuberculosis. Thus secluded, Castorp is formed, albeit inconclusively, via exposure to his fellow patients. Disease, Mann suggests, has socialising, educational and spiritual functions: 'One must go through the

Virginia Woolf: illness is something 'mystical'.

EVERYMAN

PHILIP ROTH

'THIS BOOK IS ALIVE WITH LITERARY BRILLIANCE'
SUNDAY TIMES

VINTAGE

deep experience of sickness and death to arrive at a higher sanity and health,' he declares in an afterword written for the 1927 English translation. (This is as paradoxical as it sounds, and reiterates a theme of his 1912 novella *Death in Venice*, in which Gustav von Aschenbach achieves an ecstatic apprehension of beauty at the moment of his death from cholera.)

Disease is also useful to novelists because it stokes belief in their specialness – a belief they must cling to if they are to do what they do with any conviction. Nowhere is the creative importance of sickness made clearer than in Virginia Woolf's essay 'On Being Ill', written after she collapsed at a party at her sister's house on 19 August 1925. Woolf's multiple ailments inspired multiple diagnoses. But she found liberation through illness: 'I believe these illnesses are in my case… partly mystical. Something happens in my mind.' Ill people, she writes, are dreamers, idlers, refuseniks. They take pleasure in inefficiency. They have grown used to the solitary life and now can bear no other kind. Lying on her back, Woolf gazes up at the sky and sees clouds as if for the first time, as an 'interminable experiment with gold shafts and blue shadows, with veiling the sun and unveiling it, with making rock ramparts and wafting them away'. She would later channel her 'bad nerves' into Septimus Smith in *Mrs Dalloway*, just as Dostoevsky channelled his epilepsy into Prince Myshkin in *The Idiot*.

Since their heyday in the 18th and 19th centuries, novels have tracked the awkward relationship between doctor and patient. In *Sense and Sensibility*, it seems there is little physician Mr Harris can do to help the fever-stricken Marianne Dashwood: 'His medicines had failed.' Luckily he has 'still something more to try, some fresh application' – we are not told what this is – and it triggers the 'signs of amendment' everyone is watching for. This is generous of Austen. Before sulphonamide and penicillin, GPs could do almost nothing except take the pulse and prescribe morphine: illness was, mostly, a sliproad on to the motorway of death. In Tolstoy's devastating novella *The Death of Ivan Ilyich*, Ilyich's doctors know this perfectly well, but their livelihoods depend on the bland denial of certainties. (The idea that there might be some consolation in our awareness of our mortality is similarly skewered by Philip Roth in 2006's *Everyman*.)

Yet illness can be fun too, especially when it's other people's, or silly, or specious. Gwen Raverat's *Period Piece* is a delightfully sardonic memoir of her childhood in the hypochondriacal Darwin household (she was Charles's granddaughter). Valetudinarian Mr Woodhouse in Austen's *Emma* is a comic masterpiece; likewise Jerome in Jerome K Jerome's *Three Men in a Boat*, who decides, after reading a medical encyclopedia, that he is suffering from every disease listed in it apart from housemaid's knee. He goes to see his doctor, who hits him over the chest, butts him on the side of the head, then writes him the following prescription:

'1lb beefsteak, with
1pt bitter beer every six hours.
1 ten-mile walk every morning.
1 bed at 11 sharp every night.
And don't stuff up your head with things
you don't understand.'

A book that changed my life

Matt Thorne

Reflections in a Golden Eye
by Carson McCullers

As a child and teenager, I was a wide, but not particularly discerning, reader, and I'm the same today. But I was always looking for ways into reading more difficult novels, and certain books provided gateways into areas of literature that had previously seemed inaccessible. Carson McCullers's second novel, *Reflections in a Golden Eye*, was my gateway into American literature, the book that took me from reading Stephen King (himself a McCullers fan) to tackling Herman Melville. Written when McCullers was 25 years old, this account of six people and a horse on an army base taught me that great literature can be as perverse and voyeuristic as the cheapest pulp fiction, and just how much emotion you can get into pared-down prose. It continues to be an inspiration for me as a writer and a reader, as mysterious as it is accessible, as challenging as it is engaging.

Matt Thorne's most recent novel is Cherry *(Weidenfeld & Nicolson).*

Low culture, high thought

The graphic novel has reached maturity, says **Nicholas Lezard**.

First, you have to get past the description 'graphic novel'. This is an anxious nod to the (supposedly) more venerable art form, in the hope that some of the novel's pedigree will rub off on what is, essentially, a cartoon book. Either that, or it is a way of saying 'it's a story told with more pictures than words, but we haven't come up with a proper word for it yet.'

In other words, 'graphic novel' is a marketing term indicating high intent; which, albeit with the best intentions, does the genre a disservice. Still, until someone comes up with something better, I'll stick with it. After all, it took a long time for the word 'opera' to be used of operas.

But the term changes the perceptions: do we think of the Tintin books as 'graphic novels'? We don't, and it's only in part because Hergé didn't. But they all have a narrative told in comic-strip form, and – this is the important part – qualify as successful works of art. This might surprise those who imagine that, because children like them, they're fit only for children. Indeed it's hard to shake off this heritage, which is both a strength and a weakness of the genre.

The first proper graphic novel – if we set aside, regretfully, the paintings at Lascaux or the hieroglyphs at Luxor (or Sebastian Brant's *Ship of Fools*, Hogarth's morality tales, or any number of non-Protestant church frescoes illustrating, to an illiterate audience, the lessons of the Gospels and the desirability of avoiding hell) – is, in a sense, still the purest. Published in 1919, *Mein Stundenbuch* is the work of the Belgian artist Frans Masereel, and contains 165 woodcuts and no words. It is, therefore, impossible to paraphrase, but could be said to be about a young man's adventures in a city, and elsewhere... you see how hopeless that is? You have to see it for yourself. A picture may not exactly be worth a thousand words, but the images spark a multitude of narrative possibilities. They are frames from a dream-film, by turns documentary, surreal, poignant, or erotic. And it is that last aspect, although it occupies only three or four pages of the book, that tells us most about the difference between literary and graphic narrative. A representational artist who depicts sex is going to be far more likely to incur charges of pornography than his or her word-using equivalent.

It is the demotic nature of the graphic novel that disturbs the guardians of high culture. Anyone can read one. In Masereel's hands, this is literally true for all sighted people. The form, then, is essentially humanist, inclusive, tolerant and understanding. Because its images work at such a primal level, it cannot be sophisticated. It is not genteel. Masereel understood this from the start: the hero of *Mein Stundenbuch* enjoys the license of the cartoon figure, farting, seducing, leaning back in his chair in polite company, befriending the disadvantaged – words are unnecessary because the behaviour is elemental.

This can cut two ways. While the graphic novel isn't high culture as the term is normally understood, it can nevertheless be high-falutin' or portentous on its own terms. (Although some would say, and I'd be one of them, that George Herriman's *Krazy Kat* comics are as subtle as anything endorsed by the high-cultural mavens.) As befits a young art form, familiarity with its modes is gained in youth; but being young isn't a barrier to high thought. I don't recall, as a child reading *Superman* while he dealt with

The eternally youthful **Tintin** – not just for kids.

some fairly heavy issues, getting the sense that this was a form unable to cope with anything more complex than the fight against crime, or indeed (Pow! Zok!) individual criminals, however exotic or otherworldly.

But people, and genres, grow up. The form that we now understand as the 'comic strip for grown-ups' came into being with Will Eisner, who since 1940 had been drawing an increasingly mature and disillusioned detective strip called *The Spirit*. In the 1970s he encountered the San Francisco-based comics (or 'comix') underground, whose denizens had been fans of his in childhood and were now drawing druggy, political, literary, or otherwise outrageous strips for the alternative press.

Eisner saw a mature audience, and took his chance. In the late 1970s, books such as his *A Contract with God* took the form to a whole new level, in terms of both its historically and philosophically rich content, and its groundbreaking formal innovations. This, bear in mind, when he was in his sixties. (The most prestigious American awards for the graphic novel, which have been going since 1987, are 'The Eisners'.)

The cross-fertilisation was remarkable. A colleague, Art Spiegelman, who had first had the idea in 1972, started working seriously on *Maus* in 1980: a treatment of the Holocaust in which the Jews were humans with the heads of mice (and Nazis humans with the heads of pigs). At a stroke, Spiegelman had solved, audaciously and successfully, the problem of representing humanity's greatest moral catastrophe. No one could call graphic novels immature any more.

After that, the genre flourished. How could it not? The wonder is that it took so long, after the example of Masereel. Raymond Briggs had a huge succès d'estime with the faux-naif *When the Wind Blows*, his unsettling engagement with nuclear warfare. Alan Moore and Dave Gibbons's *Watchmen* addressed one of the core iconographies of the genre, deconstructing the very concept of the superhero.

It is only now, though, that people are ceasing to apologise for the term. Posy Simmonds can even raid high culture with *Gemma Bovery* (sic), a skit, commentary and updating on and of Flaubert that would be either flat or plain inconceivable in prose. Marjane Satrapi's *Persepolis* tells us what it's like to grow up in revolutionary Iran – and makes a rebellious point by its very form, which flouts the Islamic prohibition on representational art.

Maybe the imams have a point. To tell a story with pictures is to make your message unambiguous. It fixes a truth with an image: and the cartoon image is, almost by default, a caricature. It cheeks the authority of the word, as political cartoonists have known since the days of the insurrectionary pamphlet. It's for the many, rather than the few.

Watchmen: superhero as anti-hero.

Critics' choice
Nostalgia

Brideshead Revisited by Evelyn Waugh
Waugh's swansong to the English aristocracy is a masterpiece – although he later censured it as being 'infused with a kind of gluttony, for food and wine, for the splendours of the recent past, and for rhetorical and ornamental language.'

Call It Sleep by Henry Roth
A Jewish-American classic set in the ghetto on New York's Lower East Side before World War I. Later, Roth came to wish he'd been *more* nostalgic about his own childhood, which provided the raw material for his portrayal of the six-year-old protagonist, David Schearl.

Le Château de Ma Mère by Marcel Pagnol
The chirping of cicadas, shimmering heat and seemingly endless days of childhood are vividly evoked in the playwright's elegiac tribute to Provençal rural life and to his mother. Her death, along with those of his friend Lili and little brother Paul, marks the end of his childhood.

Cider with Rosie by Laurie Lee
Laurie Lee's vivid, much-loved evocation of growing up in a remote village in the Cotswold at the turn of the century captures a way of life that was soon to be gone forever.

Death of a Salesman by Arthur Miller
Locked in a hopeless pursuit of the American Dream and unable to face up to reality, Miller's ageing anti-hero, Willy Loman, is full of nostagia for a past that – in his eyes at least – was full of promise, and for a way of life that his son Biff rejects as a 'phony dream'.

The Emigrants by WG Sebald
'When I think of Germany, it feels as if there were some kind of insanity lodged in my head.' In Sebald's first book, a wholly idiosyncratic blend of fiction, travelogue, history and memoir, the titular exiles, two of whom are Jewish, try to remember the places they used to call home.

The Enigma of Arrival by V.S. Naipaul
An immigrant's hymn to a disappearing English idyll. What once struck the narrator as 'solid and rooted in [the] earth' now seems flimsy and shoddy. The English, he laments, wallow contentedly in an 'absence of authority' and the mess of their own decay.

Ignorance by Milan Kundera
The interweaving stories of two émigrés returning to Prague after a 20-year exile provide the framework for Kundera's poignant exploration of loss, memories and 'the irrepressible yearning to return' – and what happens when you do.

Lost Worlds by Michael Bywater
A delightful compendium of reflections on what we have lost: brisk GPs with bristling moustaches, grandfather's favourite armchair and body odour. But Bywater isn't just a nostalgist; he is also a philosopher of loss.

Norwegian Wood by Haruki Murukami
Hearing the Beatles song that gives the novel its name abruptly transports its narrator, 37-year-old Toru Watanabe, back to his student days in the 1960s, and his relationship with the fragile, elusive Naoko.

Our Fathers by Andrew O'Hagan
A moving lament for a specifically Scottish ideal of working-class self-improvement. Jamie Bawn, now 35, visits his dying grandfather, a former local politician who, years before, had saved his bookish grandson from the abusive attentions of an alcoholic father.

The Sea by John Banville
Narrator Max Morden returns to the house in which he spent his childhood summers in order to mourn his dead wife. There he summons up fragmentary memories of an unsettling entanglement with a family richer and more sophisticated than his own.

A Shropshire Lad by AE Housman
Sales of Housman's lyrical, melancholic volume of poetry really took off during the Boer War and World War I, as its themes of mortality and the brief but glorious span of youth acquired a new resonance. 'And early though the laurel grows/ It withers quicker than the rose.'

Sunset Song by Lewis Grassic Gibbon
The first part of Gibbon's *A Scot's Quair* trilogy follows the early life of heroine Chris Guthrie. Gibbon draws the village of Kinraddle with loving vividness and sounds an idiomatic lament for traditional Scottish ways.

Death

'Last scene of all...
Is second childishness
and mere oblivion,
Sans teeth, sans eyes,
sans taste, sans
everything.'

The art of dying

Mark Thwaite explores what lies beyond the final curtain.

All literature is about death because, if you'll forgive the syllogism, literature is about life. Death is the great unknown. It is our common future and our shared ignorance. What happens when literature looks into the void?

Secular writers do not have available to them notions about the afterlife on to which they can graft ideas about what may come next. For Samuel Beckett, for example, we are born astride the grave, and life isn't made meaningful by anything outside it. This meagreness is all we have. Religion, by contrast, provides its followers with traditional narratives about what lies beyond. It is no surprise, therefore, that the greatest book about death in the Western literary canon belongs to a deeply religious age.

Perhaps no artist has attempted to record the Beyond as fully as Dante degli Alighieri. Indeed, some of Dante's contemporaries thought he must have actually passed over to the other side and then returned in order to record what

he had learned about the fate that awaits us all. It is said that when he passed them in the street, certain of his nervous neighbours would cower from the great writer, believing there was something otherworldly about him. In *The Divine Comedy* – the 'Divine' was added years later by admiring readers as a way of applauding the poem's inner truth – Dante descends into hell and, with his guide, the great Roman poet Virgil (author of the *Eclogues*, the *Georgics* and the *Aeneid*), walks into the Inferno to begin his difficult journey of discovery and redemption.

Robert Burton was much less ambitious and sought only to divert himself from chronic depression when he published *The Anatomy of Melancholy* in 1621. At first glance the book is simply an old-fashioned medical textbook but, like Proust's *In Search of Lost Time*, the mammoth, encyclopaedic nature of the work, into which Burton attempts to cram all of life's vicissitudes and eventualities, evokes

Emily Dickinson: 'Because I could not stop for Death,/He kindly stopped for me.'

'In the midst of life, we are in death.'

something quietly frantic. Burton continued to amend the text throughout his life, indicating both how useful and ultimately use*less* he found writing.

Life's journey, of course, begins at birth or, rather, some nine months before our bloody entry into the world. The foetus – another unknowable other – has rarely been the focus of great literature, but in Laurence Sterne's 18th-century masterpiece *The Life and Opinions of Tristram Shandy, Gentleman*, it is Tristram who speaks to us – before his physical birth – about the life and opinions principally of his father and his Uncle Toby, one of literature's most gloriously absurd creatures. *Tristram Shandy* is a bawdy, intricate ragbag of a book about lust, war, absurdity and philosophy. Like life itself, it is full of detours and digressions. In fact, the book is one long diversion. And no other literary work focuses our attention quite so clearly, and so comically, on the dark side, the back roads and byways, of our lives.

When Czech writer Milan Kundera told us that *Life is Elsewhere*, what was he saying? Perhaps that life as such is never quite graspable. Death is like that too. It lurks in the deep below the ship on which we all sail. In Herman Melville's *Moby-Dick*, Captain Ahab and his crew on the Pequod hunt for the monstrous whale. It's a ridiculously dangerous undertaking, and Melville's biblical rhythms reinforce the sense of mythic absurdity. Moby-Dick can't simply be allowed to be: he has to be harried and wrestled with. Quiescence is unthinkable. In the obsessive hunt for the death-dealing beast, life makes sense only in battle with its other.

"'Tis some visitor," I muttered, "tapping at my chamber door –
Only this, and nothing more."'

A book that changed my life

Toby Litt
The Poems of John Keats

It started with Aztec Camera. On their debut album, *High Land, Hard Rain*, Roddy Frame sang about overdosing on Keats. I thought I'd try it. Luckily, the second-hand bookshop in Bedford, Pembertons it was called, had an old copy of *The Poems of John Keats*. My first attempt at overdosing took place on the top deck of the 142 bus. I began at the equally elevated first page: 'I stood tip-toe upon a little hill...' No loss of consciousness was involved; a slight *change* of consciousness, however, did occur. Keats took me in.

I experienced his poetry as I think he intended it to be experienced – that

PENGUIN CLASSICS

JOHN KEATS
Selected Poems

is, physically – from inside his body – as if it were *my* body. Keats, for this reason, is the most sensual of poets. Up until this point, poetry had interested me, puzzled me and even excited me. But it had never *affected* me. Like most people, I couldn't see the point. Keats changed that completely. First of all, he made me want to be Keats. Then he made me want to be a poet. His best poems, the *Odes*, a couple of the sonnets, are still my absolute favourites. He's part of my funeral service.

Toby Litt's most recent novel is Hospital *(Hamish Hamilton).*

Of course, that's what we'd all like to think, along with Poe's narrator in his great poem 'The Raven' – death as just some visitor knocking at our door. But as soon as we pretend that, we see what nonsense we're speaking. Always at our shoulder, there is Nevermore. In Poe's 'The Lake', death is again invoked, alongside love, instantiated in the watery expanse:

> 'Death was in that poisonous wave,
> And in its gulf a fitting grave
> For him who thence could solace bring
> To his lone imagining –
> Whose solitary soul could make
> An Eden of that dim lake.'

Fiction has an obvious advantage over non-fiction when it comes to speaking about death: to think about death is to make an imaginative leap. We are not in empirical territory here: we can journey towards the heart of darkness, with Conrad, but if we reached our destination, we'd never return with a tale to tell.

Famously transmuted into Francis Ford Coppola's compelling film *Apocalypse Now*, Joseph Conrad's *Heart of Darkness* is his finest novel: subtle, ambiguously anti-imperialist, beautifully written and hugely intelligent. Charles Marlow tells his tale of a journey into Africa to seek out Kurtz, the great explorer. But Kurtz is lost: deranged and depraved. He is out of place in a land to which Europeans have brought only death and destruction. In a kind of ironic 'blowback', Africa is now wreaking destruction on Kurtz.

In Thomas Hardy's *Jude the Obscure* our eponymous stonemason leaves rural Marygreen for a new life, which he hopes will be filled with learning in the university city of Christminster. Soon, and contrary to his plans, Jude is saddled with responsibilities and that long dreamed-of life of learning never materialises. But Jude's life is stalked by death, as well as disappointment. Struggling to cope with his young family, Jude returns home one day to find his young son has hung himself and his two young sisters: 'Done because we are too menny.' It is one of the bleakest episodes in any great novel. But the melodrama is perhaps overdone, for death is ubiquitous and commonplace. After *Jude*, Hardy never wrote another novel, turning instead to poetry in order to investigate life, love and, of course, ageing and death.

'Fiction has an obvious advantage over non-fiction when it comes to speaking about death: to think about death is to make an imaginative leap.'

Even as we age, the sexual impulse remains with us. As Freud taught us, it is all sex and death, eros and thanatos. In Thomas Mann's *Death in Venice*, which begins with a scene by a cemetery, Gustave von Aschenbach pursues the beautiful young Tadzio as he slowly succumbs to the cholera that has affected much of the rest of the lagoon city. The very form of Mann's magnificent novella echoes and questions our lives: we look for love, and yet, as inevitably as the end of book, death haunts every moment of our life. Aschenbach knows that he can't have Tadzio and that, however much he wants to master and mould life like a great artist, he is as weak and helpless as the rest of us.

Samuel Beckett's work, so formally intricate, but with such ambiguous content, has often been used to make grandiose claims about the nature of Being. Under the influence of thinkers such as Heidegger and Blanchot, some critics have argued that Beckett's work is about the 'Big Questions' – and, as a consequence, they've missed its humour and beauty. The final work in Beckett's masterful trilogy, after *Molloy* and *Malone Dies*, is *The Unnameable*. If critics are too quick when talking about *Waiting for Godot* to equate Godot with God, they also stumble trying to explain one of Beckett's finest pieces of extended writing. There is a sense, though, in which *The Unnameable* is as profoundly clear as its title.

It was from Joyce that Beckett learned so much as he tried to find his own way. And it's worth noting that, for many, Joyce's finest work

DANTES DI ALEGIER'S FLORETINI

Dante, explorer of the afterlife.

IF THIS
IS A
MAN
·
THE
TRUCE

PRIMO
LEVI

'One of the
century's truly
necessary
books'
PHILIP ROTH

is his peerless short story 'The Dead'. Perhaps it was in the air in early 20th century? The Moderns (Joyce, Eliot, Woolf, Pound) seemed to see so much more clearly than we do now that death haunts and enables, gives our life a shape and a reason to act (if we never die, why do anything?). Virginia Woolf, in particular, writes about death exquisitely. I sometimes think that *To the Lighthouse* offers a lovely metaphor for our life's journey: we never actually get to the lighthouse, or death, but the whole novel, like our lives, points towards that terminus.

Aside from fiction, the work of the French theorist and philosopher Jacques Derrida famously took a political turn when he wrote *Specters of Marx*. Derrida's 'hauntology' saw death (vampires, spectres and ghouls) as structuring Marx's monumental critique of capitalism. When describing the circuits and flows of capital, Marx automatically reaches for phantasmagorical metaphors.

In the late 1930s, as the political situation in Germany and his native Austria grew increasingly perilous, that other great system-builder Freud wondered, in *Civilization and its Discontents*, whether a death drive, which he named 'thanatos', wasn't the dominant drive in our lives. Leaving aside the question of its dubious explanatory power, this idea certainly had a contemporary resonance. And from the catastrophe of the Holocaust that Freud just managed to avoid? Poetry. Brecht's 'Motto' reads:

'In the dark times
Will there also be singing?
Yes, there will be singing
About the dark times.'

Death had found an ideology that loved it. The experience of the camps created the conditions for some of the most powerful literature ever written. Primo Levi's *If This Is a Man* is one of the most important books we have.

World War II never went away, perhaps because war is always with us. In her poem 'Daddy', Sylvia Plath imagines her father as a Nazi ('The boot in the face, the brute/ Brute heart of a brute like you'). Plath's husband Ted Hughes, meanwhile, wrote an alternative theology in his shamanic *Crow* poems. In 'Examination at the Womb-Door', death surrounds us:

'Who owns the whole rain, stony earth? Death
Who owns all of space? Death
Who is stronger than hope? Death
Who is stronger than will? Death
Stronger than love? Death
Stronger than life? Death
But who is stronger than Death?
Me, evidently.'

Well, no, not you, Ted. Not even you.

Death in 20 books

The American Way of Death Revisited
by Jessica Mitford

Mitford's scathing, grimly satirical exposé of the sharp practises of 'the death-care industry' provoked a furore when it was first published in 1963. As the updated edition, revised shortly before Mitford's own death in 1996, reveals, not much has changed in the intervening years, with pre-paid funerals (covered in a chapter entitled 'Pay Now – Die Poorer) providing fresh fuel for the author's ire.

As I Lay Dying by William Faulkner

A poverty-stricken family in America's Deep South are bound by their mother's dying behest that they return her body to the town where she was born. The uneducated characters' outpourings of grief possess a savage, unmistakably lyrical beauty.

The Body Artist by Don DeLillo

After Lauren Hartke's husband Rey unexpectedly commits suicide, she finds a strange young man in her house who, though barely able to speak, begins to repeat fragments of conversations she had with Rey in the days before he died with eerie precision.

Chronicle of a Death Foretold
by Gabriel García Márquez

The master of magic realism turns his gaze upon an ancient honour killing, and its effects on a small Latin American town. Why did no one in the town intervene to stop the murder – and had the victim, 21-year-old Santiago Nasar, committed any crime?

Complete Poems by Emily Dickinson

The famously reclusive poet's fascination with death appears time and time again in her bleakly powerful poetry. As Conrad Aiken observed, 'She seems to have thought of it constantly – she died all her life, she probed death daily.'

The Death of Artemio Cruz
by Carlos Fuentes

A 71-year-old Mexican tycoon lies dying, haunted by the lives and loves he has destroyed. Interwoven with his painful memories of the past are the agonies of the present, as he desperately clings to life; 'this uncontrollable vomiting, this overwhelming desire to defecate without being able to […] the sensation that my blood is exploding inside me, leaking inside.'

Extremely Loud and Incredibly Close by Jonathan Safran Foer

His father's death in the World Trade Center bombing – and the final, dreadful telephone message that only he has heard – leads nine-year-old Oskar Schell on a quest for catharsis that will take him across the city.

The Famished Road by Ben Okri

As an *akibu* (spirit child), Azaro is sworn to return to the spirit world, dying and being reborn to the same mother over and over again. Seeing the grief on her 'bruised face', he decides to break his pact and stay with her. Haunted by spirits trying to lure and trick him into returning to the paradisial otherworld, he struggles to stay alive in the poverty-stricken ghetto.

Fred by Posy Simmonds

When Fred dies, the children who mourn him remember their pet cat as a sleepy, unadventurous moggy. Woken from sleep one night, however, they stumble on the funeral thrown for him by the local feline population, who worshipped him as a caterwauling rock star.

A Grief Observed by CS Lewis

The impact of his wife's death drove Lewis – one of the 20th century's most eloquent defenders of religion – to question his beliefs. 'Go to Him when your need is desperate, when all other hope is vain, and what do you find? A door slammed in your face, and a sound of bolting and double-bolting from the inside.'

If Nobody Speaks of Remarkable Things by Jon McGregor

A summer's day on a quiet suburban street is the focus of McGregor's lyrical literary debut. But as the minutae of everyday life is precisely and painstakenly evoked and the hours tick by, a sense of impending menace starts to build.

In the Springtime of the Year by Susan Hill

The protagonist, Ruth, loses her husband suddenly after he is struck by a falling tree. Hill, who wrote the book after her own fiancé, David, died, commented; 'The events and characters […] are wholly invented. The time is not the present and the death was very different. But the emotions were real. They were mine.'

Journal of a Disappointed Man by WNP Barbellion

Wilhelm Nero Pilate Barbellion (WNP for short) was the pseudonym adopted by diarist Bruce F Cummings. Declared unfit to fight in World War I, he opened his doctor's letter to the medical officer to find out why – only to discover he had multiple sclerosis, and just a few years to live. His frank, increasingly introspective diaries were published in 1919, seven months before he died, aged 30. 'I have telescoped into those few years a tolerably long life […] and when the hour comes I shall be content to die,' reads one of the final entries.

Laments by Jan Kochanowski

The 16th-century poet's laments-songs on the death of his young daughter, Urszula, are central to Polish literature. Masterfully translated by Seamus Heaney and Stanislaw Baranczak, Kochanowski's grief loses none of its raw, agonising impact.

Little Women by Louisa May Alcott

Many a readerly tear has been shed over the death of saintly Beth, from scarlet fever ('She could not say, "I'm glad to go," for life was very sweet for her. She could only sob out, "I try to be willing," while she held fast to Jo') – a tragedy second only to Jo's rejection of the handsome, rich and hopelessly devoted Laurie. Whatever was she thinking?

The Man With Night Sweats by Thom Gunn

Gunn's concise, elegant poems confront the spectre of AIDS, offering an eloquent memorial to the friends and loved ones he lost to the disease. 'You had gone on from me,' he mourns in 'Lament'. 'How thin the distance made you. In your cheek/One day, appeared the true shape of your bone/No longer padded.'

Monopolies of Loss by Adam Mars-Jones

Mars-Jones's short stories, published in 1992, describe the devasting impact of AIDS on the gay community, in terms of both the lives it claimed and its effects on those left behind, many of whom were infected and dreading the same fate.

The Old Curiosity Shop by Charles Dickens

'One must have a heart of stone to read the death of Little Nell without laughing', was Oscar Wilde's conclusion on Nell's painfully protracted end – but hundreds of readers disagreed, and wrote to implore Dickens to spare his long-suffering heroine's life.

Selected Poems by Paul Celan

Contrary to Theodor Adorno's infamous dictum, there *can* be poetry after Auschwitz – Celan, whose parents were murdered in the camps, wrote some of it. His most famous poem is 'Death Fugue': 'Black milk of daybreak we drink you at night/we drink you at noon death is a master from Germany.'

The Wings of the Dove by Henry James

Dying heiress Milly Theale's attempts to 'achieve, however briefly and brokenly, the sense of having lived' are poignantly evoked, as James returns once again to the theme of New World innocence betrayed.

DEATH

Life drawing

AC Grayling appraises the biography.

Among the principal reasons for the enduring popularity of biography are these three: that lives are narratives, and we all love a story; that lives illuminate the histories through which they are lived, and often enough for subjects of biographies – in part shape those histories; and that as organised gossip they satisfy a deep and necessary form of voyeuristic craving in us, which gives us material for understanding our own lives by peering into those of others.

The human love of narrative speaks for itself, and the trajectory of an individual life, whether long or short, is perfect as story. We know the end, which is standard for all, and for famous subjects we know the achievement (or failure) that makes the person salient. What we then wish to know is that life's texture, its struggles, the nature of its triumphs, its hopes, its intimacies and its secrets. These things – the substance, the reality – are exceedingly tempting, even if they are only seen as facts about another of our kind, albeit one considered sufficiently outstanding to be worthy of biography.

Biography is a form of history, and one of the most agreeable and accessible kinds. Michael Holroyd, a doyen of the life-writing art, once imagined a critic saying that biography had replaced history because the latter was moribund, having collapsed into the answering of questions that (as Tolstoy put it) no one was asking, for it had (as, with equal pungency, Popper put it) elevated the squabbles of politicians into the history of the world. Of course, the writing of history is anything but moribund, and it flourishes as vigorously as biography; the point should rather be that biography stands alongside other forms of historical writing, illuminating the past through the particularising lens of its principal figure, thereby rendering it vivid. Interestingly, Holroyd's own immense life of Lytton Strachey is so much a book about character and personality that it is not as much a work of history as (say) Richard Holmes's lives of Shelley and Coleridge, which are brilliant evocations of the poets' era, as well as brilliantly revelatory about the poets themselves.

But it is as the Higher Gossip that biography comes most into its own. This is not a recent phenomenon; John Dryden admired Plutarch's *Lives* because they followed their subjects into private life as well as on to the battlefield, and Boswell's *The Life of Samuel Johnson* is what it is because it seems to reveal the very man himself, the unguarded and natural living soul of a great, earnest, ponderous, lonely, fearful, sincere and vastly learned giant. Knowing how Johnson spoke to his friends and complained all the way round the Hebrides is as much a peepshow as knowing about the sexual proclivities and perversions of celebrities, as revealed in more recently written biographies that have licensed themselves to tell all.

And this is as it should be. This peep-show point, the fact that reading biography is a form of voyeurism, is not intended critically. Rather, it is a good thing that it is so, and even a necessary thing; for to repeat, if we had no insight into other real lives, we would have a poorer grasp of our own. This is a not a matter of prurient curiosity; it is a matter of self-understanding, and of being able to give a shape to our own unfolding narrative in time.

DEATH

LUDWIG
WITTGENSTEIN
THE DUTY OF GENIUS

RAY MONK

That is not to say that we can or do expressly model ourselves on the kind of people whose lives are such as to merit biographies. Except in rare instances, lives of achievement or disaster – the stuff of biography – are not unrelentingly so. Napoleon and Einstein had parents, went to school, ate lunches and dinners, fell in love, caught the flu, and did all these sorts of things far more regularly than they won great battles or hypothesised the relativistic nature of space-time. It is the quotidian as well as the remarkable that attracts readers of biography, and perhaps it is the fact of the latter that makes the former seem so interesting and so personal. It makes one feel that one could say, with Horace, *Mutato nomine de te fabula narratur*, 'change only the name and this story is about you'.

Still, the typical subject of biography is indeed usually someone famous, or occasionally infamous, in one of the spheres of activity – politics, war, literature – that most attract attention, and in this sense of course the story is very rarely *de te*. All societies hand down great names for admiration and emulation, and take pride in those they regard as ornaments of their tradition. Spain has Cervantes, Germany has Goethe and Schiller, France has Racine, Molière, and Voltaire, Russia has Pushkin, Dostoevsky and Tolstoy; each culture can name its greats – and these are just the literary ones. Generalise the point, and one sees how some greats cease to be human altogether and become emblems instead: Shakespeare, the Duke of Wellington and Winston Churchill are in England more icons than men, having been absorbed into their reputations in a way that leaves little room for a human reality that eats breakfast and goes to the lavatory.

Until, that is, someone comes along to write a biography; and then one learns how astonished anyone would have been, up until 1940, that Churchill would be venerated as a national hero for decades, because until then he was a not-very-trusted politician who had turned coat more than once in his career, and had a few egregious failures and black marks to his name. He was aged 66 in 1940, which was cutting it fine for getting a grand reputation. But in 2002 he was voted 'the greatest ever Englishman' in a BBC poll – proof of the vacuity of such polls, and of the strange chances that raise and lower individuals in the calculus of fate.

Without doubt, though, Churchill deserves his reputation as a doughty war leader, an inspiration in a dark and dangerous time, and that fact throws interesting light over Roy Jenkins's biography of him, all the more so for being written by someone of a different political persuasion. Leaving aside monuments of scholarship like John Ehrman's three-volume life of the younger Pitt, political biographies tend to attract a specialist constituency only, though some – like Mervyn Jones's biography of Michael Foot – deserve wider readerships. Far more popular, and certainly in general far better as works of literature in their own right, are literary biographies.

The names of Michael Holroyd, Richard Holmes, Richard Ellman, Hermione Lee and Claire Tomalin stand among others at the head of a distinguished list in this sphere. There are almost no major figures in the literature of the English language who do not have a constellation of biographies gathered about their names, and the greatest have secured the attention of these outstanding biographers. In the recent explosion of biography as a highly saleable literary form, the great names of the past and the great biographers of today have married one another to the vast benefit of both – and of their readers.

Paucity of information has never proved a barrier to biographers interested in writers who lived before letters and diaries accumulated – which, roughly speaking, was from the 18th century onwards. Shakespeare is well served, though at the expense of mighty detective work much aided by supposition; Anthony Holden's biography of him is one of the recent best. Curiously, Milton is less well served, though

'A good biography should satisfy the generality of its readers that its subject has come face to face with them on the page.'

there is an intriguing and angular account of him by Peter Levi, who sees the life refracted in the poetry in a striking way.

What impresses about the copiously researched, carefully thought-out and handsomely proportioned works by Hermione Lee on Virginia Woolf, Richard Ellman on Oscar Wilde and James Joyce, and Claire Tomalin on Pepys and Thomas Hardy, is their insight into motivation and relationships. One of the more convincing definitions of truth – one might better say, truthfulness – was given by CS Lewis, who likened recognising truth to hearing the sonority of a soundly cast bell as against the clank – the sound of falsehood – of a flawed bell. In these masters of the biographical art, delineation of character – that protean thing that slips like shadows between the lines of letters and the aperçus of other people's diaries and journals, and that (in the case of writers) glimmers in how they view the characters in their own creations – is caught and anatomised with the rich ring of truth. Another way of putting the point is to say that these biographers present their subjects with convincing wholeness; one is the beneficiary, so it feels, of a personal introduction.

For me, there are two additional arenas of interest: scientific and philosophical biographies. Lisa Jardine has made herself queen of the former, combining biographical skill with deep knowledge of the history of ideas. Her life of Christopher Wren is a masterpiece of that genre. Unsurprisingly, Charles Darwin is the subject of a veritable rash of biographies, most published in the last decade and a half: E Janet Browne's two-volume life leads a good pack. Here the clear presentation of ideas and discoveries is an essential, and it is a fairly recent advance to have Jardines and Brownes capable of recounting both life and thought with equal lucidity. Scientific biographies were once written by scientists for whom literary and biographical skill was an incidental; that is where the present change gratefully lies.

Philosophy has not fared quite so well, except in a couple of outstanding cases. The strange and tortured genius of Ludwig Wittgenstein would entice many biographers if it were not for the great difficulty of his work, and as a result there are only two noteworthy biographies of him, both outstanding. One is

James Boswell: the greatest biographer of them all?

Claire Tomalin: biographer of Hardy, Wollstonecraft, Mansfield, Shelley, Austen and Pepys.

A book that changed my life

George Szirtes

Collected Poems by Arthur Rimbaud

I still have the book. Arthur Rimbaud was born in 1854 and renounced literature at the age of 19, which would have been about my age when I read it. He, however, had something extraordinary to renounce: lines like 'On n'est pas sérieux quand on a dix-sept ans', which I read – because I wouldn't want to lie to you – in English as 'When you are 17 you aren't really serious'. The poet 'under the light of a pale street lamp passes a young girl... in the shadow of her father's terrifying stiff collar.' Eventually he is back in 'the dazzling café', not really serious. And you think: fine, you yourself, are you not

deep and heavy and serious? But that's not serious either. And then comes 'Une Saison en Enfer', when you are 'no longer in love with boredom', but are later startled by 'the drunken gnat in the pub urinal, in love with borage, and dissolved by a ray of sunlight'. Your breath is quite taken away. And then the wonderful obscenities 'Columbina – Que l'on pina! – Do, mi, tapote'! This eternal 17-year-old will keep you honest for the rest of your life. He will gaze at you with that violet eye and sneer at your pieties. He still does.

George Szirtes's most recent book is Budapest: Image, Poem, Film, *a collaboration with Clarissa Upchurch.*

Ray Monk's account of Wittgenstein's life, a deserved bestseller on first appearance. As a result of its success, Monk was asked to write a life of Bertrand Russell, accepted the commission, and proceeded to exemplify the truth of a view first expressed Thomas Carlyle in the 1830s in response to a new edition of Boswell's *Johnson*: namely, that biographers must have sympathy for their subjects to do their job well. Monk was certainly an admirer of Wittgenstein, and excused him much bad behaviour; he hated Russell, and his resulting two-volume account of Russell's life is marred by a determination to paint its subject in the most negative possible light.

By far the best existing philosophical biography is that other account of Wittgenstein, even though it only covers the first half of its subject's life. It is by Brian McGuinness, a distinguished philosopher and one of the translators into English of Wittgenstein's *Tractatus Logico-Philosophicus*. It is beautifully written, incisive and – because McGuinness so well understood the social and intellectual atmosphere Wittgenstein breathed in early life – richly informative. When reviewing both biographies on their first appearance,

I said that Monk's would appeal most to those who were unlikely to read Wittgenstein's own work, while McGuinness's would appeal most to those who would. The judgement stands.

Until recently, philosophers were not seen as likely candidates for biography, for did they not spend all their time uneventfully sitting and thinking? The prospect was not made more enticing by the thought that if things did not happen to them much, at least they happened to things (think of Marx's effect on the world after years of accumulating haemorrhoids in the British Library). For a long time the only major biographies of philosophers were those by David Mossner of Hume and Ronald Clarke of Bertrand Russell. But then it occurred to the cognoscenti that philosophers were not such dull fellows after all. Socrates was executed, John Locke had to flee into exile, Spinoza was excommunicated by his synagogue, Heidegger was a Nazi, Sartre a Communist, Althusser murdered his wife, Nietzsche went mad – from the biographical point of view, things look up in the face of such tumults. Perhaps in consequence there has been a sudden gush of philosophical biographies, among the best of them those by

Rudiger Safranski on Schopenhauer, Heidegger and Nietzsche.

Art has done better than music in attracting quality biography. Jenny Uglow's excellent account of Hogarth is a model of its kind, but it is hard to think of a comparable work on Brahms or Beethoven. Perhaps the reason is that illustrating art is far easier, and more generally appealing, than illustrating music.

There is no single stipulative model of what a good biography should be, other than that it should satisfy the generality of its readers that its subject has come face to face with them on the page, leaving no lingering sense of evasion or unanswered questions. The sadness of death, if poignantly felt as a farewell to an individual one has spent much time with as one turned the pages, is a mark of whether the biography has achieved its purpose – which is, simply, to be about its subject in all the senses of that ambiguous term. The magisterial biographies of Tomalin, Ellman and Holmes certainly leave one feeling sated; but quieter achievements, like PN Furbank's life of EM Forster or Robert Ferguson's life of Ibsen, also please. There are some achievements in the genre that have never been surpassed: GH Lewes's life of Goethe is the exemplar.

And there is an entire other strand of biography that is now scarcely read, perhaps dwarfed by the mighty tomes produced as standard these days: the biographical essay. A collection of forgotten classics in this line was created by Hugh and HJ Massingham in the early 1930s, under the title *The Great Victorians* (perhaps to heal wounds cut by Lytton Strachey's deliciously sharp scalpel, wielded a decade earlier); it exists now only in the stiffened and crumbling form of Pelican paperbacks, occasionally seen in a box outside second-hand bookshops, turning into dust.

That, however, is not a fate of the subjects of good biographies, preserved to life in a form of literary art that does them honour; as if indeed, as Richard Holmes once put it, they had been rowed back across the Styx by the biographer as Charon, who thus returns them to the shores of light.

Lytton Strachey: the biographer as subject.

Critics' choice
Tragedy

All My Sons by Arthur Miller
Sometimes, Miller once wrote, the 'conditions of life are hostile to man's pretensions'. His tragic hero is Joe Keller, a businessman whose firm manufactures parts for military aircraft. Joe's partner was convicted of negligence after they supplied faulty components. Joe doesn't accept his share of the blame until he learns the real reason for the death of his son Larry.

Antigone by Sophocles
Creon, the king of Thebes, orders that the body of the traitor Polynices be left unburied. When his daughter Antigone defies the order, Creon sentences her to death. Tiresias, the blind prophet, persuades Creon he is wrong. But by the time Creon reaches the cave in which Antigone is imprisoned, she has already hung herself.

Antony and Cleopatra by William Shakespeare
Antony is mesmerised by Cleopatra, the Egyptian queen. After falling out with fellow triumvir Octavius, who accuses him of neglecting his duties, Antony goes into battle on Cleopatra's behalf. Facing defeat, he runs himself through with his sword. The grieving Cleopatra presses an asp to her breast and dies.

The Birth of Tragedy by Friedrich Nietzsche
In his first published work, Nietzsche identifies in Greek tragedy the union of two contending aesthetic impulses, the Apollonian and the Dionysian. The Apollonian is associated with the formal, plastic arts, the Dionysian with the rhapsodic intoxications of music. In tragedy, the 'art-sponsoring deities' Apollo and Dionysus accept the 'yoke of marriage'.

The Death of Tragedy by George Steiner
Tragedy is a metaphysical impossibility, argues Steiner, now that we have abandoned all sense of the numinous or transcendent. 'In Greek tragedy as in Shakespeare, mortal actions are encompassed by forces which transcend man. We cannot conceive of Oedipus without a Sphinx, nor of Hamlet without a Ghost.'

Doctor Faustus by Christopher Marlowe
In this 'Tragical History', the eponymous doctor strikes a bargain with Lucifer, through the good offices of his emissary Mephistophilis. Faustus will pledge his soul to the devil in return for knowledge and power.

The Duchess of Malfi by John Webster
TS Eliot wrote of Webster that he was 'much possessed by death and saw the skull beneath the skin'. After botching an attempt to flee into exile with her husband Antonio and their children, the duchess is executed by Bosola, whom she'd previously taken into her confidence.

The Eumenides by Aeschylus
The Eumenides are the Furies, embodiments of vengeance. They gather before an Athenian jury to hear the case of Orestes, who murdered his mother. When they later submit to Athena's entreaties on Orestes' behalf, they are renamed the 'kindly ones'.

Hedda Gabler by Henrik Ibsen
Ibsen said that his aim in Hedda Gabler was to depict human beings and 'human destinies'. Hedda's destiny is to find herself trapped in an unhappy marriage with Tesman, an academic. Hedda renounces her husband's name and later betrays him when an important manuscript goes missing.

The Iceman Cometh by Eugene O'Neill
The denizens of a New York saloon bar are comfortably ensconced in their unrealisable dreams. That is, until Hickey makes his annual visit and urges them to acknowledge their delusions. But Hickey's zeal turns out to mask a dreadful secret.

Iphigeneia at Aulis by Euripedes
An attack on Troy is scuppered when the ships of the Greek fleet are becalmed. Blamed by his troops for offending the goddess Artemis, Agamemnon determines to sacrifice his daughter in return for a favourable wind.

Phaedra by Jean Racine
Drawing on Euripedes's Hippolytus, Racine unravels the disastrous consequences of Phaedra's falling for her stepson.

DEATH

Literary
haunts

Rebecca Stott on why the literary imagination is stalked by ghosts and apparitions.

Ghosts populate stories through centuries and across geographical boundaries, from the Old Testament, the *Odyssey* and the ancient tales of China, Japan and India to contemporary fiction and film. They puncture the solidity of our worlds, refusing distinctions between past and present and between the dead and the living, insisting on talking to us from beyond, below and before. Novelists and storytellers use them to make gaps in the real, to show us those places where, in Charlotte Brontë's words, 'knottings and catchings occur', where 'sudden breaks leave damage in the web'.

The poet Emily Dickinson once wrote: 'Of nearness to her sundered Things/The Soul has special times', moments when the 'the Grave yields back her Robberies', when 'The Shapes we buried dwell about,/Familiar in the Rooms'. Ghosts, these 'sundered Things', are often intermediate creatures when they appear in fiction, border-crossers; like Hamlet's father, they appear on the thresholds of buildings, between inside and outside, often on the edge of night and day, at what TS Eliot described as 'the recurrent end of the unending'. Hamlet's father appears on the ramparts at twilight and vanishes at dawn; bloodied, vengeful, he insists on a dialogue with his son and will walk the ramparts until he has been appeased and half the royal court is dead.

Writers of ghost stories show us ghosts who are familiar to those they appear to, true but out of true. Fathers, friends, children come back because for some reason they need to be pacified, appeased and laid – as shamans do in the ritual dialogues with the dead practised in some tribal cultures. Writing itself is often an act of raising and laying of ghosts. Virginia Woolf described writing *To the Lighthouse* as having laid the ghosts of her parents, and Derek Walcott in *Omeros* used his epic poem as a way of bringing classical, British and Caribbean ghosts together.

The way ghosts appear in stories changes as our rituals and ideas of the dead change. Fictional ghosts even take different colours depending on when and where they were created. The most common appearance of ghosts in classical writing is either black or smoke-like, probably because the Greeks and Romans usually cremated their dead, so dead bodies were imagined as blackened or turned to smoke from the funeral pyre. White-sheeted ghosts only began to appear when people started swaddling their dead. The whitest, most billowy ghosts of all appeared in 19th-century stories, when swaddling customs were at their most elaborate. Today, ghosts are often dressed in red, echoing Nicolas Roeg's cult 1973 film *Don't Look Now*, in which the ghost of a child drowned in a red raincoat appears to her parents in Venice.

The ghosts created by Homer and Virgil are both terrifying and vulnerable. Many are wounded and mangled; some are afraid of swords. They are anguished; they weep, like Dido with her matted, blood-tangled hair. Some return because they have not been properly buried or because they need to be avenged, like Hector as described by Virgil's Aeneas: 'There before my eyes, in a dream, appeared the desperately sad Hector, weeping many tears, torn by the chariot, as once before, and black with gory dust, walking on feet swollen by leather thongs… with a

Marley's Ghost.

A Christmas Carol, where apparitions are 'noisy, clamorous and moral'.

GHOST STORIES

©Martin Rowson 07

Critics' choice
Murders

Alias Grace by Margaret Atwood
In 1843, Canada was rocked by the trial of Grace Marks, a 16-year-old maid who was given a life sentence for her alleged role in a double murder. Taking the case as her inspiration, Atwood's fictional account asks what really happened. Just don't expect any easy answers; the smoothy duplicitous narrative is a literary tour de force.

An American Tragedy by Theodore Dreiser
Clyde is the naive son of impoverished parents, whose head is turned when he takes a job as a bell-hop. He is later forced to flee the city and eventually arrives in upstate New York, where he falls for Roberta. When she falls pregnant, Clyde resolves to murder her.

Crime and Punishment by Fyodor Dostoevsky
Raskolnikov, a handsome but penniless student, hatches a plan to murder a pawnbroker, thereby solving his financial problems. Dostoevsky's genius lies in his sifting of Raskolnikov's paranoid justifications for the deed.

Deep Water by Patricia Highsmith
Graham Greene called Highsmith a 'poet of apprehension', which is a particularly apt description of this unsettling novel. Vic Van Allen pretends to his wife that he's responsible for the murder of one of her former lovers – a deception whose consequences Highsmith unravels brilliantly.

In Cold Blood by Truman Capote
Capote claimed to have invented a brand new literary genre – the nonfiction novel – with his compelling, meticulously detailed account of the murder of Herbert Clutter and his family in 1959. Capote spent hours interviewing the killers, a pair of rootless drifters named Dick Hickock and Perry Smith.

Julius Caesar by William Shakespeare
Ignoring a soothsayer's warning to 'Beware the Ides of March', Caesar meets a grisly end at the conspirators' hands, lamenting his betrayal ('Et tu, Brute! then fall, Caesar'). But as Anthony predicts, vengeance is waiting in the wings.

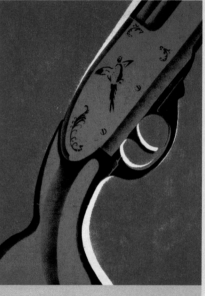

Truman Capote In Cold Blood

My Dark Places by James Ellroy
Ellroy combs the archives of the LAPD in order to reconstruct the investigation into the 1958 murder of his mother. 'I want to give you breath,' he tells his mother's ghost.

Of Mice and Men by John Steinbeck
The sweet-natured, mentally disabled Lennie is fixated by petting 'soft things', but the objects of his affections rarely survive his all-too clumsy caresses. As the novel reaches its heartbreaking denouement, not even his devoted friend George can protect Lennie.

Perfume: the Story of a Murderer by Patrick Süskind
Possessed with a superhuman sense of smell and an inhuman moral detachment, the repellent Jean-Baptiste Grenouille turns serial killer in his quest to create the ultimate perfume. The ending of Suskind's dark fable is unforgettable.

The Secret History by Donna Tartt
Julian Morrow, a charismatic teacher of classics at an exclusive New England college, has gathered around him a devoted and proudly insular coterie. The group reluctantly admits a new member, who discovers the sinister truth about their bacchanalian revels.

filthy beard and hair all stiff with blood, showing his wounds.'

Ghosts beget other ghosts – there are some, like Hector, who come back again and again in other guises; many of Shakespeare's ghosts are themselves ghosts of the paternal, larger-than-life ghosts of Virgil or Homer. They too show their wounds, demand retribution, weep and wail. And when the first ghosts appeared in the novel in the 18th century, with the rise of gothic fiction, they looked very much as they did in *The Castle of Otranto*; dead fathers returned to insist that their sons take revenge in their names.

But the ghost story proper, as we recognise it today, didn't really appear until the 1820s, with Walter Scott's 'Wandering Willie's Tale', a story inset into *Redgauntlet*. In many of these early ghost stories, the ghosts had an erotic edge. In 'The Tapestried Chamber', for instance, Scott has the narrator tell how, just as he was falling asleep, he heard the 'rustling of a silken gown' and the tapping of a pair of high-heeled shoes near his bed. Quite sure that a woman has entered his room, he describes how, 'All manhood melted from me like wax in a furnace… I sank back in a swoon.' The ghost turns around and presents features on which, to the narrator's horror, 'were imprinted the traces of the vilest and most hideous passions which had animated her while she lived.' Squatting down on his bed, she brought 'her diabolical countenance within half a yard of mine, with a grin which seemed to indicate the malice and derision of an incarnate fiend.'

While Scott's fiend might have appeared with the eroticised rustling of a silken gown, most Victorian ghosts are noisy, clamorous and moral. Throughout the 19th century, with the rise of literacy and print-culture, ghost stories proliferated in magazines, journals and Christmas supplements. For instance, the first JS Le Fanu stories, such as 'The Ghost and the Bonesetter' appeared in magazines from the 1830s on. Often written to be read aloud in family drawing rooms, they were sensational; full of skilful sound effects and suspense.

It was into this culture that Charles Dickens stepped with his host of theatrical ghosts, including Jacob Marley, who appears with his clanking chains in a wonderful passage that demands to be read aloud: 'The bells ceased as they had begun, together. They were succeeded

A book that changed my life

....

Lydia Davis

Malone Dies by Samuel Beckett

....

Beckett's *Malone Dies* was the book that startled me most profoundly with its clarity, complexity, and ostensible modesty, revealing a whole new possibility for writing. I was very young when I first read it, just 13. My diet had been, first, the good children's novels, then, at some point, romantic dramas particularly appealing to girls, such as *Jane Eyre* and a multi-volume saga that seemed rather steamy to me but was innocent enough to be included in a girls' school library: Mazo de la Roche's *Jalna* books. A novel of Dos Passos's, I think *Manhattan Transfer*, was probably the first book whose style of writing drew my attention away from its plot – though perhaps the plot had to be frankly uninteresting for me even to notice the style.

Finally, I happened upon *Malone Dies*. After the rich descriptive exuberance of Dos Passos, and the high dramas I relished, I had not imagined that the plot of a book could unfold within such a limited situation (Malone in bed), nor that unbroken paragraphs could continue for pages on end, that a story could be interrupted in mid sentence and then taken up again, a narrator admit to being discouraged with his writing, change his mind about his character right before my eyes, describe for half a page the pencil he had been writing with and had now lost, but most of all hold my complete attention merely by the twists and turns of his sharp, reasoning mind and by his entrancing precision of language.

Lydia Davis's most recent book is Varieties of Disturbance *(Farrar, Straus & Giroux), a collection of stories.*

DEATH

by a clanking noise, deep down below; as if some person were dragging a heavy chain over the casks in the wine-merchant's cellar… The cellar-door flew open with a booming sound, and then [Scrooge] heard the noise much louder, on the floor below; then coming up the stairs; then coming straight towards his door… without a pause, it came on through the heavy

Muriel Spark: ghost writer.

'Most ghost stories enact the supernatural loosening of disorder only in order to affirm the restoration of order and rationality at their close; 19th-century ghost stories tend to be conservative.'

door, and passed into the room before his eyes. Upon its coming in, the dying flame leaped up, as though it cried "I know him! Marley's Ghost!" and fell again.'

Marley's chain is made of 'cashboxes, keys, padlocks, ledgers, deeds, and heavy purses wrought in steel', which he says he made 'link by link, and yard by yard. I girded it on of my own free will, and of my free will I wore it.' And hanging on that chain is the moral of the story: Marley has made his own chains of damnation from his refusal to see beyond money, and he is determined not to let Scrooge be dehumanised in the same way. So Marley's ghost rehumanises Scrooge by making him see his past and his future; he recalls Scrooge to himself.

Oscar Wilde wonderfully satirised clanking, moralising, chain-dragging Victorian ghosts in 'The Canterville Ghost': 'Right in front of him he saw, in the wan moonlight, an old man of terrible aspect. His eyes were as red as burning coals; long grey hair fell over his shoulders in matted coils; his garments, which were of antique cut, were soiled and ragged, and from his wrists and ankles hung heavy manacles and rusty gives. […] "My dear sir," said Mr Otis, "I really must insist on your oiling those chains, and have brought for you for that purpose a small bottle of the Tammany Rising Sun Lubricator. It is said to be completely efficacious on the wrapper from some of our most eminent divines.'"

Marley's ghost may have embodied a spirit of kindness and charity chased away by dog-eat-dog capitalism, but elsewhere the prevalence of ghosts in Victorian fiction is bound up with the spread of interest in spiritualism from the mid-century onwards. In 'The Phantom Coach', Amelia B Edwards's narrator suggests that ghosts are a refutation of materialism and the enlightenment – its underside, perhaps: 'The world grows hourly more and more sceptical of all that lies beyond its own narrow radius; and our men of science foster the fatal tendency. They condemn as fable all that resists experiment. They reject as false all that cannot be brought to the test of the laboratory or the dissecting room.'

These eruptions from below may also have something to do with the political revolutions of the 19th century, plentiful in Europe and feared in Britain, quelled and then returning like a series of quakes and aftershocks. However, while the gothic novel may have had subversive leanings, most ghost stories enact the supernatural loosening of disorder only in order to affirm the restoration of order and rationality at their close. Nineteenth-century ghost stories tend to be conservative, emphasising the enduring strength of social structures.

Women writers such as Mary Braddon, Mrs Gaskell, Violet Paget and Edith Wharton wrote ghosts into their stories in the second half of the 19th century as they also began to transform the short story as a form. Their ghosts could be used to show how the oppressed might rise up, or how justice might be demanded, or else they were used to give a body to the invisible or a voice to the silenced.

Ghosts had an important role for writers trying to capture something of the horrors of World War I too – they offered a way of writing about those who had died, been left unburied, or had simply gone missing, disappearing into a kind of limbo. In Muriel Spark's 'The House of the Famous Poet', a young woman narrowly escapes death during the Blitz when a man on a train offers her a cigarette and then tries to sell her an abstract funeral, described later as a great billowing of purple along the street. At other times, ghosts of long-dead soldiers

appear as they do in Arthur Machen's 1914 story 'The Bowmen', which describes a battle in which the English are losing to the Germans. A soldier utters a Latin incantation about St George and then hears, or seems to hear, 'thousands shouting "St George! St George!"'… And as the soldier heard these voices he saw before him beyond the trench, a long line of shapes, with a shining about them. They were like men who drew the bow, and with another shout their clouds of arrows flew singing and tingling through the air towards the German hosts…'

In the great flowering of ghost stories between the wars, strange, meagre phantoms wander the interstices and labyrinths of the modern city, in railway stations or the Underground. While Victorian ghosts appear in churchyards, moors, estuaries, ruins and disused churches, ghosts in 20th-century fiction are more likely to appear in stations, suburban bungalows and country houses, and to use telephones, trains and cars.

In a post-Freudian age, fictional ghosts in modern novels are more likely to tell us something about the spectres inside our own heads. The ghosts in Henry James's chilling *The Turn of the Screw* have a way, as Virginia Woolf pointed out, of making us see 'the power our minds possess for excursions into darkness; when certain lights sink or certain barriers are lowered, the ghosts of the mind, untracked desires, indistinct intimations, are seen to be a large company.' Does James's nervy, obsessive governess, determined to keep her employer's children pure, make her own ghosts out of her fantasies about the previous governess and her lover Quint, or do they really stalk the house and gardens? James's story seems to suggest that the ghosts are inside us.

Other contemporary writers use ghosts to make us see what we have refused to see, to uncover those parts of our personal or national or cultural histories that we have buried or denied. There are two wonderful examples of this from the last 20 years. The first is a powerful ghost story by Ali Smith, 'The Hanging Girl', which tells the story of a woman who watches news footage of a girl being hanged in an unspecified war, and then finds the young woman has moved into her house and is determined to hang herself over and over again, unless she can be quietened by baths or daytime television. Smith describes it as a 'guilt parable'; the hanging girl refuses to be forgotten, and her death cannot be appeased.

The second example is Toni Morrison's extraordinary novel *Beloved*, which tells of the effects of cultural denial on a nation; specifically, the effects of the unremembered horrors of slavery on generations of survivors. In the 1870s a mother and sister live in a house in Cincinnati that is haunted by the spiteful ghost of the mother's dead baby, Beloved. The ghost breaks mirrors, turns pans of food on to the floor, overturns furniture and has driven away the other siblings. Mother and daughter are living in a state of siege. Piece by piece, the terrible story of the death of the baby emerges; the child, who wasn't properly buried, has returned for retribution. It soon becomes clear that this ghostly voice of Beloved's is one of many in this slave community, and that

'the undecipherable language clamoring around the house is the mumbling of the black and angry dead.'

Morrison built her story out of the frequent silences in slave narratives, what she calls 'proceedings too terrible to relate'. In the closing pages of the novel, she writes that there is 'a loneliness that can be rocked. Then there is a loneliness that roams. No rocking can hold it down. It is alive, on its own.' Beloved demands both acknowledgement and appeasement. In a stunning reversal of the scene of the ghost father demanding retribution from the son, this black female child, a baby, full of spite and anger, can be laid only when she is acknowledged and spoken to – and even then, even when Beloved is hushed, Morrison warns us that this is a 'not a story to pass on', for there are some histories that can't be quietened, some ghosts that won't be laid.

Ghostly child or serial killer? **Don't Look Now**

A time
to mourn

'An awful thought, a life removed,
The human-hearted man I loved'
Tennyson, *In Memoriam*

In his groundbreaking work *Bereavement*, psychologist Colin Murray Parkes argues that the 'pain of grief is just as much a part of life as the joy of love; it is, perhaps, the price we pay for love, the cost of commitment.' The loss of a loved one is an almost universal human experience. But what does it mean to be bereaved? How can we come to terms with loss and face death, 'the undiscover'd country from whose bourn/No traveller returns'?

These are questions that have exercised the literary imagination from the beginning – from classical epics, in which the hero journeys to the Underworld, to religious doctrines that seek to provide answers about what happens after death. Bereavement and mourning compel us both to try to understand what has passed, and to conceive of what will inevitably come to us in turn.

Part of that process is the reanimation of the deceased in writing. After reading *To the Lighthouse*, Virginia Woolf's elder sister, Vanessa Bell, remarked that the character of Mrs Ramsay was a startlingly accurate portrayal of their mother, Julia: 'It is almost painful to have her so raised from the dead.' And this is precisely what writing about a dead loved one achieves: it denies their evanescence and resurrects them, leaving them 'balanced between the possible and the impossible', as Thomas Hardy's biographer Claire Tomalin says of the poet's mourning verses for his wife. It's a phrase that could equally be applied to John Bayley's memoirs about Iris Murdoch (*The Iris Trilogy*),

Milton's sonnet for his wife ('Methought I saw my late espoused saint') or Ted Hughes's *Birthday Letters*, about Sylvia Plath.

That's not to say, however, that some of the world's greatest writers have not felt ambivalent about their attempts to record their mourning.

The source of the wonderful, if overexposed, line, "Tis better to have loved and lost/ Than never to have loved at all', Alfred, Lord Tennyson's *In Memoriam*, was composed as an elegy to his friend, Arthur Hallam, who died of a fever in 1833, at the age of 22. The poem is a composite of many smaller meditations, 'Short swallow-flights of song, that dip/Their wings in tears, and skim away'. Set against a sparse landscape of blurry dream-figures, the fragments, individually and cumulatively, tell the story of a 'grief as deep as life or thought'.

Yet despite the poem's emotional logic, Tennyson displays a discernible nervousness about the very act of expressing grief. For him, language is simply not capable of adequately describing his inner torment. Words merely constitute a mourning shroud, tracing an outline of the soul, while at the same time concealing its true nature.

Tennyson's uncertainty about the articulation of his mourning is illuminated by a fascinating 20th-century volume, *The Work of Mourning*, a collection of eulogies, articles and essays by Jacques Derrida. Occasioned by the loss of his friends – and what friends: Roland Barthes, Paul de Man, Michel Foucault – they are at once critical meditations on the state of bereavement and themselves expressions of grief and loss.

For Derrida, when mourning a loved one we face a virtually insurmountable problem:

DEATH

Tennyson: poet of mourning.

whether or not to monumentalise their death by speaking or writing about them. Not to do so pushes the dead further towards oblivion, of course. But if we attempt to immortalise them in writing, we risk replacing the voice of the deceased with our own. Seamus Heaney pertinently diagnosed this dichotomy when analysing *Birthday Letters*: Hughes, he said, 'was impaled on the horns of a creative dilemma: to write directly about that which most desperately craved expression could seem like an exploitation of something sacrosanct, but not to write about it must have felt like an abdication of spiritual and imaginative responsibility.'

Once a person is dead, Derrida says, they are gone and exist only in our memories. And once there, they become our property, to do with as we will. Here we might think of Robert Lowell's 'Commander Lowell' (*Life Studies*) or Plath's 'Daddy' (*Ariel*), in which each resurrects their father only to destroy them on the poet's own terms.

Sometimes, however, the dead return to reassert their rights. In Toni Morrison's *Beloved*, black slave Sethe escapes from her white masters just before the end of the American Civil War, and murders her baby daughter in order to prevent her being returned to the life of slavery she has fled. Years later, a young woman mysteriously appears, the same age as Sethe's daughter would have been and calling herself Beloved, the only name engraved on the little girl's headstone. Whether or not she is a ghost, Beloved symbolises Sethe's guilt. She allows Sethe to confront the horrors of her past, and as the narrative unfolds, we realise that the book also represents a disturbing elegy to the 'Sixty Million and more' Africans who died in the slave trade.

The most famous character in literature to come face to face with the object of his mourning is Hamlet. The Danish prince's grief for his late father is compounded by his disgust at the new king, his uncle Claudius, the passive complicity of his mother – 'A beast that wants discourse of reason/Would have mourn'd longer', Hamlet fumes – and, ultimately, by the appearance of his father's ghost, stirring him to avenge his murder.

Born on the day that Elsinore's gravedigger began work, Hamlet has lived all his life in the shadow of death. Motivated by his mourning to reflect on life, this 'quintessence of dust', he stares death directly in the face – with the aid of a skull – and recognises there the common destiny of man. He reconciles himself to a supreme if mysterious design, 'a divinity that shapes our ends,/Rough-hew them how we will', and his famous contemplation of life and death ('To be or not to be') becomes, by the final act, an acceptance of mortality: 'Let be… The readiness is all.'

However, after this apparent acquiescence in man's fate, and the final climactic scene of carnage, Shakespeare ends on an ambivalent note. Fortinbras, in his first act as ruler of Denmark, orders a military funeral for Hamlet, thereby hijacking the protagonist's character. The Hamlet we have seen is thus grossly misrepresented, though this ending neatly illustrates the fact that in the aftermath of a bereavement, the deceased may be rewritten, even reinvented. If the memory is to be kept alive, it must be reborn in the imagination of a survivor.

It is folly to speculate too much on Shakespeare's intentions, of course, though sometimes the temptation is hard to resist. Shakespeare was almost certainly writing Hamlet in 1599, if he had not completed it already. The playwright's son died of bubonic plague in 1596, aged 11. That son's name? Hamnet.

> *'When mourning a loved one we face a virtually insurmountable problem: whether or not to monumentalise their death by speaking or writing about them.'*

Further reference

WEBSITES

Arts & Letters Daily
www.aldaily.com
Make Arts & Letters your homepage and you'll never again miss that article that everyone is talking about. Witty précis and links – lots of them.

Complete Review
www.complete-review.com
A comprehensive digest of reviews from around the world, plus the peerless Literary Saloon blog.

Metacritic
www.metacritic.com/books
Mopping up anything the Complete Review misses, Metacritic provides links to book reviews from all the major newspapers and periodicals in Britain and the US.

Signandsight
www.signandsight.com
An English-language round-up of the cultural pages, or *feuilletons*, of German and other European newspapers.

BLOGS

The 'blogosphere' is no longer just the domain of narcissists, self-publicists and political obsessives. There are now hundreds of 'litblogs' out there, offering serious criticism and scholarship, 'bookchat' and publishing industry gossip. Here's a selection of the best:

Elegant Variation
www.marksarvas.blogs.com/elegvar
Reviews, the occasional interview and some internecine sniping at other critics by a Los Angeles-based writer and critic.

Grumpy Old Bookman
www.grumpyoldbookman.blogspot.com
A 'blog about books and publishing', with some superior gossip and the inside track on the latest preposterously inflated advance paid by some ailing conglomerate or other.

Litblog Co-op
www.lbc.typepad.com
An American group blog that functions as a kind of virtual book group. They are particularly interested in work published by small presses 'struggling to be noticed in the marketplace'.

Maud Newton
www.maudnewton.com/blog
One of the longest-running of the US litblogs: reviews, links, bookchat.

Peter Stothard
www.timescolumns.typepad.com/stothard
TLS editor Stothard has his own blog: a mixture of reports from the newsroom and literary jokes in Latin.

Reading Experience
noggs.typepad.com/the_reading_experience
Ruminative blog by former American academic, now freelance critic and fiction writer Dan Green.

Ready Steady Blog
www.readysteadybook.com/Blog.aspx
The blog accompanying the indispensable literary site Ready Steady Book, run by the indefatigable Mark Thwaite. Regular discussions of Gabriel Josipovici and Maurice Blanchot guaranteed.

Sam Leith
blogs.telegraph.co.uk/arts/samleith
Telegraph literary editor Leith dilates wittily on literary matters.

Valve
www.thevalve.org/go
A group blog dedicated to the recreation of the 'little magazine' (think *Partisan Review* or Eliot's *Criterion*) in blog form. Most of the contributors are academics, but use the blog format to step outside their narrow specialisms. Look out for the regular 'book events', in which the Valve critics all turn their attention towards a single recently published book, usually with a response from the author of the book in question.

CRITICISM: NEWSPAPERS

Financial Times
www.ft.com/arts/books
The *FT*'s weekend books coverage rivals the *Guardian* for breadth and seriousness. A highlight is the weekly Books Essay.

Guardian
http://books.guardian.co.uk
Just about the best books section of any newspaper in the English-speaking world.

Le Monde
www.lemonde.fr
Le Monde des livres appears every Friday and is the house journal of the Parisian intelligentsia – what remains of it.

New York Times
www.nytimes.com/pages/books/index.html
The *New York Times* Book Review is a venerable institution that has arguably been invigorated by the arrival of the internet. Still a must-read, despite editor Sam Tanenhaus's apparent uninterest in literary fiction.

CRITICISM: PERIODICALS

Areté
www.aretemagazine.com
Craig Raine's Oxford-based, bespoke literary periodical.

Believer
www.believermag.com
Part of Dave Eggers's *McSweeney*'s operation, edited by novelists Heidi Julavits and Vendela Vida. Julavits's editorial in the first issue, in which she declared war on 'snarky' reviewing, caused quite a stir.

Bookforum
www.bookforum.org
Literary sister of visual arts journal *Artforum*, *Bookforum* makes a reasonable number of its high-minded review-essays available online to non-subscribers.

London Review of Books
www.lrb.co.uk
Non-subscribers can get an online taste of the *LRB*'s distinctive mix of criticism and politics.

N+1
www.nplusonemag.com
Launched in 2004 by four young American writers, *N+1* is simply the most important literary/intellectual journal to have emerged in the past 20 years. It's modelled self-consciously on the 'little magazine' and, happily, lots of its content is freely available online.

Paris Review
www.parisreview.com
Decades' worth of the *Paris Review*'s celebrated 'Writers at work' interviews are now archived online. A treasure trove.

Times Literary Supplement
http://tls.timesonline.co.uk
The most venerable literary paper of them all has a revamped website, displaying several leading articles each week, plus a fully searchable subscribers' archive.

Time Out London
www.timeout.com/london/books
Reviews, profiles and listings for live literary events in London.

OTHER RESOURCES

British Library Catalogues
www.bl.uk/catalogues/listings.html
Search the British Library's catalogues, including newspapers and maps as well as books.

RaW
www.bbc.co.uk/raw
The BBC's literacy campaign for adults. Ring 0800 0150 950 for free advice and resources; calls are free and confidential.

Contributors

Michael Bywater's latest book is *Big Babies, Or Why Can't We Just Grow Up*. He also writes regularly for the *Sunday Times*, the *Telegraph* and the *Independent on Sunday*, and intermittently stirs himself to teach a little tragedy at Cambridge. He is currently working on *Like Brothers: On Men And Friendship*.

Lesley Chamberlain is a writer, critic and occasional broadcaster. Her books include *Nietzsche in Turin*, *Girl in a Garden* (a novel) and an edition of *Marinetti's Futurist Cookbook*.

Sarah Churchwell is a senior lecturer in American literature at the University of East Anglia. She is the author of *The Many Lives of Marilyn Monroe*, and writes regularly for the *Times Literary Supplement*, the *New York Times Book Review*, the *Independent* and the *Observer*.

Kate Clanchy's latest collection of poetry, *Newborn*, and an anthology about birth, *All The Poems You Need To Say Hello*, were published in 2004. A prose book, *What Is She Doing Here?*, will follow in 2008.

Nick Cohen began working as a journalist on the *Sutton Coldfield News*. He currently writes for the *Observer* and *Evening Standard*. His third – and most recent – book is *What's Left?*.

Jason Cowley is editor of the *Observer Sport Monthly* magazine and contributing editor of the *New Statesman*. His essays and reviews have been published in most major publications in Britain and the US.

Amanda Craig has written five adult novels, and is the children's critic of *The Times*.

Iain Dale presents *Vox Politix* on 18 Doughty Street Talk TV.

Jonathan Derbyshire is a writer and critic. His essays and reviews have appeared in the *Financial Times*, the *New Statesman*, *Prospect*, the *Times Literary Supplement* and *Time Out London*.

Brian Dillon is UK editor of *Cabinet* – a quarterly of art and culture – and author of a memoir, *In the Dark Room*. His writing has appeared in the *London Review of Books*, the *Independent*, *Frieze*, *Art Review* and the *Wire*.

Juliet Gardiner is a historian and writer. Her recent books include *The 1940s House*, *Wartime: Britain 1939-45* and *The Children's War*. She is also a regular broadcaster and historical consultant, most recently to the film of Ian McEwen's *Atonement*.

Adèle Geras has published more than 90 books for children of all ages, including *Troy* and *Ithaka*.

AC Grayling is professor of philosophy at Birkbeck, University of London. He writes regularly for the *Independent*, *Literary Review* and *Prospect*. His latest book is *Against All Gods*.

Sarah Guy is editorial director at Time Out Guides, and writes for various guides, including *1000 Things to Do in London*, *Weekend Breaks in Great Britain & Ireland* and the *London Eating & Drinking Guide*.

Sarah Hedley is the editor of *Scarlet* magazine. She also writes regularly for *Cosmopolitan*, *FHM* and the *Sun*. Her latest book is *Sex By Numbers*.

Dave Hill is a novelist, blogger and frequent writer of comment and feature articles for the *Guardian*.

Michael Hodges has reported on the Palestinian-Israeli conflict in the West Bank and on the Allied occupation of Iraq, where he was twice embedded with American forces in Baghdad and with the British Army in the south. He has written *AK47: The*

Story of the People's Gun, and is editor-at-large of *Time Out London*.

Barney Hoskyns is editor of www.rocksbackpages. com, an online archive of rock journalism. He has also edited *The Sound and the Fury: A Rock's Backpages Reader*.

John Lewis worked on the music desk at *Time Out London* for eight years and now writes about music, film and theatre for various newspapers and magazines, including *Uncut, Sight & Sound, So London*, the *Guardian, The Times, Metro* and *London Lite*.

Maxim Jakubowski was *Time Out London*'s crime fiction columnist for eight years before he moved to the *Guardian*. He is an ex-publisher and writer, and the owner of the Murder One bookshop in London. His latest books are *Confessions of a Romantic Pornographer, Fools for Lust* and *American Casanova*. He also edits annual crime and erotica anthologies and runs the Crime Scene film and literary festival.

Roz Kaveney is a writer and critic, perhaps best known for her books on TV and film. She reviews for a wide variety of periodicals including *Time Out London*, the *Independent, Sight & Sound* and the *Times Literary Supplement*.

Nicholas Lezard reviews books for the *Guardian* and radio programmes for the *Independent on Sunday*.

His latest book is *The Meaning of Fun*.

Kenan Malik is a writer, lecturer and broadcaster whose books include *The Meaning of Race* and *Man, Beast and Zombie: What Science Can and Cannot Tell us about Human Nature*.

Melissa McClements is a freelance journalist who specialises in writing about books. She has written for the *Financial Times*, the *Guardian*, the *Herald* and *Scotland on Sunday*.

Tim Newark is the editor of leading military history magazine *Military Illustrated*, and the author of several military history books and TV documentaries, including *Camouflage* and *The Mafia at War*.

John O'Connell is books editor of *Time Out London*. He is the author of *I Told You I Was Ill: Adventures in Hypochondria*.

Martin Rowson is chairman of the British Cartoonists' Association, and his work appears regularly in the *Guardian*, the *Independent on Sunday*, the *Scotsman* and the *Daily Mirror*. His first novel is *Snatches*, and his latest book is *Stuff*, a memoir of his parents, their lives, his childhood and his adoption.

Nicholas Royle is the author of five novels, including *Counterparts, The Director's Cut* and *Antwerp*, and a short story collection, *Mortality*. Widely published as a journalist, he has also edited 12 anthologies.

Forthcoming is a novella, *The Enigma of Departure*.

Ali Smith's latest novel is *The Accidental*. Her other books include *Like* and *Hotel World*.

Daniel Smith holds an MA in Renaissance literature, and is a freelance journalist and editor, who has worked on a number of Time Out city guides. He is also a contributor to the *Times Literary Supplement*.

Rebecca Stott is professor of English literature at Anglia Ruskin University in Cambridge. She is the author of historical thriller and ghost story *Ghostwalk*, and several books of non-fiction, including *Darwin and the Barnacle*.

DJ Taylor has written six novels, most recently *Kept*. His *Orwell: The Life* won the 2003 Whitbread Biography Prize. His newest book is *Bright Young People: The Rise and Fall of a Generation 1918-1940*.

Mark Thwaite is the founder and editor of the acclaimed literary website ReadySteadyBook.com. He is a regular contributor to a number of periodicals including the *Times Literary Supplement* and *PN Review*.

Peter Watts is features writer at *Time Out London*. His school experience was more like William Brown's than Billy Bunter's.

Index of titles

The following is a list of all literary works referred to in *1000 Books to change your life*. We have given the first date of publication for each book, along with a widely available edition. Poems and short stories are listed, with cross-references to the volumes in which they appear. We have also indicated where titles form part of a trilogy or series.

A

Accidental Evolution of Rock'n'Roll, The
(1997) Chuck Eddy. Da Capo Press.
Accidental Tourist, The
(1985) Anne Tyler. Vintage.
Across the Nightingale Floor
(2002) Lian Hearn. *See* Tales of the Otori.
Adam Bede
(1859) George Eliot. Oxford University Press.
Adapted Mind, The
(1992) Jerome H Barkow, Leda Cosmides, John Tooby (eds). Oxford University Press.
Addicted
(1998) Tony Adams, Ian Ridley. HarperCollinsWillow.

Adventures of Augie March, The
(1953) Saul Bellow. Penguin.
Aeneid, The
Virgil. Penguin.
Age of Innocence, The
(1920) Edith Wharton. Penguin.
Alias Grace
(1996) Margaret Attwood. Virago.
Alice's Adventures in Wonderland
(1865). Lewis Carroll. Penguin.
All My Sons
(1947) Arthur Miller. Penguin.
All Quiet on the Western Front
(1929) Eric Maria Remarque. Vintage.
All the President's Men
(1974) Bob Woodward, Carl Bernstein. Simon & Schuster.
Amber Spyglass, The
(2001) Philip Pullman. *See* His Dark Materials.
American, The
(1921) Henry James. Penguin.
American Tragedy, An
(1925) Theodore Dreiser. Signet.
American Way of Death Revisited, The
(1963) Jessica Mitford. Virago.

Among You Taking Notes
(1985) Naomi Mitchison. *See* Bull Calves.
An Equal Music
(1999) Vikram Seth. Phoenix.
Anatomy of Melancholy, The
(1621) Robert Burton. New York Review Books.
And Quiet Flows The Don
(1934) Mikhail Sholokhov. Vintage.
And When Did You Last See Your Father?

(1995) Blake Morrison. Granta.
Angel Pavement
(1930) JB Priestley. Kessinger.
Angel Stone, The
(2006). Livi Michael. Puffin.
Angela's Ashes: A Memoir of a Childhood
(1996) Frank McCourt. HarperPerennial.
Anglo-Saxon World, The: An Anthology
(1984) Kevin Crossley-Holland (ed). Oxford University Press.

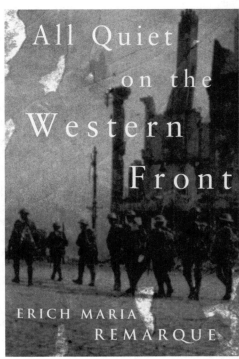

All Quiet on the Western Front

ERICH MARIA REMARQUE

INDEX

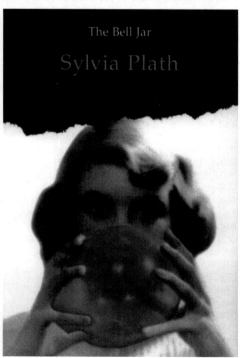

As If | Blake Morrison

'A remarkable, indispensable book.' *Sunday Telegraph*

The Bell Jar

Sylvia Plath

Animal Farm: A Fairy Story (1945) George Orwell. Penguin.

Anna Karenina (1878) Leo Tolstoy. Penguin.

Anne of Green Gables (1908) Lucy Maud Montgomery. Puffin.

Anthony and Cleopatra (1606-7) William Shakespeare. Oxford University Press.

Antichrist, The (1888) Friedrich Nietzsche. Penguin.

Antigone Sophocles. *See* Three Theban Plays.

Any Human Heart (2002) William Boyd. Hamish Hamilton.

Ape and the Sushi Master, The (2001) Frans de Waal. Basic Books.

Apostate, The (1906) Jack London. *See* When God Laughs and Other Stories.

Ariel (1965) Sylvia Plath. Faber and Faber.

Artificial Paradises (1860) Charles Baudelaire. Penguin.

As If (1997) Blake Morrison. Granta.

As I Lay Dying (1930) William Faulkner. Vintage.

Ask: Chatter of Pop (1987). Paul Morley. Faber and Faber.

Assassins' Gate, The: America in Iraq (2005) George Packer. Faber and Faber.

Astrophil and Stella (1595) Sir Philip Sidney. *See* Defence of Poesie, Astrophil and Stella and Other Writings.

Asylum (1996) Patrick McGrath. Penguin.

At Mrs Lippincote's (1945) Elizabeth Taylor. Virago.

Atomised (1998) Michel Houllebecq. Vintage.

Atonement (2001) Ian McEwan. Vintage.

Auto Da Fe (1946) Elias Canetti. Harvill Press.

Awopbopaloobop Awopbamboom: The Golden Age of Rock (1969) Nik Cohn. Grove Press.

B

Babette's Feast and Other Anecdotes of Destiny (1988) Isak Dinesen. Random House.

Babies and their Mothers (1987) DW Winnicott. Addison-Wesley.

Baby and Child Care (1955) Benjamin Spock. Simon & Schuster.

Back When We Were Grownups (2001) Anne Tyler. Vintage.

Bad Alice: In the Shadow of the Red Queen (2005) Jean Ure. Hodder.

Bad Food Britain: How a Nation Ruined its Appetite

INDEX

Critics' choice

Innocence	**p32**	Fights	**p142**
Opening lines	**p37**	Midlife crises	**p172**
Scary children	**p51**	Diaries & letters	**p177**
Siblings	**p58**	Class struggle	**p189**
Illicit liaisons	**p94**	Decay	**p206**
Drugs	**p98**	Nostalgia	**p217**
Unrequited love	**p107**	Tragedy	**p237**
Offices	**p128**	Murders	**p242**

A book that changed my life

Hari Kunzru	**p15**	Geoff Dyer	**p168**
Sarah Waters	**p19**	Nigella Lawson	**p183**
Nicholas Royle	**p24**	Ian Sansom	**p187**
Jasper Fforde	**p43**	Benjamin	
Jonathan Coe	**p55**	Markovits	**p197**
John Burnside	**p71**	M John Harrison	**p204**
Andrew O'Hagan	**p80**	Jenny Turner	**p209**
Julie Myerson	**p90**	Matt Thorne	**p213**
Maggie O'Farrell	**p100**	Toby Litt	**p223**
Will Napier	**p124**	George Szirtes	**p235**
Jonathan Franzen	**p139**	Lydia Davis	**p243**

20 books

Birth &		Men at war	**p116**
motherhood	**p20**	Food & feasts	**p158**
Children's books	**p50**	Old age	**p205**
Love & romance	**p85**	Death	**p227**

(2006) Joanna Blythman. Fourth Estate.

Bad Influence (2004) William Sutcliffe. Penguin.

Balkan Trilogy, The (1960-66) Olivia Manning. *See* Fortunes of War.

Ballet Shoes (1936) Noel Streatfeild. Puffin.

Band's Music from Big Pink, The (2005) John Niven. Continuum.

Battle Tactics of the Western Front, The (1994) Paddy Griffith. Yale.

Bear called Paddington, A (1958) Michael Bond. Collins.

Beast and Man: The Roots of Human Nature (1978) Mary Midgley. Routledge.

Beauty: A Retelling of the Story of Beauty and the Beast

(1978) Robin McKinley. Corgi.

Being Dead (1999) Jim Crace. Viking.

Bell Jar, The (1963) Sylvia Plath. Faber and Faber.

Belly of Paris, The (1873) Emile Zola. Oxford University Press.

Beloved (1987). Toni Morrison. Picador.

Beneath the Underdog (1971) Charles Mingus. Canongate.

Benn Diaries 1940-1990 (1996) Tony Benn. Arrow.

Bereavement: Studies of Grief in Adult Life (1972) Colin Murray Parkes. Penguin.

Bertrand Russell (2 vols) (1997, 2001) Ray Monk. Vintage.

Between the Acts (1941) Virginia Woolf. Penguin.

Beyond Good and Evil (1886) Friedrich Nietzsche. Penguin.

Bible, The (1611) Authorised (King James) Version. Trinitarian Bible Society.

Big Red Bath, The (2005) Julia Jarman. Orchard.

Big Sleep, The (1939) Raymond Chandler. Penguin.

Big Two-Hearted River, The (1924-25) Ernest Hemingway. *See* In Our Time.

Billy Bunter (series) (1947-65) Frank Richards. Quiller.

Birdsong (1994) Sebastian Faulks. Vintage.

Birth of Tragedy, The (1872) Friedrich Nietzsche. Penguin.

Birthday Letters (1998). Ted Hughes. Faber and Faber.

Blackberry Winter: My Earlier Years (1972) Margaret Mead. Simon & Schuster, Pocket Books.

Black Beauty (1877) Anna Sewell. Penguin.

Black Dahlia, The (1987) James Ellroy. Arrow.

Black Hawk Down (1999) Mark Bowden. Bantam.

Blank State, The (2002) Steven Pinker. Penguin.

Bleak House (1852-53) Charles Dickens. Penguin.

Bleeding London (1987) Geoff Nicholson. Orion.

Blind Needle (1994) Trevor Hoyle. Calder.

Blind Watchmaker, The (1986) Richard Dawkins. Penguin.

Bliss (1981) Peter Carey. Faber and Faber.

Blood Shelley Jackson. *See* Melancholy of Anatomy.

Blue Mars (1996) Kim Stanley Robinson. *See* Mars Trilogy.

Body Artist, The
(2001) Don DeLillo.
Picador.

**Book of Changes:
A Collection of
Interviews**
(1999) Kristine
McKenna.
Fantagraphics.

**Book of the
Duchess, The**
(1369-72) Geoffrey
Chaucer. Kessinger.

**Book of Household
Management,
The**
(1861) Isabella
Beeton. Oxford
University Press.

**Book of Lost
Things, The**
(2006) John
Connolly. Hodder.

Books of Lankhmar
(1939-88) Fritz
Leiber. Gollancz

**Book of the New
Sun** (series)
(1980-83) Gene
Wolfe. Gollancz.

Border Crossing
(2001) Pat Barker.
Penguin.

**Borrowers,
The**
(1952) Mary
Norton. Puffin.

**Bowmen and
Other Legends
of the War, The**
(1914) Arthur
Machen. Prime
Books.

Boys Beware
(2005) Jean Ure.
HarperCollins.

Brainstorm, The
(2007) Jenny Turner.
Jonathan Cape.

Brave New World
(1932) Aldous
Huxley. Vintage.

Bravo Two Zero
(1993) Andy
McNab. Corgi.

Bread Matters

(2006) Andrew
Whitley. Fourth
Estate.

Breakfast at Tiffany's
(1958) Truman
Capote. Penguin.

**Breaking the Code:
Westminster Diaries
1992-97**
(1999) Gyles
Brandreth.
Phoenix Press.

**Breaking the Spell:
Religion as a Natural
Phenomenon**
(2006) Daniel C
Dennett. Penguin.

Breathing Lessons
(1988) Anne Tyler.
Vintage.

Brideshead Revisited
(1945) Evelyn
Waugh. Penguin.

**Brief Interviews
With Hideous Men**
(1999) David
Foster Wallace.
Abacus.

Brief Lives
(1812) John Aubrey.
Penguin.

**Bright Young
People**
(2007) DJ Taylor.
Chatto & Windus.

Brighton Rock
(1938) Graham
Greene. Vintage.

**Brilliance of
the Moon**
(2004) Lian Hearn.
See Tales of the Otori.

Brokeback Mountain
(1997) Annie Proulx.
See Close Range:
Wyoming Stories.

**Brothers Karamazov,
The**
(1850-51) Fyodor
Dostoevsky. Penguin.

Budapest
(2004) Chico
Buarque. Bloomsbury.

Bull Calves, The
(1947) Naomi
Mitchison. Virago.

C
....

**C: Because Cowards
Get Cancer Too**
(1999) John
Diamond. Vermilion.

Call It Sleep
(1934) Henry Roth.
Penguin.

Camouflage
(2007) Tim Newark.
Thames & Hudson.

Cancer Ward
(1968) Alexander
Solzhenitsyn.
Penguin.

**Canterville Ghost,
The**
(1891) Oscar Wilde.
Usborne Publishing.

**Capital: Critique of
Political Economy**
(1867) Karl Marx.
Penguin.

Castle, The
(1926) Franz Kafka.
Penguin.

**Castle of Otranto,
The**
(1764) Horace
Walpole. Penguin.

**Cat in the Hat,
The**
(1957) Dr Seuss.
Picture Lions.

Catcall
(2006) Linda
Newbery. Orion.

Catch-22
(1961) Joseph Heller.
Vintage.

**Catcher in the
Rye, The**
(1951) JD Salinger.
Penguin.

**Cement Garden,
The**
(1978) Ian McEwan.
Vintage.

**Change is Gonna
Come, A**
(1998) Craig Werner.
University of Michigan
Press.

**Chapter From Her
Upbringing, A**

(2001) Ivy Goodman.
Carnegie-Mellon
University Press.

**Charlie and
the Chocolate
Factory**
(1965) Roald Dahl.
Puffin.

Charlotte's Web
(1952) EB White.
Puffin.

Charlotte Temple
(1794) Susanna
Rowson. Kessinger.

**Château de Ma
Mère, Le**
(1958) Marcel
Pagnol. Picador.

**Chick-Lit:
Postfeminist
Fiction**
(1995) Cris Mazza,
Jeffrey DeShell.
Fiction Collective
Two.

Child In Time, A
(1987) Ian McEwan.
Vintage.

Chimpanzee Politics
(1989) Frans de
Waal. John Hopkins
University Press.

Chocolat
(1999) Joanne
Harris. Black Swan.

**Christmas Carol,
A**
(1843) Charles
Dickens. Penguin.

**Chronicles of
Barsetshire, The**
(series)
(1855-67) Anthony
Trollope. Penguin.

**Chronicle of a
Death Foretold**
(1981) Gabriel Garcia
Marquez. Penguin.

**Chronicles of
Narnia** (series)
(1951-56) CS
Lewis. Collins.

**Chronicles:
Volume One**
(2004) Bob Dylan.
Simon & Schuster.

INDEX

Churchill: A Biography
(2001) Roy Jenkins. Politico's.
Cider With Rosie
(1959) Laurie Lee. Penguin.
Citadel of the Autarch, The
(1983) Gene Wolfe. *See* Book of the New Sun.
Civilization and its Discontents
(1930) Sigmund Freud. Penguin.
Clarissa, or the History of a Young Lady
(1747-48) Samuel Richardson. Penguin.
Claverings, The
(1867) Anthony Trollope. Penguin.
Claw of the Conciliator, The
(1981) Gene Wolfe. *See* The Book of the New Sun.
Climbing Mount Improbable
(1996) Richard Dawkins. Penguin.
Clockwork, or All Wound Up
(1996) Philip Pullman. Corgi.
Closer
(1997) Patrick Marber. Metheun.
Close Range: Wyoming Stories
(1999) Annie Proulx. Fourth Estate.
Clubbable Woman, A
(1970) Reginald Hill. HarperCollins.
Club of Queer Trades, The
(1905) GK Chesterton. Wordsworth Editions.
Cod
(1997) Mark Kurlansky. Vintage.

Coleridge: Darker Reflections 1804-1834
(1989) Richard Holmes. HarperPerennial.
Coleridge: Early Visions 1772-1804
(1999) Richard Holmes. Flamingo.
Cold Comfort Farm
(1932) Stella Gibbons. Penguin.
Collected Later Poems: 1988-2000
(2004) RS Thomas. Bloodaxe.
Collected Poems
(1958) John Betjeman. John Murray.
Collected Poems
(1988) Philip Larkin. Faber and Faber.
Collected Poems
(1951) Marianne Moore. Penguin.
Collected Poems
(1981) Sylvia Plath. Faber and Faber.
Collected Poems
(1994) Anne Ridler. Carcanet.
Collected Poems
(1988) EJ Scovell. Carcanet.
Collected Poems 1909-1962
(1963) TS Eliot. Faber and Faber.
Collected Poems 1934-1953
(2000) Dylan Thomas. Phoenix Press.
Comet in Moominland
(1946) Tove Jansson. Puffin.
Coming up for Air
(1939) George Orwell. Penguin.
Communist Manifesto, The

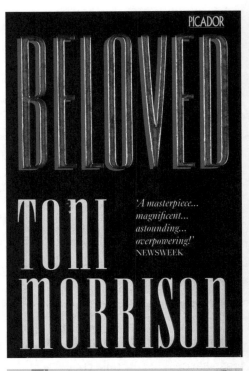

(1848) Karl Marx, Friedrich Engels. Penguin.

Company K (1933) William March. Nelson.

Compleet Molesworth, The (1958) Geoffrey Willans. Pavilion.

Complete Poems (1924) Emily Dickinson. Buccaneer.

Complete Poems (1973) John Keats. Penguin.

Complete Poems (2005) Andrew Marvell. Penguin.

Complete Ripping Yarns, The (1991) Michael Palin, Terry Jones. Mandarin.

Complete Short Stories, The (2000) Saki. Penguin.

Complete Short Stories, The (2002) Muriel Spark. Penguin.

Complete Tales and Poems of Edgar Allen Poe (2004) Edgar Allen Poe. Castle Books.

Confessions Saint Augustine. Oxford University Press.

Confessions, The (1770-72) Jean-Jacques Rousseau. Penguin.

Confessions of an English Opium Eater (1822) Thomas De Quincey. Penguin.

Conflict of Loyalty (1994) Geoffrey Howe. Politico's.

Connecticut Yankee in King Arthur's Court, A (1889) Mark Twain. Oxford University Press.

Consider the Years: 1938-46 (1946) Virginia Graham, Anne Harvey. Persephone Books.

Constance Spry Cookery Book, The (1956). Constance Spry. Grub Street.

Continental Op, The (1975) Dashiell Hammett. Macmillan.

Contract With God Trilogy: Life on Dropsie Avenue (2005) Will Eisner. WW Norton & Co.

Coquette, The (1964) Hannah Webster Foster. Oxford University Press.

Corrections, The (2001) Jonathan Franzen. Fourth Estate.

Corridors of Power, The (1964) CP Snow. Penguin.

Country (1977) Nick Tosches. Secker & Warburg.

Creation Records Story, The (2000) David Cavanagh. Virgin.

Crime and Punishment (1866) Fyodor Dosteovsky. Penguin

Crimson Petal and the White, The (2002) Michel Faber. Canongate.

INDEX

Critique of Pure Reason
(1781) Immanuel Kant. Cambridge University Press.
Crosstown Traffic
(1989) Charles Shaar Murray. Faber and Faber.
Crow
(1970) Ted Hughes. Faber and Faber.
Cucina Siciliana
(2002). Tamasin Day-Lewis. Conran Octopus.
Culinary Pleasures: Cookbooks and the Transformation of British Food
(2005) Nicola Humble. Faber and Faber.
Culture and Society: 1780-1950
(1958) Raymond Williams. Penguin.
Culture of Complaint, The
(1993) Robert Hughes. Harvill.
Curious Incident of the Dog in the Night-time, The
(2003) Mark Haddon. Vintage.

D

Daisy Miller
(1878) Henry James. Penguin.
Dandelion Wine
(1957) Ray Bradbury. Avon.
Dangerous Liaisons
(1782) Pierre Choderlos de Laclos. Penguin.
Darkness Visible: A Memoir of Madness
(1989) William Styron. Vintage.

Dark Stuff, The
(1994) Nick Kent. Penguin.
Darwin's Dangerous Idea
(1995) Daniel C Dennett. Penguin.
Darwin's Origin of the Species
(2007) E Janet Browne. Atlantic Monthly Press
Darwin Wars, The
(1999) Andrew Brown. Simon & Schuster.
David Copperfield
(1849-50) Charles Dickens. Penguin.
Day of the Sardine, The
(1961) Sid Chaplin. Flambard Press.
Dead, The
James Joyce. *See* Dubliners.
Dead and the Living, The
(1988) Sharon Olds. Knopf.
deadkidsongs
(2001) Toby Litt. Penguin.
Dead Souls
(1842) Nikolai Gogol. Penguin.
Death in the Afternoon
(1932) Ernest Hemingway. Vintage.
Death In Venice
(1912) Thomas Mann. Vintage.
Death of Artemio Cruz, The
(1962) Carlos Fuentes. Atlantic Books.
Death of Ivan Ilyich, The
(1886) Leo Tolstoy. Penguin.
Death of a Salesman
(1949) Arthur Miller. Penguin.

Death of Tragedy, The
(1961) George Steiner. Faber and Faber.
Debt to Pleasure, The
(1996) John Lanchester. Picador.
Decline and Fall
(1928) Evelyn Waugh. Penguin.
Deep Blues
(1981) Robert Palmer. Penguin.
Deep Water
(1957) Patricia Highsmith. Bloomsbury.
Defence of Poesie: Astrophil and Stella and Other Writings
(1595) Sir Philip Sidney. Penguin.
Delta of Venus
(1969) Anais Nin. Penguin.
Demonic Males
(1997) Richard W Wrangham, Dale Peterson. Bloomsbury.
Depressed Person, The
David Foster Wallace. *See* Brief interviews With Hideous Men.
Descartes
(2005) AC Grayling. Free Press.
Devotions Upon Emergent Occasions
(1624) John Donne. Vintage.
Diaries (3 vols)
(1993-2002) Alan Clark. Phoenix Press.
Diaries 1987-1992
(2002) Edwina Currie. Time Warner.
Diaries of Samuel Pepys, The – A Selection
(2003) Samuel Pepys. Penguin.

Diary of Anne Frank, The
(1947) Anne Frank. Puffin.
Diary of a Nobody
(1892) George Grossmith. Penguin.
Dino
(1992) Nick Tosches. Random House.
Discworld (series)
(1983-ongoing) Terry Pratchett. Corgi.
Disgrace
(1999) JM Coetzee. Vintage.
Dispatches
(1977) Michael Herr. Picador.
Divine Comedy, The
(1998) Dante. Oxford University Press.
Doctor Faustus
(1604) Christopher Marlowe. Oxford University Press.
Doctor Fischer of Geneva, or, the Bomb Party
(1980) Graham Greene. Penguin.
Doctor Thorne
(1878-79) Anthony Trollope. *See* The Chronicles of Barsetshire.
Doctor Zhivago
(1958) Boris Pasternak. Vintage.
Dollmaker, The
(1954) Harriette Arnow. HarperPerennial.
Dombey and Son
(1846-48) Charles Dickens. Penguin.
Don Quixote de la Mancha
(1604) Miguel de Cervantes Saavedra. Penguin.

Doors of Perception, The
(1954) Aldous Huxley. Panther.
Dorian: An Imitation
(2002) Will Self. Viking.
Downing Street Years, The
(1993) Margaret Thatcher. HarperCollins.
Downriver
(1991) Ian Sinclair. Penguin.
Dracula
(1897) Bram Stoker. Penguin.
Dubliners, The
(1914) James Joyce. Penguin.
Duchess of Malfi, The
(1623) John Webster. A&C Black.
Duel, The
(1891) Anton Chekov. Penguin.

E

Earthly Powers
(1980) Anthony Burgess. Vintage.
Earthsea Cycle, The
(1968-90) Ursula K Le Guin. Pocket Books.
East of Eden
(1952) John Steinbeck. Penguin.
Eating People is Wrong
(1959) Malcolm Bradbury. Picador.
Eclogues, The and **Georgics, The**
Virgil. Oxford University Press.
Economy and Society
(1922) Max Weber. University of California Press.

Eden Renewed
(1996) Peter Levi. Macmillan.
87th Precinct
(series) (1956) Ed McBain. Orion.
Either/Or
(1843) Søren Kierkegaard. Princeton University Press.
Embers
(2002) Sándor Márai. Penguin.
EM Forster: A Life
(2 vols) (1994) PN Furbank. Secker & Warburg.
Emigrants, The
(1996) WG Sebald. Harvill.
Emma
(1816) Jane Austen. Penguin.
Emotions Revealed
(2003) Paul Ekman. Phoenix Press.
Enchanted Wood, The
(1939) Enid Blyton. Egmont.
End of Faith, The
(2005) Sam Harris. Free Press.
End of the Affair, The
(1951) Graham Greene. Vintage.
Enduring Love
(1997) Ian McEwan. Vintage.
Endymion: A Poetic Romance
(1817) John Keats. Kessinger.
Enemies of Promise, The
(1938) Cyril Connolly. Penguin.
Energy Flash
(1999) Simon Reynolds. Picador.
England's Dreaming
(1991) Jon Savage. Faber and Faber.

England's Hour
(1941) Vera Brittain. Continuum.
English Patient, The
(1992) Michael Ondaatje. Bloomsbury.
Enigma of Arrival, The
(1987) VS Naipaul. Picador.
Enquiries Concerning Human Understanding and Concerning the Principles of Morals
(1777) David Hume. Oxford University Press.
Epicurean, The
(1894) Charles Ranhofer. Kessinger.
Eric, or Little by Little
(1858) Frederic W Farrar. Indypublish.com.
Essays
(1578) Michel de Montaigne. Penguin.
Esther Waters
(1894) George Moore. Oxford University Press.
Eumenides, The
Aeschylus. Penguin.
European Peasant Cookery: The Rich Tradition
(1986) Elizabeth Luard. Bantam Press.
Evelina: Or the History of A Young Lady's Entrance into the World
(1778) Fanny Burney. Penguin.
Everyman
(2006) Philip Roth. Vintage.
Evolution of Desire, The
(1994) David M Buss. Basic Books.

Examination at the Womb-Door
(1970) Ted Hughes. See Crow.
Excession
(1996) Iain M Banks. Orbit.
Existentialists and Mystics
(1997) Iris Murdoch. Penguin.
Exit Lines
(1984) Reginald Hill. HarperCollins.
Expensive Habits
(1986) Simon Garfield. Faber and Faber.
Explicit Animal, The
(1991) Raymond Tallis. Palgrave Macmillan.
Expression of the Emotions in Man and the Animals, The
(1872) Charles Darwin. HarperCollins.
Extended Phenotype, The
(1981) Richard Dawkins. Oxford University Press.
Extreme Europe
(2001) Stephen Barber. Reaktion Books.
Extremely Loud and Incredibly Close
(2005) Jonathan Safran Foer. Penguin.

F

Face of Battle, The
(1976) John Keegan. Jonathan Cape.
Face of Man, The
(1980) Paul Ekman. Garland Science.
Fairy Tales
(2000) Berlie Doherty. Walker.

Fairy Tales, Complete (1998) Jacob Grimm, Wilhelm Grimm. Wordsworth.

Faithfull: An Autobiography (1995) Marianne Faithfull, David Dalton. Cooper Square Press.

Famished Road, The (1991) Ben Okri. Vintage.

Fan's Notes, A (1968) Fred Exley. Modern Library.

Fanny Hill. Memoirs of a Woman of Pleasure (1748) John Cleland. Penguin.

Far Cry from Kensington, A (1988) Muriel Spark. Penguin.

Farewell My Lovely (1940) Raymond Chandler. Penguin.

Farewell to Arms, A (1929) Ernest Hemingway. Vintage.

Farmer Boy (1933) Laura Ingalls Wilder. HarperTrophy.

Farthest Shore, The (1973) Ursula Le Guin. *See* Earthsea Cycle.

Fast Food Nation (2001) Eric Schlosser. Penguin.

Fatherhood Reclaimed (1997) Adrienne Burgess. Vermilion.

Favoured Child, The (1989) Philippa Gregory. *See* Wideacre.

Fear and Loathing in Las Vegas (1971) Hunter S Thompson. HarperPerennial.

Fear and Trembling (1843) Søren Kierkegaard. Penguin.

Fear of Flying (1973) Erica Jong. Vintage.

Feast (2002) Roy Strong. Pimlico.

Feeding Frenzy (2001) Will Self. Penguin

Feel Like Going Home (1971) Peter Guralnick. Little, Brown.

Fellowship of the Ring, The (1954) JRR Tolkein. *See* Lord of the Rings.

Female Eunuch, The (1970) Germaine Greer. Flamingo.

Fermentation (1997) Angelica Jacob. Bloomsbury.

Fever Pitch (1992) Nick Hornby. Penguin.

Few Eggs and No Oranges (1976) Vere Hodgson. Persephone Books.

Fiddleback (2002) JM Morris. Macmillan.

Fifth form at St Dominic's, The (1887) Talbot Baines Reed. Hamilton.

Fight, The (1975) Norman Mailer. Penguin.

Fight Club (1996) Chuck Palahnuik. Vintage.

Fire in the Belly: On Being a Man (1991) Sam Keen. Bantam.

First Year, The EJ Scovell. *See* Collected Poems.

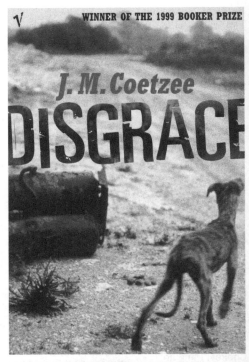

WINNER OF THE 1999 BOOKER PRIZE

J. M. Coetzee

DISGRACE

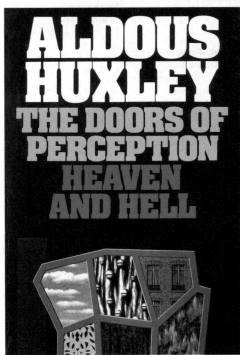

ALDOUS HUXLEY THE DOORS OF PERCEPTION HEAVEN AND HELL

Five Gates of Hell, The
(1991) Rupert Thomson. Bloomsbury.
Five on a Hike Together
(1951) Enid Blyton. Hodder.
Flea, The
(1977) John Donne. Circle Press.
Flight from the Enchanter, The
(1956) Iris Murdoch. Vintage.
Flowers of Evil, The
(1857) Charles Baudelaire. Oxford University Press.
Folded Leaf, The
(1945) William Maxwell. Harvill.
Food: A History
(2001) Felipe Fernandez-Armesto. Macmillan.
For a Child Expected
Anne Ridler. *See* Collected Poems.
Forever Amber
(1944) Kathleen Winsor. Penguin.
Forged in the Fire
(2006) Ann Turnbull. Walker.
Forgotten Cities
(forthcoming) Stephen Barber.
Forgotten Victory
(2001) Gary Sheffield. Headline.
Fortunes of Philippa, The
(1906) Angela Brazil. Blackie & Son.
Fortunes of War
(The Balkan Trilogy; The Levant Trilogy) (1960) Olivia Manning. Arrow.
For Whom the Bell Tolls
(1940) Ernest Hemingway. Vintage.

Fox in Socks
(1965) Dr Seuss. Picture Lions.
Framley Parsonage
(1878-79) Anthony Trollope. *See* The Chronicles of Barsetshire.
Frankenstein, or, The Modern Prometheus
(1818) Mary Shelley. Penguin.
Franny and Zooey
(1961) JD Salinger. Penguin.
Fred
(1987). Posy Simmonds. Puffin.
French Lieutenant's Woman, The
(1969) John Fowles. Picador.
French Provincial Cooking
(1960) Elizabeth David. Penguin.
Frog and Toad Collection, The
(2004) Arnold Lobel. HarperTrophy.
Frost at Midnight
Samuel Taylor Coleridge. *See* Collected Poems.
Funeral Blues
WH Auden. *See* Staying Alive.
Futurist Cookbook, The
(1989) FT Marinetti. Trefoil.

G

Gargantua and Pantagruel
(1532-35) François Rabelais. Penguin.
Gemma Bovery
(1999) Posy Simmonds. Jonathan Cape.
Georgics, The
Virgil. *See* Eclogues.

INDEX

Georgy Girl
(1965) Margaret
Forster. Penguin.

**Ghost and the
Bonesetter, The**
(1838) JS Le Fanu.
See Ghostly Tales.

Ghost Story
(2004) Toby Litt.
Penguin.

Ghostly Tales
(2006) JS Le Fanu.
Echo Press.

Gilead
(2004) Marilyne
Robinson. Virago.

Gilgamesh
(2004) Stephen
Mitchell. Free Press.

Go-Between, The
(1953) LP Hartley.
Penguin.

**God Delusion,
The**
(2006) Richard
Dawkins. Bantam
Press.

**God of Small
Things, The**
(1997) Arundhati
Roy. Flamingo.

**Gold Cell, The:
Poems**
(1987) Sharon Olds.
Knopf.

Golden Bowl, The
(1904) Henry James.
Toby Press.

Goldkeeper
(2004) Sally Prue.
Oxford University
Press.

Golf Dreams
(1996) John
Updike. Hamish
Hamilton.

**Gone With
The Wind**
(1936) Margaret
Mitchell. Pan.

Goodbye to All That
(1929) Robert
Graves. Penguin.

**Good Evening,
Mrs Craven**
(1999) Mollie Panter

Downes. Persephone
Books.

Good Life, The
(2006) Jay McInerney.
Bloomsbury.

Good Natured
(1996) Frans de
Waal. Harvard
University Press.

**Good Soldier
Svejk, The**
(1973) Jaroslav
Hasek. Everyman.

Go Picnic
(2004) Ted Dewan.
David Fickling.

**Gormenghast
Trilogy, The**
(1946-59) Mervyn
Peake. Vintage.

**Gospel Sound,
The**
(1975) Anthony
Heilbut. Limelight
Editions.

Grass For His Pillow
(2003) Lian Hearn.
See Tales of the
Otori.

Gravity's Rainbow
(1973) Thomas
Pynchon. Vintage.

**Great American
Novel, The**
(1973) Philip Roth.
Vintage.

Great Expectations
(1860-61) Charles
Dickens. Penguin.

**Great Fortune,
The**
(1960) Olivia
Manning. See
Fortunes of War.

Great Gatsby, The
(1925) F Scott
Fitzgerald. Penguin.

**Great Victorians,
The**
(1932) Hugh
and Harold John
Massingham (eds).
Penguin.

Green Eggs and Ham
(1960) Dr Seuss.
Picture Lions.

Green Mars
(1992) Kim Stanley
Robinson. See
Mars Trilogy.

Grief Observed, A
(1961) CS Lewis.
Faber and Faber.

Groupie
(1969) Jenny Fabian.
Omnibus Press.

**Growth of the
Novelist, The**
(1977) PN Furbank.
See EM Forster:
A Life.

Gruffalo, The
(1999) Julia
Donaldson, Axel
Sheffler. Macmillan.

Gulliver's Travels
(1726) Jonathan
Swift. Penguin.

H

Hamlet
(1602) William
Shakespeare.
Penguin.

**Hanging Girl,
The**
Ali Smith. See
Other Stories
and Other Stories.

Harry Potter (series)
(1997-2007) JK
Rowling. Bloomsbury.

**Harsh Cry of
the Heron**
(2006) Lian Hearn.
See Tales of the Otori.

**Heartbreaking
Work of Staggering
Genius, A**
(2000) Dave Eggers.
Picador.

Heart of Darkness
(1902) Joseph
Conrad. Penguin.

Heat
(2006) Bill Buford.
Vintage.

Heat of the Day
(1949) Elizabeth
Bowen. Vintage.

**Heavier Than
Heaven: Biography
of Kurt Cobain**
(1997) Charles
Cross. Sceptre.

Hedda Gabler
(1890) Henrik Ibsen.
Methuen.

**Hellfire: The Jerry
Lee Lewis Story**
(1982) Nick Tosches.
Penguin.

Henrik Ibsen
(1996) Robert
Ferguson. Richard
Cohen.

Henry V
(1599) William
Shakespeare.
Penguin.

**Here is Where
We Meet**
(2005) John Berger.
Bloomsbury.

**Here Today Gone
Tomorrow**
(2002) John Nott.
Politico's.

**Hey Yeah Right
Get a Life**
(2000) Helen
Simpson. Jonathan
Cape.

His Dark Materials
(trilogy)
(1995-2000) Philip
Pullman. Scholastic.

**His Worship
The Mayor**
(1934) Walter
Greenwood. Chivers.

**History of the
English-Speaking
Peoples since
1900, A**
(2006) Andrew
Roberts. Weidenfeld
& Nicolson.

**History of Mr
Polly, The**
(1910) HG Wells.
Penguin.

History Man, The
(1975) Malcolm
Bradbury. Picador,
Penguin, Vintage.

INDEX

Hitch Hiker's Guide to the Galaxy, The (1996) Douglas Adams. Heinemann.

Hitler's Willing Executioners (1996) Daniel Jonah Goldhagen. Little, Brown.

Hit Men (1990) Fredric Dannen. Vintage.

Hogarth: A Life and a World (1997) Jennifer Uglow. Faber and Faber.

Homage to Catalonia (1938) George Orwell. Penguin.

Honey from a Weed (2002) Patience Gray. Prospect.

Horned Man, The (2002) James Lasdun. Jonathan Cape.

Horrid Henry (series) (1994-2006) Francesca Simon, Tony Ross. Orion.

House of the Famous Poet, The Muriel Spark. *See* Complete Short Stories.

House of the Seven Gables, The (1851) Nathaniel Hawthorne. Oxford University Press.

House of the Spirits, The (1985) Isabel Allende. Everyman.

House Mother Normal (1971) BS Johnson. Picador.

How I Live Now (2004) Meg Rosoff. Puffin.

How the Mind Works (1998) Steven Pinker. Penguin.

How to Eat (1999) Nigella Lawson. Chatto & Windus.

H.R.H. (2006) Danielle Steel. Corgi.

Human Nature After Darwin (2000) Janet Radcliffe Richards. Routledge.

Human Stain, The (2000) Philip Roth. Vintage.

Hungry Years, The (2005) William Leith. Bloomsbury.

I

I Capture The Castle (1948) Dodie Smith. Vintage.

I Remember (1970) Joe Brainard. Granary.

I Remember More (1972) Joe Brainard. Angel Hair.

Ice Storm, The (1994) Rick Moody. Abacus.

Iceman Cometh, The (1941) Eugene O'Neill. Jonathan Cape.

Idiot, The (1869) Fyodor Dostoevsky. Vintage.

Idle Thoughts of An Idle Fellow (1886) Jerome K Jerome. Dodo Press.

Idylls of the King, The (1885-86) Alfred, Lord Tennyson. Penguin.

If I Die in a Combat Zone (1973) Tim O'Brien. Flamingo.

If Nobody Speaks of Remarkable Things (2002) Jon McGregor. Bloomsbury.

If This is a Man (1947) Primo Levi. Vintage.

Ignorance (2002) Milan Kundera. Faber and Faber.

Iliad, The Virgil. Penguin.

Illness as Metaphor (1978) Susan Sontag. Farrar, Straus & Giroux.

I'm With the Band: Confessions of a Groupie (1988) Pamela Des Barres. Helter Skelter Publishing.

Image of a Society (1956) Roy Fuller. Hogarth Press.

In A Station of the Metro Ezra Pound. *See* Selected Poems 1908-69.

In Cold Blood (1966) Truman Capote. Penguin.

In Every Face I Meet (1995) Justin Cartwright. Sceptre.

In Gods We Trust (2002) Scott Atran. Oxford University Press.

In Memoriam, Maud and Other Poems (1850) Alfred, Lord Tennyson. Kessinger.

In Our Time (1924-25) Ernest Hemingway. Scribner.

In Search of Lost Time (1913-27) Marcel Proust. Penguin.

In the Country of Country (1997) Nicholas Dawidoff. Faber and Faber.

In the Springtime of the Year (1973) Susan Hill. Long Barn Books.

Indecision (2006) Benjamin Kunkel. Picador.

Independence Day (1995) Richard Ford. Harvill.

Indian Summer of a Forsyte (1918) John Galsworthy. Oxford University Press.

Infants Without Families (1944) Anna Freud, Dorothy Burlingham. Hogarth.

Information, The (1995) Martin Amis. HarperPerennial.

Inheritors, The (1955) William Golding. Faber and Faber.

Innocence (1986) Penelope Fitzgerald. Flamingo.

Inside the Whale and Other Essays (1969) George Orwell. Penguin.

Intimacy (1998) Hanif Kureishi. Faber and Faber.

Invisible Man (1952) Ralph Ellison. Penguin.

Iphigeneia at Aulis Euripedes. Penguin.

Iris Trilogy, The (2003) John Bayley. Abacus.

INDEX

Iron John: A Book about Men
(1990) Robert Bly. Rider.

Islington
John Berger.
See Here is Where We Meet.

Ivanhoe
(1819) Sir Walter Scott. Penguin.

J

Jalna (series)
(1927-57) Mazo de la Roche. Kessinger.

James and the Giant Peach
(1961) Roald Dahl. Puffin.

James Joyce
(1959) Richard Ellmann. Oxford University Press.

Jane Eyre
(1847) Charlotte Brontë. Penguin.

Je Me Souviens
(1998) Georges Perec. Hachette.

Jennings Goes to School
(1950) Anthony Buckeridge. House of Stratus.

Jizzen
(1999) Kathleen Jamie. Picador.

John Major: The Autobiography
(1999) John Major. HarperCollins.

Journal of a Disappointed Man, The
(1919) WNP Barbellion. Sutton.

Joy of Sex, The
(1972) Dr Alex Comfort. Mitchell Beazley.

Jonathan Strange and Mr Norrell
(2004) Susanna Clarke. Bloomsbury.

Jude the Obscure
(1895) Thomas Hardy. Penguin.

Julie, or the New Héloïse
(1761) Jean-Jacques Rousseau. Dartmouth College.

Julius Caesar
(1623) William Shakespeare. Penguin.

Jungle, The
(1906) Upton Sinclair. Sharp Press.

Jungle Book, The
(1894) Rudyard Kipling. Penguin.

Just William
(1922) Richmal Crompton. Macmillan.

K

Kama Sutra
Mallanaga Vatsyayana. Oxford University Press.

Keep the Aspidistra Flying
(1936) George Orwell. Penguin.

Kenneth Williams Diaries, The
(1993) Kenneth Williams. HarperCollins.

Kept
(2006) DJ Taylor. Vintage.

King Dork
(2006) Frank Portman. Delacorte Press.

King Lear
(1603-06) William Shakespeare. Penguin.

King Oedipus

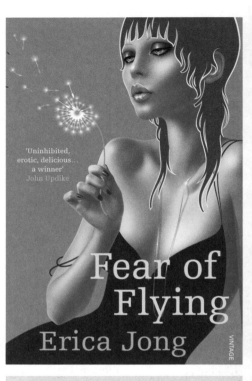

'Uninhibited, erotic, delicious… a winner'
John Updike

Fear of Flying
Erica Jong

VINTAGE

PENGUIN CLASSICS
SØREN KIERKEGAARD
FEAR AND TREMBLING

INDEX

'The ultimate book in every way. It is brilliant reading, enthralling and exciting, as well as great cookery'
Gary Rhodes,
The Times

Elizabeth
David
French Provincial Cooking

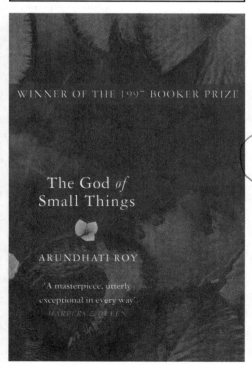

WINNER OF THE 1997 BOOKER PRIZE

The God *of* Small Things

ARUNDHATI ROY

'A masterpiece, utterly exceptional in every way'
HARPERS & QUEEN

Sophocles. *See* Three Theban Plays.

King of the World (1999) David Remnick. Picador.

Kipps (1905) HG Wells. Penguin.

Kitchen Confidential, The (2000) Anthony Bourdain. Bloomsbury.

Krapp's Last Tape (1959) Samuel Beckett. Faber and Faber.

Krazy and Ignatz: The Komplete Kat Komics 1925 and 1926 (2001) George Herriman. Fantagraphics.

L

LA Confidential (1990) James Ellroy. Arrow.

Lady Chatterley's Lover (1928) DH Lawrence. Penguin.

Lake, The Edgar Allan Poe. *See* Complete Tales and Poems.

Laments (1580) Jan Kochanowski. Faber and Faber.

Larousse Gastronomique (2001) Prosper Montagne. Hamlyn.

Last Bus to Woodstock (1975) Colin Dexter. Pan.

Last Cage Down (1935) Harry Heslop. Lawrence & Wishart.

Last Chronicle of Barset, The (1878-79) Anthony Trollope. *See* The Chronicles of Barsetshire.

Last Orders (1996) Graham Swift. Picador.

Last Post, The (2006) Max Arthur. Cassell.

Laughter in the Dark (1961) Vladimir Nabokov. Penguin.

Led Zeppelin (2005) Erik Davis. Continuum.

Left Hand of Darkness, The (1969) Ursula K Le Guin. Orbit.

Lemon Table, The (2004) Julian Barnes. Jonathan Cape.

Let the Good Times Rock (2004) Bill Millar. Music Mentor Books.

Letters from a Lost Generation – First World War Letters of Vera Brittain and Four Friends

Letters of Abélard and Héloïse, The (1616). Penguin. (1999) Alan Bishop, Mark Bostridge (eds). Abacus.

Letters of Kingsley Amis, The (2000) Kingsley Amis. HarperCollins.

Levant Trilogy, The (1977-1980) Olivia Manning. *See* Fortunes of War

Lewes on Goethe: The Life of Goethe (2002) GH Lewes. HarperCollins.

Life After Birth (1998) Kate Figes. Penguin.

INDEX

Life and Fate (1984) Vasily Grossman. Vintage.

Life and Opinions of Tristram Shandy, Gentleman, The (1759) Laurence Sterne. Penguin.

Life at the Centre, A (2006) Roy Jenkins. Politico's.

Life is Elsewhere (1974) Milan Kundera. Faber and Faber.

Life of Bertrand Russell, The (1975) Ronald Clarke. Jonathan Cape.

Life of David Hume, The (1954) Ernest Mossner. Oxford University Press.

Life of Hunger, The (2006) Amelia Nothomb. Faber and Faber.

Life of Pi, The (2002) Yann Martel. Canongate.

Life of Samuel Johnson, The (1791) James Boswell. Kessinger.

Life's Work, A (2001) Rachel Cusk. Fourth Estate.

Lights Out For the Territory (1997) Iain Sinclair. Penguin.

Like Water for Chocolate (1989) Laura Esquivel. Black Swan.

Line of Beauty, The (2004) Alan Hollinghurst. Picador.

Lion, the Witch and the Wardrobe, The (1950) CS Lewis. *See* Chronicles of Narnia.

Lisboa John Berger. *See* Here is Where We Meet.

Lisbon: A Cultural and Literary Companion (2002) Paul Buck. Signal.

Little Dorrit (1855) Charles Dickens. Penguin.

Little Lord Fauntleroy (1886) Frances Hodgson Burnett. Puffin.

Little Prince, The (1943) Antoine de Saint-Exupéry. Penguin.

Little Princess, A (1905) Frances Hodgson Burnett. Penguin.

Little Women (1868) Louisa M Allcott. Penguin.

Lives Plutarch. Modern Library.

Lolita (1955) Vladimir Nabokov. Penguin.

London Blood Michael Moorcock. *See* Time Out Book of London Short Stories.

London Fields (1989) Martin Amis. Vintage.

London Revenant (2004) Conrad Williams. Do Not Press.

London War Notes, 1939-1945 (1971) Mollie Panter Downes. Longman.

Loneliness of the Long Distance Runner, The (1959) Alan Sillitoe. Flamingo.

Long Distance Call (2000) Richard Williams. Aurum Press.

Long Good-bye, The (1953) Raymond Chandler. Penguin.

Look At It This Way (1990) Justin Cartwright. Sceptre.

Lord of the Flies (1954) William Golding. Faber and Faber.

Lord of the Rings, The (trilogy) (1954-55) JRR Tolkien. HarperColllins.

Lost Happy Endings (2006) Jane Ray. Bloomsbury.

Lost Highway (1979) Peter Guralnick. Mojo Books.

Lost Worlds (2004) Michael Bywater. Granta.

Love and War in London (2005) Olivia Cockett. Wilfrid Laurier University Press.

Love in the Time of Cholera (1985) Gabriel Garcia Marquez. Penguin.

Love is Blue: A Wartime Diary (1986) Joan Wyndham. Flamingo.

Love Lessons: A Wartime Diary (1985) Joan Wyndham. Virago.

Love on the Dole (1933) Walter Greenwood. Vintage.

Love, Poverty and War (2004) Christopher Hitchens. Atlantic Books.

Love Story (1970) Erich Segal. Coronet.

Love's Work (1995) Gillian Rose. Vintage.

Loving (1945) Henry Green. Vintage.

Loving, Living, Party Going (1978) Henry Green. Vintage.

Lucky Jim (1953) Kingsley Amis. Penguin.

Lud-in-the-Mist (1926) Hope Mirrlees. Gollancz.

Ludwig Wittgenstein (1990) Ray Monk. Vintage.

L-Shaped Room, The (1960) Lynne Reid Banks. Vintage.

Lytton Strachey: A Critical Biography (1967) Michael Holroyd. Vintage.

M

Machiavellian Intelligence (2 vols) (1988, 1997) Andrew Whiten, Richard Byrne. Oxford University Press.

Macbeth (1623) William Shakespeare. Penguin.

Machine Gunners, The (1975) Robert Westall. Macmillan.

Madame Bovary (1857) Gustave Flaubert. Penguin.

Mafia at War, The: Mussolini, Hitler and the Mob (2007) Tim Newark. Greenhill Books.

INDEX

Magic Mountain, The (1924) Thomas Mann. Vintage.

Mainlines, Blood Feasts and Bad Taste (2003) Lester Bangs. Serpent's Tail.

Making Babies: Stumbling into Motherhood (2004) Anne Enright. Vintage.

Making of the English Working Class, The (1963) EP Thompson. Penguin.

Malone Dies Samuel Beckett. See Three Novels.

Malory Towers (series) (1946-51) Enid Blyton. Egmont.

Man With Night Sweats, The (1992) Thom Gunn. Farrar, Straus & Giroux.

Man Who Ate Everything, The (1998) Jeffrey Steingarten. Headline.

Man who Travelled on Motorways, The (1983) Trevor Hoyle. Calder.

Manhattan Transfer (1925) John Dos Passos. Penguin.

Manhood in America: A Cultural History (1996) Michael Kimmell. Free Press.

Mansfield Park (1814) Jane Austen. Penguin.

Mars Trilogy, The (1992-96) Kim Stanley Robinson. Collins.

Martin Chuzzlewit (1843-44) Charles Dickens. Penguin.

Martin Heidegger: Between Good and Evil (1998) Rüdiger Safranski. Harvard University Press.

Mary Barton (1848) Elizabeth Gaskell. Penguin.

Masculinities (1995) RW Connell. Polity.

Master, The (2004) Colm Toibin. Picador.

Master of Go, The (1951) Yasunari Kawabata. Vintage.

Maus (Part 1 & Part 2) (1980) Art Spiegelman. Penguin.

Mein Stundenbuch (1928) Frans Masereel. Kurt Wolff.

Melancholy of Anatomy, The (2002) Shelley Jackson. Anchor.

Memoirs (1978) Richard Nixon. Simon & Schuster.

Meridon (1990) Philippa Gregory. See Wideacre.

Metamorphosis and Other Stories (1937) Franz Kafka. Penguin.

Mezzanine, The (1988) Nicholson Baker. Vintage.

Michael Foot (1994) Mervyn Jones. Gollancz.

Michael Rosen's Sad Book (2004) Michael Rosen. Walker.

Microserfs (1995) Douglas Coupland. HarperPerennial.

Middlemarch (1871-72) George Eliot. Penguin.

Middlesex (2002) Jeffrey Eugenides. Bloomsbury.

Midnight Bell, The (1929) Patrick Hamilton. See Twenty Thousand Streets under the Sky.

Midnight's Children (1981) Salman Rushdie. Vintage.

Midsummer Night's Dream, A (1600) William Shakespeare. Penguin.

Midwich Cuckoos, The (1957) John Wyndham. Penguin.

Military Philosophers, The (1969) Anthony Powell. Arrow.

Military Revolution, The (1988) Geoffrey Parker. Cambridge University Press.

Mill on the Floss, The (1860) George Eliot. Penguin.

Millstone, The (1965) Margaret Drabble. Penguin.

Mind of an Ape, The (1983) David Premack. Norton.

Misconceptions (2001) Naomi Wolf. Vintage.

Moby Dick (1851) Herman Melville. Penguin.

Molesworth Geoffrey Willans. See Compleet Molesworth.

Molloy Samuel Beckett. See Three Novels.

Money: A Suicide Note (1984) Martin Amis. Vintage.

Moneyball: The Art of Winning an Unfair Game (2003) Michael Lewis. WW Norton & Co.

Monopolies of Loss (1994) Adam Mars-Jones. Vintage.

Moral Minds (2006) Marc Hauser. Little, Brown.

More I Remember More (1973) Joe Brainard. Angel Hair.

Morning for Flamingos, A (2005) James Lee Burke. Phoenix Press.

Morning Songs Sylvia Plath. See Ariel.

Morte d'Arthur, Le (1485) Sir Thomas Malory. Cassell.

Most Dangerous Enemy, The (2000) Stephen Bungay. Aurum.

Mother Goose Treasury, The (1966) Raymond Briggs. Hamish Hamilton.

Mother London (1988) Michael Moorcock. Scribner.

Mr Phillips (2000) John Lanchester. Faber and Faber.

Mrs Dalloway (1925) Virginia Woolf. Penguin.

Much Depends on Dinner (1986) Margaret Visser. Penguin.

My Dark Places

(1996) James
Ellroy. Arrow.
My Life
(2004) Bill Clinton.
Arrow.
**My Magpie Eyes are
Hungry for the Prize**
David Cavanagh.
See Creation
Records Story.
My Own Life
(1776) David Hume.
Mermaid Turbulence.
My Secret Garden
(1973) Nancy Friday.
Quartet.
My Secret Life
(1888) 'Walter'.
Wordsworth Editions.
**Mysteries of
Udolpho, The**
(1794) Ann Radcliffe.
Oxford University
Press.
**Mysterious Affair
at Styles, The**
(1920) Agatha
Christie.
HarperCollins.
Mystery Story
(1980). David Pirie.
Frederick Muller.
Mystery Train
(1975) Greil Marcus.
Faber and Faber.

N
....
**Naked and the
Dead, The**
(1948) Norman Mailer.
HarperPerennial.
**Naked Civil
Servant, The**
(1968) Quentin Crisp.
HarperPerennial.
Naked Lunch
(1959) William
Burroughs.
HarperPerennial.
Natural, The
(1952) Bernard
Malamud. Vintage.
**Natural History:
A Selection**

Pliny the Elder.
Penguin.
Nausea
(1938) Jean-Paul
Sartre. Penguin.
**Nella Last's War:
A Mother's Diary
1939-45**
(1981) Nella Last.
Sphere.
Neon Rain
(1987) James Lee
Burke. Phoenix.
Neuromancer
(1984) William
Gibson. Voyager.
**New Confessions,
The**
(1987) William
Boyd. Penguin.
**New York Trilogy,
The**
(1986) Paul Auster.
Faber and Faber.
Newborn
(2004) Kate
Clanchy. Picador.
Next To You
(2005) Gloria
Hunniford. Penguin.
Nickel and Dimed
(2002) Barbara
Ehrenreich. Granta.
**Nico: Songs They
Never Play on the
Radio**
(1992) James
Young. Bloomsbury.
**Nietzsche: A
Philosophical
Biography**
(2000) Rüdiger
Safranski. Granta.
**Night Dances,
The**
Sylvia Plath. *See* Ariel
Nineteen Eighty-Four
(1949) George Orwell.
Penguin.
No Logo
(1999) Naomi Klein.
Flamingo.
No Shame, No Fear
(2003) Ann Turnbull.
Walker.
Noblesse Oblige

INDEX

The Heat of the Day
ELIZABETH BOWEN
WITH AN INTRODUCTION BY ROY FOSTER

'I have long considered
The Heat of the Day her
masterpiece'
ROSAMUND LEHMANN

Julian Barnes
THE LEMON TABLE

(1956) Nancy Mitford (out of print).

Northern Lights (1995) Philip Pullman. *See* His Dark Materials.

Norwegian Wood (1987) Haruki Murakami. Vintage.

Nose to Tail Eating (1999) Fergus Henderson. Bloomsbury.

Not in our Genes (1984) Richard Lewontin, Stephen Rose, Leon Kamin (out of print).

Notes on a Scandal (2003) Zoe Heller. Viking.

Nowhere to Run (1984) Gerri Hirshey. Southbank Publishing.

No. 1 Ladies' Detective Agency, The (1998) Alexander McCall Smith. Abacus.

O

Oaken Heart, The (1941) Margery Allingham (out of print).

Ocean of Sound (1996) David Toop. Serpent's Tail.

Ode on Melancholy John Keats. *See* Complete Poems.

Odyssey Homer. Penguin.

Oedipus At Colonus. Sophocles. *See* Three Theban Plays.

Of Love and Hunger (1947) Julian Maclaren-Ross. Penguin.

Of Mice and Men

(1937) John Steinbeck. Penguin.

Old Curiosity Shop, The (1841) Charles Dickens. Penguin.

Old Goriot (1835) Honore de Balzac. Penguin.

Old Man and the Sea, The (1952) Ernest Hemingway. Vintage.

Old School (2003) Tobias Wolff. Bloomsbury.

Oliver Twist (1838) Charles Dickens. Penguin.

Omeros (1990) Derek Walcott. Faber.

On a Grander Scale (2004) Lisa Jardine. HarperPerennial.

On Being Ill (1930) Virginia Woolf. Continuum.

On Hashish (2006) Walter Benjamin. Belknap.

On Men: Masculinity in Crisis (2000) Anthony Clare. Vintage.

On Murder, Mourning and Melancholia (1917) Sigmund Freud. Penguin.

On Royalty (2006) Jeremy Paxman. Viking.

On the Natural History of Destruction (2003) WG Sebald. Hamish Hamilton.

On the Origin of Species (1859) Charles Darwin. Penguin.

On The Road (1957) Jack Kerouac. Penguin.

On the Side of the Angels

INDEX

(1945) Betty Miller. Virago.

Once
(2005) Maurice Gleitzman. Puffin.

Once On A Time
(1917) AA Milne (out of print).

One Fine Day
(1947) Mollie Panter Downes. Virago.

120 Days of Sodom
(1784) Marquis de Sade. Arena.

One Voice
(2005) Vera Brittain. Continuum.

Operation Shylock
(1993) Philip Roth. Vintage.

Orlando Furioso
(1516) Ludivico Ariosto. Oxford University Press.

Orwell: The Life
(2003) DJ Taylor. Chatto & Windus.

Oscar and Lucinda
(1988) Peter Carey. Faber and Faber.

Oscar Wilde
(1989) Richard Ellman (out of print).

Other Stories and other Stories
(2004) Ali Smith. Penguin.

Our Fathers
(1999) Andrew O'Hagan. Faber and Faber.

Outsider, The
(1942) Albert Camus. Penguin.

Oxford Companion to Food
(1999) Alan Davidson. Oxford University Press.

Oxygen
(2001) Andrew Miller. Sceptre.

P

Pacifist's War, A
(1978) Frances Partridge. Phoenix Press.

Palgrave's Golden Treasury
(1861) Frances Turner Palgrave. Oxford University Press.

Pamela
(1740) Samuel Richardson. Oxford University Press.

Paradise Lost
(1667) John Milton. Penguin.

Passion, The
(1987) Jeanette Winterson. Vintage

Path to Power, The
(1995) Margaret Thatcher. HarperCollins.

Patrimony
(1991) Philip Roth. Vintage.

Peacock Spring, The
(1975) Rumer Godden. Macmillan.

Pedant in the Kitchen, The
(2003) Julian Barnes. Atlantic Books.

Penalty, The
(2006) Mal Peet. Walker.

People's Music, The
(2003) Ian MacDonald. Pimlico.

Perfect Tense
(2001) Michael Bracewell. Vintage.

Perfume: the Story of a Murderer
(1985) Patrick Süskind. Penguin.

Period Piece: The Victorian Childhood of Charles Darwin's Grandaughter
(1952) Gwen Raverat. Clear Press.

Permanent Rose
(2005) Hilary McKay. Hodder.

Perrault's Fairy Tales
(1969) Charles Perrault. Dover Publications.

Persepolis
(2003) Marjane Satrapi. Jonathan Cape.

Persuasion
(1818) Jane Austen. Penguin.

Peter Pan
(1911) JM Barrie. Penguin.

Phaedo
(360 BCE) Plato. Oxford University Press.

Phaedra
(1677) Jean Racine. Penguin.

Phantom Coach, The: Collected Ghost Stories
(1864) Amelia B Edwards. Ash Tree Press.

Phantom Tollbooth, The
(1961) Norton Juster. Puffin.

Physiology of Taste, The
(1825) Jean-Anthelme Brillat-Savarin. Penguin.

Pickwick Papers
(1836-37) Charles Dickens. Penguin.

Picture of Dorian Gray, The
(1890) Oscar Wilde. Penguin.

Pig Who Saved the World, The
(2006) Paul Shipton. Puffin.

Pirates!
(2003) Celia Rees. Bloomsbury.

Plague, The
(1947) Albert Camus. Penguin.

Plains of Cement, The
(1931) Patrick Hamilton. See Twenty Thousand Streets under the Sky.

Please Kill Me: The Uncensored Oral History of Punk
(1997) Legs McNeil, Gillian McCain. Abacus.

Poems of Thomas Hardy
(2006) Thomas Hardy. Penguin.

Poetical Works of Christina Georgina Rossetti, The
(1906) Macmillan.

Poetics
(350 BCE) Aristotle. Penguin.

Point of View of My Work as an Author, The
(1851) Søren Kierkegaard. Princeton University Press.

Polycrate's Ring: 1914-1970
(1978) PN Furbank. See EM Forster: A Life

Porterhouse Blue
(1974) Tom Sharpe. Arrow.

Portrait of the Artist as a Young Man, A
(1916) James Joyce. Penguin.

Possession
(1990) AS Byatt. Vintage.

Post Office
(1971) Charles Bukowski. Ecco.

INDEX

Post-Partum Document
(1983) Mary Kelly. University of California Press.

Pride and Prejudice
(1813) Jane Austen. Penguin.

Primate's Memoir, A
(2001) Robert Sapolsky. Jonathan Cape.

Prison Diaries
(3 vols)
(2002-04) Jeffrey Archer. Pan.

Project For a Revolution in New York
(1970) Alain Robbe-Grillet (out of print).

Prolegomena to Any Future Metaphysics
(1783) Immanuel Kant. Hackett.

Proper Little Nooryeff, A
(1982) Jean Ure. Puffin.

Provoked Wife, The
(1697) Sir John Vanbrugh. A&C Black.

Prozac Nation: Young and Depressed in America
(1994) Elizabeth Wurtzel. Quartet.

Prufrock and Other Observations
(1917) TS Eliot. Faber and Faber.

Psychopathology of Everyday Life, The
(1914) Sigmund Freud. Penguin.

Psychotic Reactions and Carburetor Dung: The Work of a Legendary Critic
(1987) Lester Bangs. Serpent's Tail.

Q

Quality of Light, The
(2001) Christopher Kenworthy. Serpent's Tail.

Quarrel of the Age, The: The Life and Times of William Hazlitt
(2000) AC Grayling. Weidenfeld & Nicolson.

Quiet American, The
(1955) Graham Greene. Vintage.

Quigleys, The
(2002) Simon Mason, Helen Stephens. Corgi.

R

Rabbit Angstrom: A Tetralogy
(1995) John Updike. Everyman.

Radetzky March, The
(1932) Joseph Roth. Granta.

Radon Daughters
(1994) Iain Sinclair. Vintage.

Ragged-Trousered Philanthropists, The
(1914) Robert Tressell. Penguin.

Railway Children, The
(1906) E Nesbit. Puffin.

Rainbow, The
(1915) DH Lawrence. Penguin.

Rape of Nanking, The
(1998) Iris Chang. Penguin.

Raven and Other Poems and Tales, The
(1845) Edgar Allan Poe. Little, Brown.

Rebecca
(1938) Daphne du Maurier. Virago.

Recording Angel, The
(1987) Evan Eisenberg. Yale University Press.

Red Badge of Courage, The
(1895) Stephan Crane. Penguin.

Red Harvest
(1929) Dashiell Hammett. Orion.

Red Mars
(1992) Kim Stanley Robinson. See Mars Trilogy.

Red Queen, The
(1993) Matt Ridley. Viking.

Redgauntlet
(1824) Walter Scott. Everyman.

Reflections on a Ravaged Century
(1999) Robert Conquest. John Murray.

Reflections on the Revolution in France
(1790) Edmund Burke. Oxford University Press.

Regeneration Trilogy
(1996) Pat Barker. Viking.

Relish
(2006) Rosemary Cowen. Weidenfeld & Nicolson.

Remains of the Day
(1989) Kazuo Ishiguro. Faber and Faber.

Remaking History and Other Stories
(1991) Kim Stanley Robinson. Tor Books.

Remind Me Who I Am Again
(1998) Linda Grant. Granta.

Report On Male Sexuality
(1981) Shere Hite. Ebury.

Republic, The
(c360 BC) Plato. Penguin.

Return, The
(1898) Joseph Conrad. Hesperus Press.

Return of the King, The
(1954) JRR Tolkien. See Lord of the Rings.

Reverse Revolution
Angelica Jacob. See Time Out Book of London Short Stories Vol 2.

Revolution in the Head
(1994) Ian MacDonald. Pimlico.

Rhythm and the Blues
(1993) Jerry Wexler, David Ritz. Jonathan Cape.

Rice Book, The
(1993) Sri Owen. Doubleday.

Ring-a-Ring o' Roses: A Picture Book of Nursery Rhymes
(1962) Raymond Briggs. Coward, McCann.

Rip It Up and Start Again
(2005) Simon Reynolds. Faber and Faber.

Rights of Man, The
(1791) Thomas Paine. Penguin.

River Out of Eden: A Darwinian View of Life
(1995) Richard Dawkins. Phoenix.

Road of Bones
(2006) Anne Fine. Doubleday.

Road of Death, The

(2006) Kevin Brooks. Push.

Road to Wigan Pier, The
(1937) George Orwell. Penguin.

Roast Chicken and Other Stories
(1994) Simon Hopkinson. Ebury.

Robinson
(1994) Chris Petit. Viking.

Rock Dreams
(1973) Nik Cohn, Guy Peellaert. Taschen.

Roland Barthes
(1989) Roland Barthes. Palgrave Macmillan.

Roofworld
(1988) Christopher Fowler. Warner.

Room Temperature
(1990) Nicholson Baker. Granta.

Romeo and Juliet
(1597) William Shakespeare. Penguin.

Room on the Broom
(2001) Julia Donaldson, Axel Sheffler. Macmillan.

Room With A View, A
(1908) EM Forster. Penguin.

Route 666
(1993) Gina Arnold. St Martin's Press.

Royal Flash
(1970) George Macdonald Fraser. HarperCollins.

S

Samuel Pepys
(2002) Claire Tomalin. Penguin.

Saplings, The
(1945) Noel Streatfeild. Persephone Books.

Satan Says
(1980) Sharon Olds. University of Pittsburgh Press.

Satanic Verses, The
(1988) Salman Rushdie. Vintage.

Saturday
(2005) Ian McEwan. Vintage.

Saturday Night and Sunday Morning
(1958) Alan Sillitoe. HarperPerennial.

Satyricon, The
(AD 61) Petronius. Oxford University Press.

Scanner Darkly, A
(1977) Philip K Dick. Vintage.

Scarlet Letter, The
(1850) Nathaniel Hawthorne. Penguin.

Scarlet Pimpernel, The
(1905) Baroness Emmuska Orczy. Hodder & Stoughton.

School Friend, The
(1920) Hilda Richards (out of print).

Schopenhauer and the Wild Years of Philosophy
(1989) Rüdiger Safranski. Harvard University Press.

Screwtape Letters, The: Letters from a Senior to a Junior Devil
(1942) CS Lewis. Fount.

Sea, The
(2005) John Banville. Picador.

Seabiscuit: The True Story of Three Men and a Racehorse
(2001) Laura Hillenbrand. HarperPerennial.

Secret Garden, The
(1909) Frances Hodgson-Burnett. Penguin.

'This year's most sumptuously enjoyable book'
Sunday Times Books of the Year

Middlesex
JEFFREY EUGENIDES

'A triumph' Sunday Telegraph
'Truly compelling' Daily Mail
'Superb' Independent on Sunday

Winner of the 2003 Pulitzer Prize for Fiction

PENGUIN CLASSICS

HOMER

The Odyssey

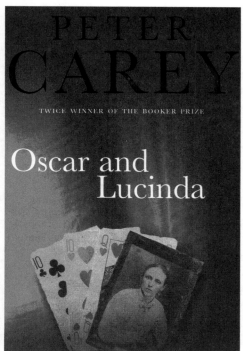

Secret History, The
(1992) Donna Tartt. Penguin.

Secret History of Tom Trueheart, The Boy Adventurer
(2006) Ian Beck. Oxford University Press.

Secret Life of Sally Tomato, The
(2001) Jean Ure. HarperCollins.

Seeds of Chaos
(1944) Vera Brittain. See One Voice.

Selfish Gene, The
(1976) Richard Dawkins. Oxford University Press.

Selected Poems
(1979) WH Auden. Faber and Faber.

Selected Poems and Prose of Paul Celan
(2001) Paul Celan. WW Norton & Co.

Selected Poems 1908-69
(2004) Ezra Pound. Faber and Faber.

Selected Poems
(2005) Sharon Olds. Jonathan Cape.

Selected Poems
(1976) William Carlos Williams. Penguin.

Sense and Sensibility
(1811) Jane Austen. Penguin.

Seven Pillars of Wisdom, The
(1935) TE Lawrence. Penguin.

Severed Head, A
(1961) Iris Murdoch. Vintage.

Sex Revolts, The: Gender, Rebellion and Rock 'n' Roll
(1995) Simon Reynolds, Joy Press. Serpent's Tail.

Shadow of the Torturer, The
(1980) Gene Wolfe. See Book of the New Sun.

Shakespeare: His Life and Work
(1999) Anthony Holden. Little, Brown.

Shakey: Neil Young's Biography
(2002) Jimmy McDonough. Random House.

Shawl, The
(1991) Cynthia Ozick. Jonathan Cape.

Sheik, The
(1919) EM Hull. Virago.

Shelley: The Pursuit
(1974) Richard Holmes. HarperPerennial.

Ship of Fools
(1494) Sebastian Brant (out of print).

Short History of Decay, A
(1949) EM Cioran. Arcade.

Short Life and Long Times of Mrs Beeton, The
(2005) Kathryn Hughes. Fourth Estate.

Shropshire Lad, A
(1896) AE Housman. Penguin.

Siege of Pleasure, The
(1931) Patrick Hamilton. See Twenty Thousand Streets under the Sky.

Sign of Four, The
(1891) Arthur Conan Doyle. Penguin.

Sign on Rosie's Door, The
(1960) Maurice Sendak. Harper Collins.

Silence of the Lambs, The

INDEX

(1988) Thomas Harris. Arrow.

Silver Sword, The
(1956) Iain Serraillier. Red Fox.

Slaughterhouse Five
(1969) Kurt Vonnegut. Vintage.

Sleeping Beauty in the Wood, The
Charles Perrault. *See* Perrault's Fairy Tales.

Slow Motion: Changing Masculinities, Changing Men
(1990) Lynne Segal. Palgrave Macmillan.

Small House at Allington, The
(1878-79) Anthony Trollope. *See* The Chronicles of Barsetshire

Small Island
(2004) Andrea Levy. Review.

Soapbox: Essays, Diatribes, Homilies and Screeds 1980-1997
(1998) Glen O'Brien. Imschoot.

Social Contract, The
(1762) Jean-Jacques Rousseau. Penguin.

Sociobiology: The New Synthesis
(1975) Edward O Wilson. Harvard University Press.

Soft City
(1974) Jonathan Raban. Harvill.

Soho Black
(1998) Christopher Fowler. Time Warner.

Something Happened
(1974) Joseph Heller. Vintage.

Song of Ice and Fire
Series (1996-present) George RR Martin. Voyager.

Songs of Innocence and Experience
(1789) William Blake. Oxford University Press.

Sons and Lovers
(1913) DH Lawrence. Penguin.

Sophie's Choice
(1979) William Styron. Vintage.

Sorrows of Young Werther, The
(1774) JW Goethe. Penguin.

Sound and the Fury, The
(2003) Barney Hoskyns (ed). Bloomsbury.

Sound Effects
(1981) Simon Frith. Constable.

Sound of the City, The
(1970) Charlie Gillett. Souvenir Press.

South of the Border, West of the Sun
(1992) Haruki Murakami. Harvill.

Speak, Memory: An Autobiography Revisited
(1950) Vladimir Nabokov. Penguin.

Spectres of Marx
(1994) Jacques Derrida. Routledge.

Spies
(2002) Michael Frayn. Faber and Faber.

Spire, The
(1964) William Golding. Faber and Faber.

Spirit, The (series)
(1940-52) Will Eisner. Taylor & Francis

Spleen
Charles Baudelaire. *See* Flowers of Evil.

Spoilt City, The
(1962) Olivia Manning. *See* Fortunes of War.

Sportswriter, The
(1986) Richard Ford. Bloomsbury.

Stage Fright
(1995) Lisa Natalie Pearson. *See* Chick-Lit: Postfeminist Fiction.

Stairway to Hell
(1991) Chuck Eddy. Da Capo Press.

Stalky & Co
(1899) Rudyard Kipling. Oxford University Press.

Stand on Zanzibar
(1968) John Brunner. Gollancz.

Starlust
(1985) Fred & Judy Vermorel (out of print).

Stars My Destination, The
(1956) Alfred Bester. Gollancz.

Stasi Files, The
(2003) Anthony Glees. Free Press.

Staying Alive: Real Poems for Unreal Times
(2002) Neil Astley (ed). Bloodaxe.

Stepping Westward
(1966) Malcolm Bradbury. Picador.

Stiffed: The Betrayal of Modern Man
(1999) Susan Faludi. Vintage.

Stig of the Dump
(1963) Clive King. Puffin.

Stones of Venice, The
(1851) John Ruskin. Pallas Athene.

Story of Babar, The
(1933) Jean de Brunhoff. Metheun.

Story of My Life, The
(1790) Giacomo Casanova. Penguin.

Straight Life: The Story of Art Pepper
(1979) Art Pepper, Laurie Pepper. MOJO Books.

Strangeland
(2005) Tracey Emin. Sceptre.

Struggles of Albert Woods, The
(1952) William Cooper. Methuen.

Studs Lonigan: A Trilogy
(1932-35) James T Farrell. Library of America.

Subtle Knife, The
(1997) Philip Pullman. *See* His Dark Materials.

Sum of Things, The
(1980) Olivia Manning. *See* Fortunes of War.

Summer of Love
(1994) Joel Selvin. Cooper Square Press.

Sunset Song
(1932) Lewis Grassic Gibbon. Canongate.

Supernatural Short Stories
(1986) Walter Scott. J Calder.

Swallows and Amazons
(1930) Arthur Ransome. Red Fox.

Sweet Soul Music
(1987) Peter Guralnick. MOJO Books.

Sword of Honour (trilogy)
(1952-61) Evelyn Waugh. Penguin.

Sword of the Lictor, The
(1981) Gene Wolfe. *See* Book of the New Sun.

Sybil: Or The Two Nations

(1845) Benjamin Disraeli. Oxford University Press.

Symposium, The
Plato. Penguin.

Synners
(1991) Pat Cadigan. Four Walls Eight Windows.

T

Tale of Peter Rabbit, The
(1902) Beatrix Potter. Frederick Warne.

Tale of Two Cities, A
(1859) Charles Dickens. Penguin.

Tales of a Fourth-Grade Nothing
(1972) Judy Blume.

Tales of the Otori (series).
(2002-06) Lian Hearn. Macmillan.

Talking Heads
(1988) Alan Bennett. BBC Books.

Tamar
(2005) Mal Peet. Candlewick Press.

Tapesteried Chamber, The
Walter Scott. *See* Supernatural Short Stories.

Tea
Saki. *See* Complete Short Stories.

Tehanu
(1990) Ursula Le Guin. *See* Earthsea Cycle.

Ten Seconds From the Sun
(2005) Russell Celyn Jones. Abacus.

Tess of the D'Urbervilles
(1891) Thomas Hardy. Penguin.

Testament of Experience

(1957) Vera Brittain. HarperCollins.

Testament of Youth
(1933) Vera Brittain. Virago.

Thank You, Jeeves
(1934) PG Wodehouse. Penguin.

Then We Came to the End
(2007) Joshua Ferris. Penguin.

They Do It With Mirrors
(1952) Agatha Christie. HarperCollins.

They Do Things Differently There
(1994) Jan Mark. Red Fox.

Third Eye, The
(2000) David Knowles. Random House.

This Sporting Life
(1960) David Storey. Vintage.

Thomas Hardy: The Time-Torn Man
(2006) Claire Tomalin. Viking.

Thousand Acres, A
(1991) Jane Smiley. HarperPerennial.

Three Men in a Boat (To Say Nothing of the Dog)
(1889) Jerome K Jerome. Penguin.

Three Novels: Molloy; Malone Dies; The Unnameable.
(1994) Samuel Beckett. Grove Press.

Three Soldiers
(1921) John Dos Passos. Penguin.

Three Theban Plays
(428-441 BC) Sophocles. Penguin.

Three Women
(1968) Sylvia Plath. *See* Collected Poems.

Through Our Eyes Only?
(1999) Marian Stamp Dawkins. Oxford University Press.

Through the Looking-Glass, and What Alice Found There
(1871) Lewis Carroll. Penguin.

Time of My Life, The
(1989) Denis Healey. Politico's.

Time Out Book of London Short Stories, Volume 2
(2000). Penguin.

Time Traveller's Wife, The
(2005) Audrey Niffenegger. Vintage.

Timaeus
(360 BC) Plato. Hackett.

Tin Drum, The
(1959) Günter Grass. Vintage.

Titan, The
(1914) Theodore Dreiser, Kessinger.

Titus Alone
(1959) Mervyn Peake. *See* Gormenghast Trilogy.

Titus Groan
(1946) Mervyn Peake. *See* Gormenghast Trilogy.

To Bed with Grand Music
(1946) Marghanita Laski (out of print)

To His Coy Mistress
(1681) Andrew Marvell. *See* Complete Poems.

To the Finland Station
(1940) Edmund Wilson. Phoenix Press.

To the Lighthouse
(1927) Virginia Woolf. Oxford

University Press.

Toast
(2003) Nigel Slater. HarperPerennial.

Tom Brown's Schooldays
(1856) Thomas Hughes. Oxford University Press.

Tom Jones (The History of Tom Jones, A Foundling)
(1749) Henry Fielding. Wordsworth Classics.

Tombs of Atuan, The
(1971) Ursula Le Guin. *See* Earthsea Cycle.

Tomkinson's Schooldays
Michael Palin & Terry Jones. *See* Complete Ripping Yarns.

Tom's Midnight Garden
(1958) Philippa Pearce. Puffin.

Tortilla Curtain, The
(1995) T Coraghessan Boyle. Bloomsbury.

Towards the End of Morning
(1967) Michael Frayn. Faber and Faber.

Tractatus Logico-Philosophicus
(1922) Ludwig Wittgenstein. Routledge.

Tracy Beaker (series)
(1991) Jacqueline Wilson. Corgi.

Trainspotting
(1993) Irvine Welsh. Vintage.

Treasure Island
(1881-82) Robert Louis Stevenson. Penguin.

Treatise of Human Nature, A
(1738) David Hume. Oxford University Press.

Trial, The
(1925) Franz Kafka.
Penguin.
Tropic of Cancer
(1934) Henry Miller.
HarperPerennial.
**Trouble at Willow
Gables and
Other Fictions**
(2002) Philip Larkin.
Faber and Faber.
**Trouble With Being
Born, The**
(1976) EM Cioran.
Viking.
**Truth About
Babies, The**
(2002) Ian Sansom.
Granta.
**Turn of the
Screw, The**
(1898) Henry James.
Penguin.
**Twelve Days on
the Somme**
(1933) Sidney
Rogerson. Greenhill.
**Twenty Thousand
Streets under the
Sky** (trilogy)
(1929-35) Patrick
Hamilton. Vintage.
253
(1998) Geoff Ryman.
Saint Martin's Press
Two Towers, The
(1954) JRR Tolkien.
See Lord of the
Rings.

U

Ultima Thule
Gareth Evans.
See Time Out Book
of London Short
Stories Vol 2.
Ulysses
(1922) James Joyce.
Penguin.
**Unbearable Lightness
of Being, The**
(1984) Milan
Kundera. Faber
and Faber.

Under Fire
(1916) Henri
Barbusse. Penguin.
Unheralded Victory
(1999) Mark W
Woodruff.
HarperCollins.
Unless
(2002) Carol
Shields. Fourth
Estate.
**Unnameable,
The**
Samuel Beckett.
See Three Novels.
**Unquiet Western
Front, The**
(2002) Brian
Bond. Cambridge
University Press.
**Unsung Heroes of
Rock and Roll**
(1991) Nick Tosches.
Da Capo Press.
Upwardly Mobile
(1988) Norman
Tebbit. Futura.
**Urchin in the
Storm, An**
(1987) Stephen
Jay Gould. Penguin.

V

Vail
(1984) Trevor
Hoyle. Abacus.
**Varieties of
Disturbance**
(2007) Lydia Davis.
Farrar, Straus &
Giroux.
**View from No.11:
Memoirs of a
Tory Radical**
(1993) Nigel Lawson.
Corgi.
**View in Winter:
Reflections on
Old Age**
(1979) Ronald
Blythe. Penguin.
Vile Bodies
(1930) Evelyn
Waugh. Penguin.

INDEX

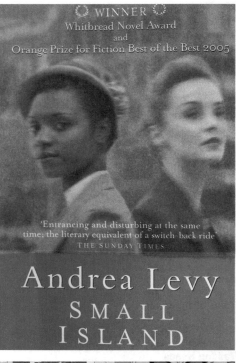

WINNER
Whitbread Novel Award
and
Orange Prize for Fiction Best of the Best 2005

'Entrancing and disturbing at the same
time; the literary equivalent of a switch-back ride'
THE SUNDAY TIMES

Andrea Levy
SMALL
ISLAND

Vladimir Nabokov
Speak, Memory: An Autobiography Revisited

To the Lighthouse
VIRGINIA WOOLF
WORDSWORTH CLASSICS

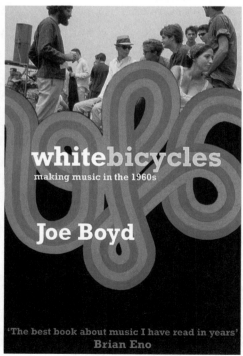

whitebicycles
making music in the 1960s

Joe Boyd

'The best book about music I have read in years'
Brian Eno

Villette
(1853) Charlotte
Brontë. Penguin.
**Vindication of
the Rights of
Women, A**
(1792) Mary
Wollstonecraft.
Penguin.
Virginia Woolf
(1997) Hermione
Lee. Vintage.
Viriconium
(2000) M John
Harrison. Gollancz.
Vita Nuova, La
(1292-94). Dante.
Oxford University
Press.
**Volcano Lover,
The: A Romance**
(1992) Susan
Sontag. Vintage.
**Voyage Round
My Father, A**
(1971) John
Mortimer. Oberon.

W

Waiting for Godot
(1952) Samuel
Beckett. Faber
and Faber.
Waking The Moon
(1995) Elizabeth
Hand. HarperCollins.
Wanderer, The
anon. *See* Anglo-
Saxon World.
**Wandering Willie's
Tale**
(1824) Sir Walter
Scott. *See*
Redgauntlet.
War and Peace
(1865-69) Leo
Tolstoy. Wordsworth
Classics.
**War and Peace
Memoirs, The**
(series)
(1971-1992)
Spike Milligan.
Penguin.

**War of the
Worlds, The**
(1898) HG Wells.
Penguin.
**War Memoirs of
David Lloyd George**
(1933-36) David
Lloyd George. Simon
Publications.
War Poems, The
(1994) Wilfred Owen.
Chatto & Windus.
**Warden and
Barchester
Towers, The**
(1878-9) Anthony
Trollope. *See*
Chronicles of
Barsetshire.
**Wartime Chronicle:
1935-1945**
(1989) Vera Brittain.
Gollancz.
Watchmen
(1986-87) Alan
Moore, Dave Gibbons.
DC Comics.
**Water-Babies,
The**
(1862-63) Charles
Kingsley. Puffin.
Watership Down
(1972) Richard
Adams. Puffin.
**Way I Found Her,
The**
(1998) Rose Tremain.
Vintage.
**We Need To Talk
About Kevin**
(2003) Lionel Shriver.
HarperPerennial.
We Were One
(2006) Patrick K
O'Donnell. Da Capo
Press.
**Weather in the
Streets, The**
(1936) Rosamund
Lehmann. Virago.
**Well of Loneliness,
The**
(1928) Radcliffe Hall.
Virago.
**Western Way
of War, The**

(1989) Victor David Hanson. Hodder & Stoughton.

What Maisie Knew (1897) Henry James. Penguin.

What's Become of Waring (1939) Anthony Powell. Mandarin.

When God Laughs and Other Short Stories (2004) Jack London. Prometheus Books.

When Knighthood was in Flower (1898) Charles Major. Wildside Press.

When the Wind Blows (1982) Raymond Briggs. Penguin.

Where Are You, Blue Kangaroo? (2001) Emma Chichester Clark. Dragonfly.

Where Dead Voices Gather (2002) Nick Tosches. Jonathan Cape.

Where Did Our Love Go? The Rise and Fall of Tamla Motown (1986) Nelson George. Omnibus Press.

Where I'm Calling From: Selected Stories (1988) Raymond Carver. Harvill.

Where The Wild Things Are (1964) Maurice Sendak. Red Fox.

Whispering Road, The (2005) Livi Michael. Puffin.

White Bicycles: Making Music in the 1960s

(2005) Joe Boyd. Serpent's Tail.

Whitelaw Memoirs, The (1989) William Whitelaw. Headline.

Why the Allies Won (1995) Richard Overy. Jonathan Cape.

Wide, Wide World, The (1850) Susan Warner. The Feminist Press.

Wideacre (trilogy) (1986-7) Philippa Gregory. Penguin.

Widower's House (2001) John Bayley. See Iris Trilogy

Wind in the Willows, The (1908) Kenneth Grahame. Penguin.

Wind-up Bird Chronicle, The (1994-95) Haruki Murakami. Vintage.

Wine and War (2001) Don and Petie Kladstrup. Hodder & Stoughton.

Wings of the Dove, The (1902) Henry James. Penguin.

Winnie-the-Pooh (1926) AA Milne. Egmont Books.

Winter Dreams (1922) F Scott Fitzgerald (out of print).

Winter's Tale, A (1623) William Shakespeare. Arden.

Wish House, The (2005) Celia Rees. Macmillan.

With Bold Knife and Fork (1968) MFK Fisher. Vintage.

Wizard of Earthsea, A (1968) Ursula K Le Guin. See Earthsea Cycle.

Woodlanders, The (1887) Thomas Hardy. Penguin.

Woolworth Madonna (1976) Elizabeth Troop. (out of print).

Women in Love (1920) DH Lawrence. Penguin.

Work of Mourning, The (2001) Jacques Derrida. University of Chicago Press.

Working For Victory (2001) Kathleen Church-Bliss, Elsie Whiteman. Sutton.

World of Girls, A (1992) Rosemary Auchmuty. Women's Press.

Writer's Diary, A (1953) Virginia Woolf. Harvest.

Written In My Soul (1986) Bill Flanagan. Music Sales Ltd.

Wuthering Heights (1847) Emily Brontë. Penguin.

Y

Year of Magical Thinking, The (2005) Joan Didion. HarperPerennial.

Yellow Wallpaper, The (1892) Charlotte Perkins Gilman. Virago.

Young Ludwig: Wittgenstein's Life 1889-1921 (2005) Brian McGuinness. Oxford University Press.

Younger Pitt, The (3 vols) (1969-96) John Ehrman. Constable & Robinson.

Z

Zurich (1991) Kim Stanley Robinson. See Remaking History and Other Stories.

INDEX